Race Against Time

David Bolton has spent much of his life
on or around the water. He grew up in
Cambridge, where punting and rowing
came as naturally as riding a bicycle. For
years he lived in Surrey at the confluence of
the rivers Mole and Thames, and sailed
boats on the south coast. Seven years ago he
gave up a successful career in public relations consultancy and moved from Islington
(a house close to the Regent's canal) to fulfil
an ambition to live on a narrowboat and
travel around the inland waterways. He now
divides his time between his boat and a
house situated between the Stratford canal
and the river Avon, and he writes about
many aspects of water activity for national
newspapers and magazines.

By the same author
available from Mandarin Paperbacks

Journey Without End

RACE AGAINST TIME

How Britain's Waterways were Saved

DAVID BOLTON

Mandarin

A Mandarin Paperback
RACE AGAINST TIME

First published in Great Britain 1990
by Methuen London
This edition published 1991
by Mandarin Paperbacks
Michelin House, 81 Fulham Road, London SW3 6RB

Mandarin is an imprint of the Octopus Publishing Group,
a division of Reed International Books Limited

A CIP catalogue record for this title
is available from the British Library
ISBN 0 7493 0994 6

Printed and bound in Great Britain
by Cox & Wyman Ltd, Reading, Berks

This book is dedicated
to everyone who has made
some personal contribution
to the restoration and revival
of the waterways.

'From the start it has been a race against time,
and a continuous crisis. It is generally considered
that at the best it takes a generation (twenty years)
to change the prevailing opinion on any subject;
and we have had to work against the background
of an endless series of emergencies and disappointments.'

Robert Aickman, April 1956

Contents

Illustrations

The author and publishers are grateful to Felice Pearson for allowing them to reproduce these photographs from the collection of the late Robert Aickman. The map on p. xii was drawn by Neil Hyslop.

Acknowledgements

I have particular cause to be grateful to Felice Pearson for her warm support and assistance, and for her kind permission to reproduce extracts from Robert Aickman's literary works and collection of photographs. This is closely coupled with my gratitude to David Hutchings, MBE.

My sincere thanks are due to many people who gave their time in recalling memories from the past and in retrieving papers and records. They include: Barbara Balch; the late Douglas Barwell, OBE; Marion Benedict; Audrey Bowley; L. A. 'Teddy' Edwards; Charles Hadfield, CMG; Sir Peter Hall, CBE; Audrey Harrison; the Rt. Hon. Lord Harvington (formerly Wing Commander Grant Ferris, MP); Elizabeth Jane Howard; Eric de Maré; Brian Morgan; Ann Pym; Jean Richardson; the late Sir Peter Scott, CH, CBE; Rosemary Shaw; Dr Graham and Heather Smith; Michael Streat; Anthea Sutherland; and the late Cyril Taplin.

I am also grateful to the chairman and general secretary of the Inland Waterways Association for giving me access to the council's minutes; to Robert Cotton and British Waterways; and to the Keeper and staff of the Public Record Office.

Sonia Rolt has given her kind permission to allow me to quote from *Narrow Boat* and *Landscape with Machines*, and for the use of copyright material drawn from the Aickman Papers (PRO 30/82) deposited with the Public Record Office. She wishes it to be known that she is not in total agreement with the interpretation of the events described in the early chapters.

Finally, although by no means least, my gratitude to Lynda for her constant encouragement through the struggles of compiling the book and her ardent support in processing the manuscript.

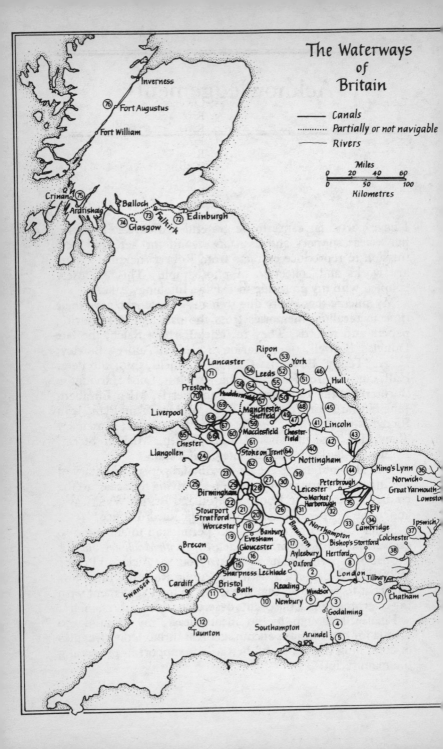

The Waterways
of
Britain

— Canals
.... Partially or not navigable
— Rivers

Miles
0   20   40   60
0   50   100
Kilometres

Introduction

It seems inconceivable now that, only a generation ago, Britain's immense heritage of inland waterways was in such a state of neglect and decay that a great part of the system was nearly lost for ever. This book tells the story of how our river and canal navigations fell into such disuse and how a small band of enthusiasts fought long and hard to save them by alerting an indifferent public and challenging an unseeing bureaucracy.

The idea of forming a consumer society to fight for the preservation of the environment was, in 1945, a bold and original one. It began when Robert Aickman, who later became a successful writer of ghost stories, approached Tom Rolt, whose book *Narrow Boat* had stimulated public awareness of the plight of waterways. Together with their wives, Ray and Angela, they called a meeting at the Aickmans' London home and set up the Inland Waterways Association. Although this book covers the Association's first twenty years, it is not in any sense an 'official' history – it is the story of individuals of vision and enterprise.

I first thought of writing about this during the three years that I spent living on my seventy-foot narrowboat *Frederick* and travelling around the country, described in part in my first book, *Journey Without End*. I had become vaguely aware that the canals and rivers which I had come to enjoy and love so much had not always been in such a reasonable state of repair as I had found them, and I had picked up some reference to the part played by Rolt and Aickman in campaigning for waterways restoration. I thought that other people who, like myself, had in recent years simply gone out and hired or bought a boat and enjoyed the amenity would be interested to learn more about the past – how, in fact, many little known enthusiasts had devoted much of their lives to fighting for the survival of a system threatened with extinction.

David Hutchings, whom I had met briefly in the course of writing about the reopening of the Stratford canal, pointed me in the right direction when I explained my initial idea to him, and through him I met Felice Pearson, a close friend of Robert Aickman, and his literary executor. She very kindly gave me unlimited access to personal papers and records. I have also been greatly helped by Sonia Rolt and by many other people who were involved in the early years of the campaign.

Aickman was an extraordinary hoarder of materials. His files contained not only every letter and communication that he received, but also copies (usually typed on the back of other documents and often wandering from sheet to sheet) of his own replies. Since he, virtually single-handed, ran the waterways campaign for many years and enthusiasts all over the country kept him informed, these hundreds of files provide a nearly complete record of what happened both in London and throughout Britain: a day-to-day record that is as alive as the day on which it was written. In the late 1970s, Robert and Felice devoted a great deal of time to sorting the files into chronological order, and they were deposited with the Public Record Office at Kew.

The other important source of information is the IWA *Bulletin*, started in November 1946 by Aickman as a simple stencilled sheet, and gradually growing into a more professional and sophisticated publication over the years. During the twenty years covered in this book, more than seventy issues of the *Bulletin* appeared (largely written by Aickman, drawing on his vast correspondence) and they give a running account of the campaign within the framework of political policy and national events.

As I started to read and turn over the pages of history, a far more fascinating and dramatic story began to emerge than I had originally expected. In the early post-war years, when Rolt and Aickman started to awaken the interest of a dormant public, the object was simply to keep open a system that had fallen into almost total decay; at this stage the fight concentrated on forcing the statutory right of navigation along such canals as the Stratford, the Kennet and Avon and the Huddersfield, which had become virtually impassable.

As the campaign started to bite in the 1950s, the problem escalated rapidly into a far more serious situation when government and nationalised industry adopted a policy of trying to abandon waterways on a major scale: more than half the navigations (including most of the canals which have since become popular cruising routes) were threatened with extinction.

The following decade saw the focus return to saving particular canals as the government slowly came around to recognising the public's desire – pressed by a substantial number of Parliamentarians from all parties – to preserve and improve this national heritage, and as individuals with vision pioneered the way by reopening the lost navigations of the river Avon and the Stratford canal. It took twenty years to change official attitudes towards the waterways – initially they were seen as an outdated liability, and only later as an environmental asset that could bring great pleasure to many people.

There had never before been a campaign like it and there has not been one since so successful in saving such a vital part of the countryside. Today, millions of people each year enjoy sightseeing and walking along the canals, most of them without paying a penny. Britain's 3,000 miles of inland waterways offer a fascinating glimpse of the past, a unique opportunity to see a transport system established 150 years ago and little changed today, yet now more widely used than at any time in the past, though by a very different type of boater.

The campaign of the 1950s and 1960s succeeded in achieving the retention of an exceptional segment of the environment that would otherwise have been submerged beneath still more roads, offices, factories, houses and refuse dumps. The Kennet and Avon, the Stratford, the Maccles-field, the Staffordshire and Worcestershire and countless others would have disappeared in the way in which the Forth and Clyde and the Huddersfield have been lost as navigations.

The threat to the environment remains, and has in fact intensified over recent years as Britain returned to a period of economic growth with its adherent property boom. The tide has turned so fully that waterways, far from being unwanted, have become so popular and desirable that there is a fresh danger that they will be engulfed under a mass of new developments which often have little relevance to the true purpose of the waterways as navigations.

Throughout the country property developments are taking place or being planned which appear on the one hand to be bringing back a past prosperity to the waterways, yet on the other rarely have any genuine connection with the use of the waterways other than the fact that they are drawing upon a pretty location. While it is unrealistic to think of preserving waterways in the charming, evocative and partially derelict state of the last two decades, it is vital that future developments should retain their historic character and atmosphere, and make a contribution towards their authentic purpose as *navigations*.

All of us who use the waterways – walkers, fishers, boaters, sightseers, and the people who live or work in the neighbourhood – owe a debt to the founders of the movement. The best way in which we can repay our debt to the past is by continuing to fight for the protection of the environment and ensuring its survival, unblemished and in first-class condition, for the enjoyment of future generations.

Meeting at Tardebigge

It was a warm Sunday afternoon in August 1945. The war in Europe had ended only three months earlier; fighting still raged around the Pacific. Britain was in a weary, battle-torn state, its resources depleted from excessive demands and little renewal.

An aging train from Birmingham rumbled into Bromsgrove and, as passengers alighted to form a long queue for non-existent taxis, the Aickmans broke away from the crowd and set off on foot down a minor road. The railway station lay on the outer rim of the grey sprawling Midlands town. Robert and Ray, a good-looking couple in their mid-thirties, smartly attired in clothes that bespoke London rather than the provinces, soon left behind the last of the plain red-brick cottages and arrived in open fields.

After about a mile they reached a hump-back bridge, only wide enough for a single vehicle and too high to see over to the far side, and they turned, as they had been instructed, off the road and on to the canal towing-path, immediately reaching a lock. The structure was much as it was when it had been built over a century earlier, yet it exuded a sad atmosphere of decay and neglect. The neat Victorian brickwork had crumbled in many places where wild purple flowers had gained a foothold and flourished, and water jetted from cracks in the rotting timber of the gate.

Above the lock there was a short level pound of water, about three hundred yards in length, and then the bottom gates of another lock of identical design and similarly disused condition; this was followed by the same sequence, pound and lock, as the Aickmans climbed steadily uphill. They were never able to see more than one or two locks ahead as the canal wove between hedges so that at no time was it possible to see much of the flight. Its scale was deceptive; the longest flight in England, it comprised thirty-five locks, carrying the water step by step from an escarpment at Tardebigge, 450 feet high, down into the Severn valley and, after another twenty locks, to Worcester.

After passing seventeen locks of the Worcester and Birmingham canal, the Aickmans reached the much longer pound below the summit. The waterway had been strangely quiet and deserted, but here at last they saw the first boats – three pairs of seventy-foot narrowboats tied to the bank, their cargo holds empty and lying open to the sky like gutted fish, though there was bustling, noisy activity among the families living in the minute stern cabins.

So close now to their destination, they must have shared a sense of expectancy and anticipation, intuitively feeling that they were nearing a moment in their lives which would bring about a fundamental change in direction. About a month earlier, Robert had written a letter which began: 'Dear Mr Rolt, We are literary agents but seldom encounter a new manuscript at once so distinctive and so penetrating.'

It had been addressed to L. T. C. Rolt, whose book *Narrow Boat* had appeared a few months earlier, care of his publishers, Eyre and Spottiswoode. It told the story of how Tom Rolt had acquired an old working boat called *Cressy* in 1939 and converted it into a home for his new wife Angela, so that they could live in it and travel around the English waterways. The book had drawn attention to the almost unknown and forgotten world of the waterways and to their present sorry state, some abandoned, many neglected and decaying to a stage where they were becoming unusable, and even the best canals suffering from lack of trade and investment.

'For many years I have been interested in canals, and distressed both by the neglected condition of many of them and by a certain lack of enterprise . . . with which the remainder are too commonly administered,' Robert's letter had continued. 'I think, as you say, there is a real danger of the canals merely being allowed to die; and for no good reason as, properly administered, they could still occupy a perfectly sound place in the national economy.'

This was no idle comment. Aickman went on to make the revolutionary proposal that a body should be formed to promote the regeneration of canals. He suggested that it should be somewhere between the Light Railway Transport League, which was championing the case for trams, and supporter groups like the Friends of Canterbury Cathedral. It should be a 'disinterested body of enthusiasts (not fanatics)'.

The proposal had struck an immediate chord with Rolt and, by return post, he replied enthusiastically. 'Six months ago I would have doubted whether such a project would receive adequate response but now, judging by the number of letters I have received, I am inclined to think otherwise,' he wrote. He was prepared to help Aickman in setting up such a society. Rolt had always preferred the country to the city, and refused the Aickmans' offer of hospitality in London at their Gower Street flat. Instead, he invited Robert and Ray to visit the Rolts on *Cressy* at Tardebigge. The Aickmans welcomed the opportunity as it would be their first opportunity to see such a boat that had been converted into a home.

They walked under a narrow bridge and ascended the side of the last lock of the flight. A few hundred yards ahead they could see the black half-circle of a tunnel entrance, and to the right the land rose steeply to a small hillock on which, surrounded by a clump of pine trees, stood an immaculate church with a slender, fragile spire. Just beyond the lock they saw *Cressy* moored on the left of the canal where the land fell away from the escarpment, opening on to an expansive view of Bromsgrove in the middle distance and, across the patchwork of fields, the misty blue foothills of the Welsh mountains.

Their first impression of the boat was its impressive length at seventy feet, compared with its slender width of seven feet, emphasised by the low rounded bow and open front deck, and the dark colours of the hull and cabin. There was a series of white framed windows, higher than they were wide, along the side of the cabin, and on top of this was a single black cylindrical chimney, bound by three bright brass rings, placed in the middle of the boat.

It was the first time that the two couples had met. The men were of fairly similar physical stature, medium height and weight, though Tom was slightly taller and had the lean appearance of a man who has spent much time living and working in the open air. His thin moustache and flattened hair gave an almost military precision to his appearance. In contrast, the pallor of Robert's rather boyish face, and his well-groomed hair, betrayed the life of a city-dweller. He had a set and serious expression, emphasised by heavy hornrimmed spectacles, yet this changed and became start-lingly alive the moment he spoke.

The two women were both attractive, though in different ways. The fair-haired Angela was slim and vivacious, while Ray, slightly more heavily built, had dark hair and large violet-blue eyes.

They entered the boat through double doors from the front well, and came first into the spare cabin which con-tained a dining table fixed to one wall and seats which doubled as berths. Passing through the galley, with a cooker on one side and a sink on the other, they arrived at the saloon in the middle of the boat, comfortably furnished with loose chairs, the walls deeply lined with books and, at the far end, the fixed desk where Tom had sat and written *Narrow Boat*.

A large double berth took up most of the space in the next cabin, allowing a narrow passage into Tom's prized pos-session, the bathroom. When fitting out at Banbury in 1939 he had been determined to provide this comfort for his new bride, although it was an unknown luxury on boats at the time. After an extensive search, he had found a deep bath which was sufficiently narrow to be carried on board, and he had placed it on a base high enough to allow the waste water to drain out without having to use a hand-pump.

Beyond the bathroom Tom had his all-important working space, a bench and racks of carpentry and mechanical tools for carrying out repairs and improvements. Finally, steps led out on to a wide stern deck under which he had fitted a Model-T Ford engine, suitably geared and adjusted to the slow speed of the canals.

The boat had had a chequered history. It had been built during the First World War on the Llangollen canal for the Shropshire Union Canal Carrying Company; it was then just an open, finely shaped wooden hull with a small stern cabin, and was drawn by a horse. The original fleet was disbanded around 1920, and *Cressy* had been used for carrying grain between Ellesmere Port and Welshpool until it was laid up in 1930. A close friend of the Rolt family, Kyrle Willans, who was an experienced steam engineer, had bought it and fitted it with steam power. Tom himself had taken part in the original trial cruise and had immediately fallen in love with the beauty and tranquillity of the waterways.

Robert's own first awareness of the waterways – and their present deplorable condition – stemmed from a very different experience. As a keen theatre-goer, he had been staying in Stratford-upon-Avon before the war during the annual Shakespeare festival season, and he had decided to explore the old canal, starting from the ornamental gardens, once the trading wharves, alongside the new, ultra-modern theatre.

He had made his way with difficulty along the broken and overgrown towing-path, puzzled and distressed by the derelict state of the canal, lock gates hanging from their stanchions, the entire cut virtually dry, the mud sides and bottom cracked, and full of stinking refuse. He had walked as far as Wilmcote, five miles north of Stratford, where the house of Mary Arden, Shakespeare's mother, was situated, and it was the same sad and forlorn scene all the way up the long flight of locks.

As he wrote later in his autobiography *The River Runs Uphill*, the walk had been like a nightmare. 'It struck me as being not so much a region of the dead, but a region of which I knew nothing. There was not a boat in sight, but I did not at the time realise that no boat could pass.' The whole experience had seemed an unreal fantasy:

Everywhere there were threatening notices, all stamped out
on iron plates, and all in the name of the Great Western
Railway Company. I was at a loss to understand how the
GWR could come into the scene at all . . . I recall feeling
that everything around me was, as I have said, fantasy:
unreal and unlike the rest of the world, though I had no idea
how or why: and not the least of all those black notices.

He discovered much later the reality behind his fantasy.
Britain's waterways had been constructed in an incredibly
short span of about sixty years from the late eighteenth
century until around 1830, when the first commercial railways started to operate. Within another two decades, railway
mania had seized the country and, in an attempt to stifle
competition, many of the burgeoning rail companies bought
out the canals, introducing penal conditions and charges that
killed off the trade.

As the afternoon progressed, the two couples agreed that
a waterways protection body of some kind would have to be
formed, and as soon as possible, if the inevitable decline was
to be reversed. How they would tackle it and what degree of
support would be forthcoming seemed highly problematical.
Would anyone share their concern for such a little-known
feature of the environment when the nation was faced with
the daunting task of social and economic reconstruction after
five years of war?

Tom, having lived among some of the boaters who still
found work, added a cautionary rider that the campaign's
aim should be to support the traditional trade of the canals,
as he feared that anything just preserved for 'pleasure' would
tend to become a precious and 'arty cult'.

One of the readers who had written to him expressed the
fear that his book, by popularising the canals, would spoil
the traditional atmosphere. As he told him, however, 'I
recognised this when I wrote it, but accepted it as the lesser
of the two evils, the evil of neglect and abandonment being
much greater. I feel that I could put up with swarms of the
most ill-behaved holidaymakers on a canal if by such means
it could be kept open. Then at least it would be available for
future generations who might put it to better use.'

Within the enclosed, womb-like atmosphere of *Cressy*'s narrow cabin ideas were generated and discussed. By the time the Aickmans left to catch their train back to Birmingham the two couples found that they shared a liking and respect for each other beyond the few hours of acquaintance. Tom and Robert discovered that they had a common philosophy of life in their desire to see mankind triumph over the threatening 'machine age'. Tom, who was a trained engineer by profession and loved nothing better than working on an intricate piece of machinery, hated the destruction of craftsmanship by modern mass production; while Robert, who could not tell a petrol engine from a diesel engine, feared that man's increasing dependence on technology would expunge individual ideas and initiative.

There were other similarities between the two men. Both were only children and had grown up during the difficult inter-war years in middle-class families which had once enjoyed a wealthy way of life, rooted in the Edwardian past, with servants and large houses. Both their fathers had failed to live up to the lifestyle of their forebears, suffering from declining fortunes and the lowering of standards at home. The sons carried some of these scars on their personalities, Robert more than Tom.

'My father remains the oddest man I have ever known,' wrote Robert Aickman later in his life. One of the oddest things about him was that he had no known relations at all. His age was also uncertain, but it was assumed that he was eighty-one when he died in 1941. Although the name could have suggested German, and perhaps Jewish, ancestry, Robert maintained that Aickman was a common name in Scotland and that the 'c' had been added accidentally to a legal document in the past and the style had persisted.

The German origins derived, in fact, from his mother's family, her grandfather having been a Mr Heldmann who had fled from Bavaria to Nottingham in 1848 and made money out of textiles. The family eventually settled in a fine and historic country house, Worton Court, near Isleworth,

Middlesex, and their elegant lifestyle made a deep
impression on Robert's childhood.

He was also much influenced by his grandfather, Richard
Marsh, who had been educated at Eton and Oxford, and
became a prolific and popular author, producing almost a
hundred titles ranging from boys' adventure stories to
romances. His most successful book, *The Beetle*, was a horror
story ranked at the beginning of the twentieth century
second only to *Dracula*, and reprinted many times as a cheap
paperback.

It was Richard Marsh who was responsible for bringing
together Robert's father and mother. His father, William
Arthur Aickman, had a predilection for the grand hotels that
flourished at British seaside resorts before the First World
War, and this was shared by Richard Marsh. Both of them
were staying at the Hydro Hotel, Eastbourne, and happened
to meet in the gentleman's lavatory.

As there was little difference in their ages and they
discovered similar tastes in wining and dining, the two men
became firm friends and before long Aickman was a regular
visitor at Marsh's home at Haywards Heath. It could have
been little surprise when the eldest of his two daughters,
who had had a very repressed upbringing, became engaged
to her father's friend. She was twenty-three when she
married and, on signing the register, learned that her
husband's declared age was fifty-three (though Robert
believed he could have been older).

The marriage of an eccentric, mid-fifties bachelor of fixed
ways to an inexperienced and ill-prepared maiden was
doomed from the start. Robert claimed that, when he was
thirteen, his mother told him that the wedding night was
'worse than I could ever have believed possible', and she
specifically implied that he had been conceived from a single
and never repeated consummation.

Most of Robert's early years were spent in Stanmore, then
a village in countryside north of London, where they lived
in a substantial five-bedroomed house, Langton Lodge. His
father practised as an architect, but his working procedures
were most haphazard as he had no sense of time. He would

rise from his bed at about ten or eleven, and potter painstakingly for hours over his toilet and dressing before departing to his office in Bloomsbury, not returning until about 10 p.m. and sometimes, if he missed the last train, not until the early hours of the morning. These unsociable habits were exacerbated by his insistence that he would be 'down for breakfast' and 'back for dinner', so that his wife was forced into the impossibly frustrating position of preparing meals that were invariably ruined.

His unpunctuality spoiled all other aspects of the family life. Robert, from the age of five, was taken often to the theatre, but the occasions were always overshadowed by the uncertainty of his father's arrival, frequently only after the curtain had risen. 'My father always rationalised the situation by saying that late arrival gave one the extra enjoyment of trying to work out what had happened on the stage in one's absence. Similarly, he was against the purchase of a programme.'

The same erratic behaviour dominated their other social activities as a family: departure on holiday, Sunday walks in the country, and their frequent dinners in London restaurants, when sometimes the situation would be compounded by his father's failure to have sufficient money to settle the bill.

The young Robert grew up in a household dominated by his father, of whom he lived in dread. He feared, particularly, his father's late returns from work when long quarrels with his wife usually concluded with his coming upstairs and creeping stealthily into Robert's bedroom, where he would stand breathing heavily until his son admitted to being awake. The morning custom was even more terrifying. His father would hammer on the floor of his bedroom with a special wedge of wood until Robert reluctantly appeared, when he would be harangued about his unruly hair and lazy ways.

Many years later Robert realised that his father had 'sought in me the love he failed to find in his wife. It was a particularly dangerous thing to do for all parties; especially as my mother also sought in me the love she missed in her husband.'

Growing up an only child in this traumatic, strife-torn household inevitably turned Robert into a recluse, and he had no close friends of either sex until his late teens. His education, on the other hand, was certainly not neglected, his mother no doubt channelling her energies into trying to mould a son who would be different from his father. She taught him to read by the age of three, and by five he started on Shakespeare. After local preparatory schools, where he did well academically, he won one of two Gladstone scholarships to an élite London school, Highgate. He became a weekly boarder and was fortunate in joining a residential house that seems to have been an exception in such single-sex schools of the time in that it was run in a liberal style with lax discipline and little bullying.

At Highgate he excelled at classics, partly because of his admiration for a young, elegant master called T. L. Twidell, who was in charge of the Classical Fifth form, and encouraged his flair for writing. He set a weekly essay on a variety of challenging subjects which had to be written over the weekend, and Robert devoted most of his time at home to this project, producing sometimes three thousand words, and never in two years receiving less than the highest mark.

The tragedy of Robert Aickman's life was that, after this preparation, no master at school and no parent seems to have pushed him into obtaining a place at Oxford or Cambridge, for which he was undoubtedly qualified. The idea was mentioned by his father, but Robert stoically rejected the suggestion as he felt that there was no way it could be afforded. By this time his father's practice, not unnaturally, had declined to a minimal level, while his mother had been undergoing months of expensive treatment in nursing homes for some painful ailment, probably arthritis.

At the age of seventeen Robert concluded his formal education, leaving Highgate in an embarrassed silence unable, like other boys, to say what he was going 'to do'. At the same time his mother decided to leave his father, and it later emerged that she had formed some kind of relationship with a viscount who had been resident at the same convalescent home. She moved to Hastings, where she received some income from working for the viscount.

'I had no job, no money, no friends, and no expectations. Some people may add that I had no spirit, I do not know,' Robert recalled about this nadir of his life.

In the absence of any alternative, he drifted into helping his father with the remnants of the architectural practice, mainly designing lavatories for London public houses owned by H. H. Finch, a prominent London caterer, and he found that his father, in fact, sorely needed his assistance. But he had no inclination towards this kind of work: the only thought in his mind was that he might become an author. His father's comment was that the time to write was in the evenings after work.

During the later part of the 1930s his father became ill from a severe ulcer and after a period in nursing homes, died in December 1941. He never returned to Langton Lodge, leaving his son alone in the large house with a minute allowance to keep it going. The architectural practice virtually closed on the office lease being terminated in 1937, and Robert obtained a small income from writing theatre reviews for a periodical called the *Nineteenth Century and Afterwards*.

Freed, at last, from the suffocating parental ties that had dominated his early years, Robert began to shape his own life. He went to his first opera at Covent Garden, met two Jewish girls in the gallery queue and 'went home happy for the first time in years'. He became addicted to opera and a regular member of the queue, which, for star productions, meant placing a folding stool in the line forty-eight hours before the performance; a strong camaraderie evolved among the fans as they took turns at looking after each other's place.

Robert's life, suddenly, was transformed from one with no friends of his own age into an existence overflowing with female companionship of an avant-garde nature. There was a dark girl in a blue shirt and trousers, who painted glowing but unsalable ikons and prided herself on possessing neither a skirt nor a dress. There was a large red-haired girl who invited him back to her smart West End flat and immediately asked him to participate in 'a particular erotic exercise'. He once went to the opera with a girl wearing a fur coat and shiny black shoes and nothing else. He fell in love with a woman, nine years older, with whom he shared a beautiful relationship which made him inordinately happy for the first time in his life until she departed, quite suddenly, on official duties to the Caribbean at the outbreak of war.

The most lasting friendship that Robert formed in the opera queue was with Audrey Linley, a nineteen-year-old Royal College of Music student, who came from a well-endowed family and lived in a formidably splendid house in Lower Sloane Street. He believed himself to be in love with her; he was almost certainly in awe of her and her rich connections, and her opinions and attitudes moulded much of his future life. Audrey did not find him particularly attractive in a physical way, yet she was mesmerised by his brain and personality.

Robert described himself at this time as 'impecunious, unconnected, less than well dressed, dubiously occupied, blatantly without prospects. I was also opinionated about things I cared for, and silent about other things. I was desperately earnest and aggressive about art and its importance. I saw women in terms of poetry and free love, not in terms of responsibility.' It was hardly surprising that Mrs Linley did not encourage this particular friendship of Audrey's, and actively dissuaded her from thoughts of marriage.

On one occasion, Audrey was unable to accept Robert's invitation to the opera, and suggested that instead he should take her own great friend, Ray Gregorson, whom she had met on holiday at Dinard, then the exclusive French resort for rich British families. Her mother had remarked on this lonely child playing by herself on the beach and encouraged Audrey to make friends with her – later, they discovered that Ray's mother had already left her husband and was living with her chauffeur (tragically, the relationship ended with a suicide pact).

The outbreak of war brought this bohemian way of life to an end and Audrey departed to Bristol, though they were to keep in touch as close friends for the rest of their lives. The butterfly days of the opera queue were over and Robert turned to Ray, starting a relationship based more on their intellectual interests than on any genuine feeling for each other. In 1941, when they were both twenty-seven, they married, a disastrous union for two people who both came from unhappy and traumatic backgrounds. Robert wrote to Audrey, explicitly stating that he had married not for love, but out of sympathy. Audrey was desperately upset and feared the worst, as Robert had always deplored marriage for its 'Noah's Ark aspect' – the fact that married couples were expected to appear everywhere together.

During the months of tension over the Munich crisis, as international events led inexorably towards war, one of Robert's most strongly held views had been in favour of pacificism and against fighting. When war finally broke, he declared himself a conscientious objector and made such a convincing presentation of his own case before the tribunal that he was one of only a handful of applicants granted total immunity from any kind of war work.

Whatever one's beliefs, there was no protection from a war that knew no frontiers, and Robert's own life was as directly affected as any other when in 1943 his mother was killed by a direct hit on her house in Hove by a stray German plane returning from a raid with unused bombs. It so happened that Robert and Ray were staying there for the weekend, and they had left the house to take a cliff walk only an hour or so before they heard the explosion.

Robert, who had failed so far to find a publisher for his writing, and Ray, who had worked as a secretary to Ronald Jeans, the playwright, decided to set up a literary agency in partnership with Howard Coster, a well-known photographer. It was called the Richard Marsh agency, after Robert's grandfather. They let Langton Lodge and took a large, two-storey flat in Bloomsbury so that they could work as well as live there.

*

Tom Rolt's decision to live in Tardebigge during the war years was no accident as it brought him within sight of the Welsh border country where he had grown up as a boy, deeply implanting its character on his personality. He had been born in Chester in 1910, but four years later his parents moved to a brand new, ornate Edwardian villa on an estate designed to appeal to gentlemen of leisure but limited means on the outskirts of Hay-on-Wye, made accessible by a new branch railway line.

His father, Lionel, had spent a foot-loose career around the world on an Australian cattle ranch and an Indian plantation before failing to make his fortune in the Yukon gold rush in 1898. He returned to England and married at the age of thirty-nine, retaining the desire to live in the style of his ancestors, but unfortunately the family's wealth had already been dissipated by the previous generation.

The house was situated in the foothills of the Black Mountains, and the wild grandeur appealed to the small boy who loved to go for drives in a horse-trap deep into the mountains. The First World War seemed to have no impact on this remote, rural retreat.

It came as a bitter blow when, at the age of ten, he was sent away as a boarder to Cheltenham College and found that, instead of the sweep of the mountains, his vision was confined to barrack-like buildings within an enclosed brick wall. A worse blow was to come, however, when his father lost a sizable investment out of his dwindling capital (on the mistaken advice of a favourite brother) and drastic economies had to be made. It was decided that the family should move closer to Cheltenham and to a smaller property which could be run without servants.

They settled in the tiny hamlet of Stanley Pontlarge on the lower slopes of the north Cotswolds near Winchcombe, and bought two cottages which had been converted into one dwelling. Although Tom found the Cotswolds tame after the rugged Welsh mountains, the charming stone-built house, the oldest part dating back to the fourteenth century, made such a strong impression on him that it was to become home for his own family over the last twenty years of his life.

Tom was never able to come to terms with the restricted life at school, and was happy when at the age of sixteen he persuaded his father to take him away. He had shown a fascinated interest in his father's motor vehicles, an early and unreliable Belsize and a recently purchased and much admired Alvis sports car, so it was natural for the family to seek the advice of Kyrle Willans, married to Tom's godmother, Hero Taylor, and regarded as 'uncle'.

Kyrle was a natural engineer of the old school, who devoted his time to inventing and developing new machinery, but his skill was unfortunately coupled with an uncompromising individualism so that, throughout his life, he moved from job to job, and place to place. 'He had a delightful sardonic sense of humour which made him a pastmaster in the art of deflating self-esteem,' Tom recalled in later years. 'When he was in a mellow mood there could be no more delightful companion, but he was self-opinionated to a degree and extremely touchy. Quick to take offence, often where none was intended, he would suddenly become inexplicably morose.'

Kyrle arranged for Tom to begin training with his friends the Bomford brothers, who ran an agricultural engineering business alongside their farm outside Evesham. It was a marvellous start to his new life. In a small workshop with seven men he learned craft engineering from the rudiments upwards, and he loved the atmosphere of working alongside skilled individuals. They had the satisfaction of building and repairing machinery that was actually used on the surrounding farms, especially the great steam-powered engines used for ploughing and threshing.

It was a shock to Tom when, at the age of eighteen, he transferred to the alien urban environment of the Potteries to begin a three-year apprenticeship with a leading firm of locomotive builders, Kerr, Stuart and Company, which Kyrle Willans had just joined to develop his ideas for a new high-speed oil pressure-engine. After the intimate, rural atmosphere of Bomford's workshop, he began a new existence of living in a sombre terraced house under the pall of smoke belching from surrounding chimneys, summoned by a steam hooter to work in a production line amid the heat of furnaces and the noise of machinery.

After Saturday-morning work, he would escape from these depressing surroundings and head off on his motorcycle to his favourite Welsh border country, where the Willanses were now living at Dovaston in Shropshire. Before long there was the added attraction of sharing in Kyrle's new passion for converting an old working boat, *Cressy*, over to steam power.

No sooner was *Cressy* ready for use than the Willans family made one of their frequent moves of house, this time to Barlaston, closer to Kyrle's work at Stoke-on-Trent. Tom and his cousin Bill joined Kyrle on the momentous voyage to move the boat from the Llangollen to a more convenient mooring on the Trent and Mersey canal. On a cold, dark night in March 1930 Tom slept on a narrowboat for the first time and, on the following day, was immediately won over by the pleasures of gliding along a tranquil canal, the boat hardly intruding on the landscape, and he had a premonition that this would provide a way of life in which his love of engineering and of the environment could be combined.

Six months before his apprenticeship was due to be completed, yet another blow hit Tom's career when Kerr, Stuart was unexpectedly confronted with a bank order for compulsory closure. It emerged that the chairman, a City man with no other interest in the company, had illegally used the company's resources to float another operation which had failed. The company secretary shot himself and the chairman disappeared. Kyrle Willans made frantic efforts to save the company but, within weeks, work ceased and the assets were sold. Kyrle, once again, had to look for another appointment and was forced to sell *Cressy*, while Tom was fortunate in finding a Gloucestershire firm with which he finished his training.

The 1930s was a bad era for a young man trying to establish a career for himself and for four years Tom went from depressing job to depressing job as firms collapsed in the recession and employees were made redundant. Finally, in 1935, he decided to go into business on his own account and, in partnership with John Passini, a sports-car racing friend, acquired a run-down garage and workshop, the Phoenix at Hartley Whitney, Hampshire. At around the same time they decided to form the Vintage Sports Car Club, and its headquarters became the Phoenix Green garage.

The garage's position on a very busy trunk road between London and the West Country attracted a variety of customers, including some rather flashy characters, and during the next four years Tom learned a great deal about the seamier side of running a business, with its wheeling and dealing and side-fiddles on petrol. Meanwhile, the club became more demanding as Tom took the lead in setting up, in conjunction with the Bugatti Owners Club, the famous speed hill climb at Prescott, near Stanley Pontlarge. Although it was a busy and fascinating life in many ways, he was still not completely satisfied.

'On hot summer days, when traffic surged endlessly past the garage and the air was full of the stench of petrol fumes and hot tarmac, I would think of *Cressy* gliding along some narrow ribbon of still water between green fields as a traveller in the desert dreams of a oasis,' he later wrote.

When *Cressy* had been sold Tom had written to the purchaser, asking him to contact him if he ever thought of parting with the boat. Only eighteen months later, Tom heard that the new owner's wife had died tragically and he wished to sell the boat that held such sad memories for him. As Tom could not afford to buy it he told Kyrle, who once again acquired *Cressy*, then moored at Leicester, and together they moved it to Braunston, then to Banbury.

Not all the customers at the garage were local farmers or fly-by-nights. One summer morning in 1937 a white Alfa Romeo swooped into the forecourt driven by a lovely young girl in a white polo-necked sweater, blonde hair flying in the wind. This 'combination of exotic motor-car and beautiful blonde' seemed like something out of a Hollywood film until Tom discovered that the car did not live up to its initial image – it had just been rescued from a scrapyard.

The driver was another story. Angela Orred was a sophisticated 22-year-old girl-about-town who had her own London flat. She claimed descent from the Earl of Clarence, illegitimate son of King William IV, and her father, a retired army major, enjoyed a wealthy and luxurious life at a substantial house near Ascot. Over the following months they started to see each other often, and the next spring took a holiday on *Miranda*, a converted ship's lifeboat which they hired from Wyre Piddle on the river Avon, partly to test out an idea already discussed between them of living on the waterways.

Tom's 'design for living' had been brewing in his mind for some time; he had already written an unpublished novel and had formulated the idea of living on a boat, travelling around the inland waterways and earning his way as a writer. When the Phoenix garage needed an injection of capital early in 1939 he sold his share to his partner and set out on this adventure. He found, much to his surprise, that Kyrle Willans was willing to part with *Cressy* for £100.

In April 1939 Tom moved on to *Cressy* at Banbury with a camp-bed and started on a total conversion to turn it into a habitable home. Angela and he wanted to marry, but this was violently opposed by her father, who savagely harangued Tom at their only meeting at a London club. A few weeks later Angela arrived in the middle of the night, having been thrown out of her parents' house, and in July they married at Caxton Hall with only two friends as witnesses. There was never any reconciliation between Angela and her father.

With conflict at home and the war brewing in Europe, the newly married couple set out at an inauspicious time to explore the canals. They had travelled for only a few weeks as far as Stoke-on-Trent when Neville Chamberlain made his fateful broadcast announcing that Britain was at war. From Nantwich Tom caught a bus into Crewe and joined Rolls-Royce as a fitter, but he soon realised that he could not survive working in a vast mass-production plant with no exterior daylight.

Six weeks later – after converting *Cressy* to burn paraffin – they made the long trek south and reached Hungerford, on the almost unnavigable Kennet and Avon, where Tom spent a year helping to recondition tractors. This work was more to his liking, but poorly paid, so in March 1941 they were

again on the move, heading towards Bromsgrove where Tom
had been offered a temporary civil servant's appointment
with an engineering inspectorate of the Ministry of Supply.

Tardebigge became their home mooring for eighteen
hundred days. In the evenings, after Tom had travelled in
an Austin Seven to engineering plants in Birmingham,
Wolverhampton and other Midlands towns, he sat down at
the little fixed desk in the saloon and, in the light of paraffin
lamps, wrote his account of their attenuated travels on
Cressy. After it had been rejected by countless publishers,
Tom despaired and pushed the manuscript under a berth. A
few months later he was in correspondence with H. J.
Massingham, the esteemed writer on the English scene, who
suggested that Tom should write a book about the canals.
The text was retrieved and, with Massingham's influence,
the book was published by Eyre and Spottiswoode in 1944.

He concluded in *Narrow Boat* that:

The future of the English canals . . . depends no less than
that of the countryside on the order we build after the war.
In a society framed to cherish our national heritage the
canals can play their part not only as a means of transport
and employment, but as part of an efficient system of land
drainage and a source of beauty and pleasure. But if the
canals are left to the mercies of economists and scientific
planners, before many years are past the last of them will
become a weedy, stagnant ditch, and the bright boats will rot
at the wharves, to live on only in old men's memories. It is
because I fear that this may happen that I have made a
record of them.

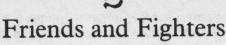

Friends and Fighters

It took a further six months after their initial meeting, despite their enthusiasm for the cause, for the Aickmans and the Rolts to arrange for an inaugural meeting to set up the proposed waterways protection body.

The time was not wasted. The two couples corresponded frequently and with ever increasing warmth; and they met again, this time in London. The tentative contact made at Tardebigge started to grow and flourish into a personal and intimate friendship, between the two men and the women, and across the sexes. Tom and Robert built up a firm understanding of each other, laying the foundations of what was to be a formidable team, each of them gaining an increasing respect for the other.

In an initial exchange of letters following the Tardebigge meeting Angela already felt confident enough to write in her beautifully rounded hand a light-hearted, slightly ironic letter to Robert which was to be typical of many to be sent over subsequent years. Referring back to a conversation they had had about the Society of Individualists, she thought that Tom was well qualified to become a member. 'His outfit of corduroy and one gold ear-ring might cause a stir at an otherwise sticky meeting – also he would be an advertisement for the Society.'

In the autumn the Rolts pressed the Aickmans to come and join *Cressy* on its spring cruise to Banbury, where it was scheduled to have a long-overdue postwar refit at Tooley's old-established boatyard while Tom and Angela took time off to explore the Irish canals.

Robert was thrilled with the chance of having his first genuine canal-boating experience, and he invited the Rolts to stay at the Gower Street flat soon after Christmas. 'Whatever happens, *don't* make up TWO beds for Tom and me. We can quite well sleep in one and have done so for the past six years!' Angela begged Ray in reply, adding that she would bring butter, eggs and sausages to alleviate the tough food rationing still in force.

Robert and Ray were excellent hosts. They loved entertaining and going out to restaurants and the theatre. Tom and Angela, coming from the relatively isolated and unsophisticated circumstances of *Cressy*, were swept off their feet. In the evening, as was his practice when guests were staying, Robert roped everyone into taking part in a dramatic reading of one of his own plays (none of which, sadly, ever achieved public performance).

'Robert's play haunts me. I can remember whole bits, which is a good sign as I have a bad memory. It really *should* be produced,' enthused Angela to Ray, signing off, for the first time, 'love'.

Tom had been equally impressed. 'I have not forgotten your piece of Grand Guignol. I think it is masterly and feel something must be done. Next time we pay you a visit I shall have to see if I can't curdle *your* blood!' he wrote, sitting by the blazing stove on *Cressy*, encased in snow and ice.

The next time, an altogether different event, was to be the inaugural meeting of the new association, arranged, finally, for 8 p.m. on 15 February 1946 at Gower Street. Tom and Robert corresponded about the people who should be invited to this occasion, since, from the outset, they were anxious to restrict it to those who had shown a keen and positive interest in the project. One of these was Charles Hadfield, then working for Oxford University Press, whose schoolboy enthusiasm for West Country canals had been developed by wartime work on the Thames for London's fire brigade; he had been inspired, like Aickman, to make contact with Rolt after the publication of *Narrow Boat*.

Tom thought that Hadfield should be invited, but he advised Robert not to ask him to bring along any other guests 'because I feel that anyone he is likely to produce might have too strong a "left-wing" bias for my liking or yours. While the society itself would be non-political, we want people with our views (approximately) at the centre with Hadfield as the indispensable liaison with the powers-that-be.'

Charles Hadfield, in fact, brought along Frank Eyre, who was his assistant at OUP and had an interest in yachting and canoeing. Robert had invited Commander Luard, who had started the Little Ship Club, a successful venue in the City of London for sailing enthusiasts, and Dr R. K. Kirkland.

The meeting was to be momentous, yet none of those who had been invited could have guessed this at the time they reached the door of 11 Gower Street, a finely proportioned Georgian house on the Bedford estate in Bloomsbury, formerly the home at different times of the actress Violet Tree and Dean Inge of St Paul's. They climbed two staircases, passing an odd assortment of small business offices, some representing eastern European countries, and were then confronted by a door bearing the plaque *Richard Marsh Literary Agency*. After ringing the doorbell and being admitted, they entered an entirely different environment, first ascending a lovely curving flight of stairs, richly lined with a vast and varied collection of paintings and drawings, some representing the architectural work of Robert's father.

They arrived at the main living-room on the third floor of the house. One wall was entirely filled from carpet to ceiling with part of Robert's immense collection of books that he had assembled throughout his life, reflecting his dynamic interest in theatre, opera, ballet and the visual arts. More books filled the shelves around the fireplace, and the whole room seemed to be bulging with collected items, including – in its place of honour above the door leading to the bedroom – a traditionally painted Buckby can and pitcher, used by working boaters to contain fresh drinking water. Beyond the door, there was a bathroom with an ornate Edwardian bath on pedestal legs.

Another door from the living-room gave on to a second flight of stairs, again lined with pictures, that led to the top floor under an elegant domed, oval ceiling light, still retaining its remnants of wartime black-out curtains. Here, over the view of the drab rooftops of central London, the dining-room, kitchen and two spare rooms had a delightful and sunny aspect.

As the oddly assorted guests eyed each other, rather cautiously and curiously, the doorbell rang one more time. Robert and Tom exchanged puzzled glances since no one else was expected by invitation. A stranger stood on the step. 'Is this the meeting of the Inland Waterways Association?' he asked, and then he introduced himself as Captain R. L. H. Smith.

'The name of the organisation had not by then been formally agreed upon. No one ever admitted to having invited Captain Smith, and I do not think anyone had . . . his advent among us was part of the waterways fantasy; the first occurrence in what became known as "the best traditions of the IWA",' Robert reflected afterwards.

The name – Inland Waterways Association – was adopted and its aims were defined as 'advocating the maintenance, development and use of our rivers and canals both for waterborne trade and as national amenities'. The original select band formed themselves into an executive committee which they called the 'council'. Robert Aickman and Charles Hadfield became respectively chairman and vice-chairman of the Association, and Tom Rolt assumed the role of honorary secretary with Frank Eyre as treasurer. Ray wrote out the minutes of this historic meeting in her own neat, exact, script.

The waterways which were considered to be particularly at risk were identified and allocated to individuals for future monitoring. Tom undertook the task of looking after the Warwickshire Avon valley, while the Kennet and Avon – the canal linking the Thames with the Severn, on which there was still some traffic, though seriously impeded by endless repair stoppages – fell to Robert.

Tom returned to *Cressy* and immediately started to plan his spring trip to Banbury. He calculated that the shortest of two alternative routes would cover 159 miles, passing

through 175 locks, and consume 53 gallons of fuel (still at
this time strictly rationed and in very short supply). He
planned to leave Tardebigge on 12 April, arriving in Banbury
nine days later.

All this talk of boating had fired Robert's imagination,
and he began to search up and down the country for a craft
of his own. From an advertisement in *The Times* he learned
of a converted narrowboat called *Imagen*, which he asked
Tom to have a look at. The seller, however, was obviously
waiting for the highest offer, and eventually the boat went
for the 'wicked price' of £1,500. Tom's view was that it was
certainly not worth it.

Phosphorus was the next prospect. Formerly owned by the
Grand Union Canal Company, it had an open hull, and was
now lying at Southall. Robert succeeded in buying it for
£264, and made some play of its being available for the use
of IWA members. He gave much thought to the interior
design (for which he always had a flair), but the conversion
was never carried out because he found that it was too time-
consuming and distracted him from the campaign. In any
case, he had little interest in practical and mechanical matters
(he never, for instance, learned to drive a car, relying instead
on the goodwill of his friends).

The trip to Banbury was successfully completed and the
Aickmans travelled part of the way, giving Robert his first
actual taste of boating. The Rolts then left *Cressy* for its refit
at Tooley's boatyard and departed for Ireland, spending a
long and leisurely summer exploring the Irish canals, which
were in about the same state of neglect as the English ones.
This gave Tom the material for his book *Green and Silver*.

Robert, now on his own, wrote letters to *The Times* and
many other publications announcing the formation of the
Association and asking for support. The initial subscription
had been set at one guinea and it remained at this low level
for several years. By the end of July Robert reported to Tom
that they had passed the 50 mark; by October, this had
trebled to 150 members.

It was not entirely smooth-going, however, since Charles
Hadfield decided to resign from the council in September,

ostensibly because of possible conflict of interests arising from his new appointment as Director of Publications at the Central Office of Information. Privately, he confessed that he and Aickman had taken an instant dislike to each other and Hadfield decided that they could not work together.

'It turned out that the three of us had quite different ideas – Rolt wanted to preserve an old way of life and traditional ways,' he now recalls. 'What Aickman wanted was rather difficult to say; what he seemed to want was a little bit of paradise, a touch of William Morris, a shelter from the modern world – and I didn't think for a moment there would be anything in it.'

Even though Frank Eyre stayed on for a while as treasurer and Richard Smith joined the council, Tom was upset by the resignation. 'The council seems to be dwindling to a dictatorship. Who remains?' he wrote to Robert.

There was by now a new aspect to their relationship in that Tom had placed his literary work in the hands of Robert's agency. After a slow start to his new career, Tom was writing books at the rate of about one each year. His philosophical treatise on modern society, *High Horse Riderless*, caused endless problems: the cover design was considered to be 'too sexy'. A collection of ghost stories, *Hear Not My Steps* (subsequently published as *Sleep no More*), had been doing the rounds of publishers, so Robert was delighted when he succeeded in placing it with Constable – though as he himself was a putative, as yet unpublished, writer of ghost stories it might have caused a ripple of jealousy.

At around this time two attractive and intelligent women became involved with the IWA who were to have a profound and far-reaching effect on the personal lives of the Rolts and the Aickmans. They were Sonia Smith and Elizabeth Jane Howard.

After their return from Ireland the Rolts lived in a caravan while work (which had fallen badly behind schedule) continued on *Cressy*. It was at this time that they met Sonia Smith, a former actress, who had become one of the unusual band of boating women during the war. The romantic, though extremely tough, life of working a pair of narrow-boats to aid the war effort seemed to appeal to actresses – Susan Wolfit, wife of the famous actor-manager Sir Donald, had been another volunteer. The recruits were given a little basic training before being teamed up with two other women and put in charge of their own pair of boats.

Sonia had met and married a strong, fair and handsome life-long boatman called George Smith, and in October the Rolts came across them on their boat *Halifax*. They spent an interesting evening, sitting in the compact, though beautifully fitted, traditional stern cabin. Mrs Smith and her husband were 'mines of information', Tom told Ray, and suggested that a special class of membership should be created since working boaters could not afford to pay a guinea a year from their low and uncertain earnings.

Tom was fascinated by Sonia (who was to become his second wife some years later) from the moment of their first meeting. He made a particular point of telling Robert about her knowledge of the ghost stories along the cut and of Crick tunnel's reputation as a haunted spot.

Mrs Smith's attractive, extrovert personality made her an excellent representative of working boaters' interests (few of them had any literacy). She soon became involved, as much as her peripatetic life style allowed, with the Association and joined the council in 1948.

With correspondence rapidly building up as new members joined and reports filtered through about threats to individual waterways, it became necessary to take on a part-time secretary to help at Gower Street. A girl recommended by Charles Hadfield lasted only a few weeks, no doubt because she could not satisfy Robert's exacting standards.

Robert turned to a friend, Elizabeth Jane Howard, who was looking for some income while she struggled to write her first novel. Although she was only twenty-four, she had already had a career as an actress – she trained at the London Mask Theatre and played repertory in Devon and Stratford-upon-Avon – and an unsuccessful marriage with Peter Scott, the naturalist and painter, who was also a friend of Robert's.

Robert – and not Robert alone – was entranced and

captivated by her striking good looks combined with a rare sensitivity and intelligence. 'Jane Howard was so beautiful that continuous problems arose,' he wrote afterwards. 'Little in the way of completely normal business was possible or sensible when she was in the room. I had previously thought that the power of Zuleika Dobson was exaggerated. I now learnt that it was not. Jane's presence had the effect of making everything else in life seem worthless and absurd beside her radiant identity. By merely existing, she promoted loves and hates which, through no fault of hers, left some who felt them fevered and wasted.'

Robert was passionately attracted to her, yet the work had to go on, starting with two mornings a week and increasing to several days, for which Jane, as she was always known, was paid a nominal amount. The administration was very efficient; since she did not have shorthand, Robert dictated his letters on to the typewriter. He never faltered, never made a mistake or changed his mind or the punctuation; after being interrupted by the telephone, he was quite capable of going straight on.

'The Association had no money in those days; most people regarded the whole enterprise as a non-starter – a few cranks who were only going to make a fuss about something which wasn't going to lead to anything,' she now recalls. 'The combination of Tom and Robert, while they were getting on with and approved of each other, was absolutely unbeatable because they were both highly coherent, filled with energy. Robert had the most amazing energy: he could work nearly all day and most of the night. They both really worked for the cause, although they weren't either of them easy men.'

One of Jane's early tasks was to produce the first IWA *Bulletin*, five pages of text closely typed on to a stencil and run off on absorbent paper – the first of an impressive series of newsletters to keep members informed, mostly written by Robert personally, which over the years were to become highly influential and one of the most effective campaigning weapons of the Association. By the time he retired, Robert estimated that the number of words he had contributed to the *Bulletins*, then numbering seventy, amounted to the equivalent of six or seven full-length novels.

The first *Bulletin* was, in fact, published only as a stop-gap awaiting the launch of a monthly magazine that Tom Rolt had agreed to edit with the intention of improving the Association's prestige, as well as helping to raise funds. Although the forthcoming publication was announced as the main item of news in the *Bulletin*, it was never produced, appearing to founder over the first difference of opinion between the two men.

They were unable to agree on the choice of name. Tom was set upon a workmanlike title such as *The Boatman* or *The Cut*, whereas Robert fancied something altogether more grandiose such as *Horizon* or *Voices* and petulantly refused to write for any magazine with a title that he compared with *The Builder and Plumber*.

'This conflict of wills regarding our title is really most distressing,' Tom wrote to Robert. 'In my opinion it is revealing the snag of having too small a council where the personal element counts to an extent that (a) members don't vote according to their honest judgement for fear of giving offence, or (b), if they do, the member outvoted feels unconvinced and may even smell some sinister connivance at work against him.'

This, written before the Association was a year old, foreshadowed the gulf that was to separate the two founders over the coming years in which Robert's deliberately auto-cratic, forceful style of leadership – aimed at achieving positive decisions from committees that he found meddle-some and ineffective – clashed with Tom's natural desire for a democratic movement.

Even so, this particular difference of opinion did not cloud their personal relationship and the friendship between the foursome continued to flourish. The Rolts stayed frequently at Gower Street, encouraged to use the spare room on the top floor whenever they needed to visit London – to see *Lady Windermere's Fan* in June, Benjamin Britten's *Peter Grimes* (highly prized seats) in October and for a pre-Christmas party which led Angela to rave over the Aickmans' 'bounteous hospitality'.

The end of 1946 brought ominous signs of threat to the existence of the waterways that seemed certain to increase as the legislation to establish the British Transport Commission passed through Parliament. 'Great Western Railways have come into the open with their aspiration to abandon the Kennet and Avon,' Robert told Tom before Christmas. 'Coming just before nationalisation, I feel that this step may pressage, or indeed accompany, a similar step with regard to the Stratford and possibly others.'

In the first *Bulletin* he had already identified three waterways as being particularly threatened: the Kennet and Avon (providing an unrivalled broadbeam route between the Thames at Reading and the Severn at Bristol and passing through superb countryside); the south Stratford (offering the only link between the Grand Union and the Avon since the river itself had become partially unnavigable); and the river Stour in Suffolk (made for ever memorable in the paintings of Constable). He urged all members living near any of these waterways 'to do everything in their power to arouse interest in the present disgraceful condition of the navigations and our efforts to have them improved'.

Robert himself had been bombarding the government with letters drawing attention to the deplorable state of the canals, and this resulted in the first significant political breakthrough when the IWA, still less than a year old, was invited to send a deputation to discuss their views on the Transport Bill, then at Select Committee stage in the House of Commons. The deputation would be received by Alfred Barnes, Minister of Transport in the Labour government led by Clement Attlee, after winning an enormous majority against Winston Churchill's Conservatives in the post-war general election.

Under the Bill Britain's entire railway and docks system – which had been controlled by the Ministry of Transport during the war – was to be nationalised and brought under a single mammoth organisation, the British Transport Commission. Since most of Britain's canals were owned by the railways, they were also to be nationalised, perhaps more by accident than design.

The Association's public profile had also been raised when Sir Alan Patrick Herbert, MP – universally and fondly regarded as the average man's politician with an unusual sympathy for the environment and a renowned sense of humour – agreed to become president. At the same time Peter Scott became vice-president along with the Earl of Portsmouth, who had campaigned for the use of waterways in agriculture, and Algernon Newton, RA, famous for his painting of waterscapes. It was decided that the Association's deputation would be led by Sir Alan and would consist of Aickman and Rolt, Captain Richard Smith and Sonia Smith. Tom undertook to find Sonia wherever she might be on her travels around the canals, to tell her that she had been appointed a member of the deputation. He came across her and George on the pair of boats *Cairo* and *Warwick*, refuelling at Braunston, the major boating centre near Daventry, Northamptonshire.

As the exact date and time of the meeting with the Minister of Transport were not yet known, Tom made elaborate arrangements for keeping in touch. Whenever the Smiths were in London they were to telephone Robert; otherwise, their progress would be monitored by Bill at Cowroast (on the Grand Union near Tring) and by Mr Veater at Sutton Stop (the junction at Hawkesbury of the Coventry and north Oxford canals).

In the end, this system of canal telegraph was frustrated by the exceptionally bitter winter that hit the country, paralysing not only the canals, but also for a time the roads and railways. This fearful winter was etched into people's minds for years to come, as the prolonged power cuts and fuel shortages produced a return to near wartime conditions. Many blamed this winter, during which canal transport was halted for weeks, for hastening the collapse of the remaining waterways traffic.

In late February 1947 Tom drove over to Bugbrooke junction, Warwick, and found the Smiths ice-bound at the Cape, below Hatton's flight of twenty-one widebeam locks, the longest in Britain. Reports confirmed that the whole canal system was impassable except for one vital coal route from Atherstone to Coventry power station – this had been smashed clear by ice-breakers preceding a convoy of a dozen boats, pulled by an impressive team of horses.

On the morning of the meeting, 5 March, Tom was particularly unlucky. Having to catch an early train from Banbury, he was awoken by the alarm clock in the cold dark of the winter morning, dressed in his unfamiliar city clothes and staggered out into the boatyard to find that there had been a fresh fall of snow overnight. Floundering through it, he discovered that the yard gate was still locked and, instead of climbing it, decided to take a short-cut across the frozen canal.

His left leg immediately disappeared through the new blanket of snow into an icy hole – he had picked the one place where the surface had been broken the previous evening to water a horse. With no time to spare, he had to continue with a trouser leg and shoe soaking in freezing water – hardly the ideal way in which to approach his first meeting with a Minister of the Crown.

The Minister was presented with a memorandum (see Appendix A) drafted by Tom and approved by the IWA council, which pressed for assurance and action on ten straightforward, practical points – this laid the foundations of the Association's policy for many years ahead, in particular the demand that no single navigation should be abandoned until its potential for recreational as well as commercial use had been studied. Even at this early stage the IWA was virtually alone in foreseeing the potential of the waterways for leisure and tourism, with the possibility of attracting visitors from overseas. They also pressed for a rationalisation of the hopelessly outdated system of tolls still applied to the canals (equivalent to the road tolls abolished long ago) which prevented the commercial carriers from competing fairly with road hauliers.

The deputation came away reasonably satisfied with the courteous hearing that they had received. Alfred Barnes told them that the Association might be invited to join a Users' Consultative Council that he proposed to attach to the future Canals and Docks Executive, and he emphasised that 'this would not be a mere façade but would play a real and vital part in the management of the industry'. Being still novices in political negotiation, the delegates did not then realise how many more times in the future they were to hear similar blandishments before eventually, after many years of fierce campaigning, any positive action would be taken.

In the House of Commons, questioned by two MPs, Elwyn Jones and Ian Mikardo, the Minister refused to give a general assurance that no waterway would be abandoned before the setting-up of the Transport Commission; he added, however, that the Kennet and Avon specifically was not being considered. Concern about the future of this canal had become so widespread that a public meeting was held at Newbury Town Hall, packed to capacity, at which Aickman shared the platform with four local MPs and gave a highly praised speech – the first of many hundreds that he was to give over the next two decades.

In the spring the Aickmans felt that they needed to take a break away from the growing pressures on their time and went on holiday to the Isle of Man – it nearly turned into a tragic disaster in which Ray could easily have lost her life. At Port Soderick on Easter Sunday Robert was standing on a ridge of rock when a wave suddenly broke right over him, carrying away his glasses and leaving him with little vision as he was so short-sighted. As Ray went to his rescue, an even more formidable wave crashed over them, hurling Robert to the ground.

As he recovered he found blood coming from various gashes on his body but, far more worrying, he looked around for Ray, who was nowhere to be seen. She emerged from below the rocks 'looking like a Catholic martyr' with blood pouring from a bad head wound, having been lifted by the wave and hurled twenty feet away into a lagoon.

'Her escape without other injury, even her escape with her life, verges on the miraculous,' Robert explained to Tom. 'She appears to have been thrown through the air instead of rolling down the jagged rock, and to have been deposited more or less exactly into a small pool of sufficient depth to break her fall.'

'It seems quite clear to me that you have somehow contrived to upset the Island gods,' Tom replied. 'I would advise you to keep away from the foreshore until you have performed some sort of propitiation.'

Despite their frightening experience, which caused an immediate return to London for Robert's spare glasses, the Aickmans were enthralled by the majestic, mountainous scenery and booked for a return visit in July with the Rolts. Over this period there was an almost uninterrupted exchange of letters between the two couples – as often about personal incidents as IWA business – reflecting their desire, as close friends, to share each other's plans and thoughts, and a natural inclination on the part of both men to express their views in writing, occasionally verging on verbosity, sometimes erupting into spontaneous witticisms. In an age when the telephone was already overtaking the post as the method of communication for many people, this almost daily correspondence was encouraged by the Rolts' lack of ready access to any telephone and Robert's own preference for the written word.

One of Tom's letters contained exciting news. The Great Western Railway had, after repeated requests, at last granted permission for him to navigate the north Stratford canal, which had become impassable a year or so earlier when a former lift bridge at Lifford Lane, near King's Norton, had been replaced by a fixed bridge at too low a level to allow the passage of boats. A well-disposed member of the House of Lords, Lord Methuen, obtained an assurance from the Transport Ministry that the bridge would be lifted, subject to twenty-four hours' notice of intention to travel along the route. It had become imperative that the IWA now demonstrated that a demand existed and tested GWR's ability to meet this undertaking.

Plans were put in hand for the first great campaigning cruise by the Association. The past months of letter-writing to the national newspapers, coupled with the outstanding success of the Newbury meeting, had confirmed the public's dormant, yet potentially enormous, interest in the long-neglected waterways. Robert had already revealed a natural flair for publicity and sensed that the Lifford Lane bridge-lifting exercise would appeal to the media – he appreciated that this first victory over bureaucratic indifference in forcing GWR to carry out their statutory obligation to provide navigation could be turned into a newsworthy event and focus public attention on the deplorable state of the canals.

Tom reacted violently against the proposal to turn his voyage on *Cressy* into a publicity stunt. 'Personally, I loathe anything of this sort,' he told Robert. 'It is also extremely difficult to organise because it is impossible to say at which time we shall reach the King's Norton end . . . A greater objection is that in my experience, local reports, even if they do make a story, always contrive to treat it in the worst possible way, and would probably do more harm than good.'

Robert joined *Cressy* at Kingswood, the junction with the Grand Union, on Monday 19 May, and they set out along the north Stratford canal preceded by an empty working boat, *Bilster*, which GWR had chartered in their eagerness to be seen to be helpful. The idea was that *Bilster* would clear a passage along the disused, heavily silted route, but this proved to be a disaster. Although *Bilster* left four hours earlier, it soon ran aground and was overtaken by *Cressy*, which had a shallower draught. After strenuous efforts by twelve railwaymen and a farm tractor it was refloated, only to become jammed again. This time *Cressy* was able to tow it off, but then it became completely wedged under a bridge. The IWA party continued, leaving *Bilster* to be set upon by vandals.

The following day Lifford Lane was reached at 5 p.m., the exact time planned by Tom. Spectators lined the towing-path all the way, eager would-be helpers were on hand, and the excited noise of the crowd at the bridge could be heard some distance away. Ignoring Tom's objections, Robert had alerted the media and widely promoted the event. Three Birmingham daily papers covered the entire voyage; four national dailies devoted two columns to their reports together with pictures (this at a time when severe shortage of newsprint restricted newspapers to only a few pages).

'As to general publicity, however distasteful it may be to

me personally, I am bound to admit that the Stratford episode has proved the force of your argument,' Tom acknowledged. Lifford Lane bridge itself had been jacked up just enough to permit *Cressy* to pass underneath, and Tom prepared a thorough report, illustrated by Angela's photographs, which proved beyond doubt that the canal was being maintained far below the required statutory standard. The report was delivered to the Ministry of Transport.

A week later, IWA's first annual general meeting was held: the original brave band of six had swollen to the sixty people who attended out of the still larger membership. With Peter Scott in the chair, Aickman reminded members that the Association had been run without any kind of payment from his own flat and almost entirely by voluntary effort; while offering to continue in this way for one further year, he urged them to find a better solution.

This small, badly under-funded body which had not existed a year earlier, and for which there had been no precedent in this field of activity, had achieved a measure of recognition for the waterways – a great, yet decayed national heritage – in Parliament and in the media, and through them in the eyes of a public that was becoming increasingly concerned about the problem.

Last Passage through Standedge Tunnel

After the assault on the Stratford canal, Tom continued in *Cressy* westwards on an ambitious voyage for the summer which would take him back to his boating roots. He was determined to fulfil a youthful dream formed seventeen years earlier to take *Cressy* back along the Llangollen, across Telford's immense and awe-inspiring aqueduct spanning the Dee valley at Pont Cysyllte, and to return to the place on the far side where the boat had been built during the First World War.

He had been on board *Cressy* – his first boating experience ever, and one that was to shape his future career – on a Sunday in 1930 when Kyrle Willans had taken the boat on its initial steam trials after being converted at a yard near Frankton junction. Frustratingly, they had to turn back before reaching Pont Cysyllte, although they had come tantalisingly close to it. Shortly afterwards the Willans family moved from the Welsh Borders to the Potteries, and *Cressy* was transferred to the Trent and Mersey, leaving the Llangollen far away.

By 1947 the return voyage to the Llangollen had become a daring and uncertain venture. No boats had travelled to Llangollen since the beginning of the war, and in 1944 the London, Midland and Scottish Railway had obtained Parliamentary powers to abandon the navigation. The canal remained in limited water only because it continued to be used as a feeder from the Horseshoe Falls at Llantisilio, above the town of Llangollen where water was taken from the river to supply reservoirs at Hurleston junction, providing the main source for the Shropshire Union to Chester and

Ellesmore Port. Monsanto Chemicals in North Wales also drew on substantial quantities of water from the canal.

The railway company granted permission to the Rolts to use the canal, but only on the strict understanding that it was at their own risk – if *Cressy* suffered damage resulting from the poor conditions or became totally stranded, then it would be entirely the Rolts' own responsibility and they would have no redress against the company. Knowing that it was going to be a difficult, if not impossible, journey, Tom equipped the boat with new spare strong lines and a set of pulley blocks.

At Nantwich he was delighted to find that a small cabin cruiser called *Heron*, owned by the Grundy family of Liverpool, was also planning an attack on the Llangollen. Their two sons Christopher and Martin would provide additional muscle power, and both of them were to become intensely involved with the waterways movement over the next decades.

The progress of the two boats over the lower part of the route was extremely slow and hazardous, with everything against them: the sides of the lock chambers had caved in, the water level was very low, and the canal was totally overgrown with weed. For much of the way *Cressy* was physically bow-hauled, towing *Heron* behind. The block and pulleys were frequently used to force the boats out of the locks. At one point, wide enough to wind (turn) *Cressy*, Tom seriously considered abandoning the attempt, but he decided to press on as far as the flight of locks at Grindley Brook.

The conditions here deteriorated still further. 'The locks here are in a shocking state. Narrower than most when built, frost had pushed in the walls and copings so that they are all shapes,' Tom wrote to Robert. *Cressy* wedged firmly at the entrance of the bottom lock and had to be pulled out backwards with the block and pulley. They spent the day chipping the 'high spots' off the hull with a hammer and wood chisel, and then smeared it all over with grease. Finally, by charging the locks at speed, they managed to make the ascent.

The effect on *Cressy*'s wooden hull of using it as a

battering-ram may well have been part of the reason for its subsequent decline. At the time, however, it seemed worth the risk as the pound above the flight proved to be easier and free from weed as the canal passed through the glorious open countryside of the Shropshire lake district and, at last, they made a steady pace to Ellesmere. Here they were stranded again by weed so thick that only a horse could have pulled the boat through it, and later their problems were compounded when they found that a burst culvert at Chirk had caused the water supply to be cut off.

'This canal makes a shocking and lamentable sight, the more so as the dereliction is not yet fundamental, though it soon will be unless something is done,' Tom reported from Ellesmere.

The two craft were now stuck for many weeks before there was sufficient water to make the return passage. Fortunately, they enjoyed superb summer weather and Tom took the opportunity to explore on foot the conditions further up the canal. He became acquainted with the local engineer, who was canal-minded and 'talks hopefully of the canal being used again when it is nationalised'.

The local man complained that bureaucracy had taken over to such an extent that all important decisions were made by a railway manager based at Crewe, and he cited the way in which the adjoining Montgomery canal had been abandoned between Newtown and Welshpool. There had been a small leak on an aqueduct which the local engineer knew that he could prevent by pumping cement into the masonry: Crewe counter-ruled that the water was to be piped permanently over the aqueduct, a far more expensive and complex task, involving sub-contractors and preventing navigation.

Tom visited the Chester office, which also proved to be understanding and, 'speaking unofficially', hopeful of improvement to the canal after nationalisation. They arranged for sufficient water to be let down from Llantisilio for the two boats to return eventually to Hurleston. Tom remained determined in his ambition to try again to reach Pont Cysyllte, probably the next year.

Travelling along the Trent and Mersey, *Cressy* now

crossed to the far side of the country, reaching Gayton, the junction of the Grand Union and Northampton arm, on 4 September. Within an hour of tying they were passed by George and Sonia Smith, carrying a load south. Gayton had been chosen as the Rolts' winter mooring; they had a very busy period ahead in making the final preparations for the first ever waterways exhibition, due to open on 14 October at the Mansard Gallery of Heal's renowned furnishing store in Tottenham Court Road, London.

The Mansard Gallery was at that time one of the most popular and best known venues for staging exhibitions of arts and crafts, and it was fortunate that Aickman had run across one of the store's employees, who recalled that Antony Heal was an old friend of Tom Rolt, going back to the earliest days of the Vintage Sports Car Club at the Phoenix. Both Tom and Angela seized on the idea as a marvellous opportunity to interest the wider public in the traditional life of the narrowboat people, and the timing proved to be perfect.

No one had ever before tried to bring together a representational display of canal life and the Rolts picked on Gayton as the best point to tackle this task as it remained one of the busiest places on the canals and had a good train link to London. They hoped to persuade passing boats to loan suitable items, and the local district engineer, Charles Hadlow, had had an interest in the history of waterways for a long time. He subsequently played a major role in setting up the first national waterways museum at Stoke Bruerne (on the far side of Blisworth tunnel from Gayton).

Tom and Angela moved to London a few days before the exhibition's opening, and physically assembled and placed the materials on display. They had achieved a marvellous collection representing the colourful and traditional ways of narrowboat life, never before seen by the general public. There was a large triangular wooden cratch, picked out in a sharp red, green and yellow diamond pattern, from the bow of a boat, where it would have held up the line of planks running back to the stern, providing both a walkway and support to sheets of canvas protecting the cargo. As an example of an ornament from the tiny stern cabins that were home to generations of boating families, there was the Rolts' own much prized Measham teapot; these were large ornate ceramic pots, decorated with a favourite motto like 'Love at Home', produced at Measham on the Ashby canal. Similarly, there was a can and pitcher from Buckby on the Grand Union, painted with stylised roses and castles; these contained fresh drinking water and usually stood on the cabin roof.

There were also glittering horse brasses and an intricately patterned lace cap for the horse; a motor boat's brightly polished brass tiller bar and pin and its butty's painted wooden tiller, curved like a scimitar; painstakingly woven ropework that hung from the tillers; right-angled metal windlasses, each with a different size of eye to fit the varied paddle gear of the locks; a wooden shaft painted in red, white and blue stripes that followed the round contours like a barber's pole; a stunning collection of women's prim bonnets, tiered skirts and lace shawls and men's neat and practical corduroy jackets, trousers pulled in like leggings, and thick leather belts into which a windlass could be tucked.

These examples of canal artefacts, still then in everyday use, were displayed on one side of the exhibition. On the other were dramatic black-and-white photographs (taken by Angela and James Sutherland, who had become IWA treasurer) contrasting the fascinating and thriving life of the working boats on busy canals with those in the last stages of decay and neglect.

Sir Alan Herbert opened the exhibition – the first major public event of the IWA's own creation – and the public flocked to see it. Heal's claimed that it broke all records for the gallery, attracting as many as a thousand people on some days. The impact of its message, displayed in the centre of London, was immense, and the organisers were pressed into keeping the collection together so that it could be toured around the country. For a year it proved to be just as big a draw in Birmingham, Bristol, Stoke, Luton and other cities, but it was a constant drain on the energies of the Rolts and others, who often had to make repairs to the displays damaged in transit.

The atmosphere of goodwill and congratulation generated by the exhibition was soon shattered when Robert received an unexpected and highly personal inquiry from Tom. After protesting in the opening paragraph that he did not believe 'in concerning myself with the private affairs of those around me', he complained that he, as honorary secretary, had been 'deliberately misled' into believing that the paid secretary, Elizabeth Jane Howard, had been working in the office as usual. 'On the question of how Jane spent her canal holiday and who with, I could not care less,' he added.

Robert replied that there had been no deception, though admitted that he had been at fault in not telling Tom exactly where Jane was and what she was doing. 'The case was a very difficult one; and I hope that you know me well enough to give my actions the benefit of the doubt, knowing, as I must do, more about the circumstances.'

Jane, he explained, had been working for more than a year without any break, going far beyond the services which a typist receiving two pounds ten shillings a week could be expected to give. He praised her initiative in bringing in the Association's president and vice-president and claimed that she had recruited a quarter of the members. Despite this, Jane had no personal experience of boating and was very keen to take a waterways holiday, so Robert and she had hired a thirty-foot motor boat and cruised the Thames as far as Lechlade.

Robert acknowledged that Tom and Angela would not be completely happy about the situation. 'I, on the other hand, could hardly refuse to help her with the project,' he added, referring to the 'exceptionally difficult state' of her personal affairs which, he believed, would be sorted out before long to her own and everyone else's relief.

Correspondence about such a sensitive, personal matter should have been terminated then, but Tom was not satisfied and wrote back, complaining that he still felt that he had been misled. 'I do not think that this was right and, as I said before, it damages the feeling of mutual confidence without which a concern like IWA cannot carry on, at least not happily.'

The matter rumbled on between the two men until two weeks later Angela decided to intervene in the most bitter terms: 'I *do not hate* Jane. Indeed I admire her brain and her beauty immensely but, from the day we all four went to the opera together, Jane has never spoken a civil word to me . . . Apart from one conversation with Ray (which I now regret) I have never discussed Jane with anyone . . . Why you should think that Tom and I want to interfere in your affairs, God only knows.'

The relationship between Tom and Robert was now showing definite signs of strain. Tom had previously raised some nagging doubts about the accuracy of the Association's book-keeping which, after Robert's explanation, he was obliged to retract. Next, he complained rather pettily that a meeting in London had been arranged without prior consultation about the exact date so that, inconveniently, he would be forced to travel to the city twice within a few days.

There had, in fact, been four months' notice of the meeting, which was not the kind of occasion that could be moved to suit everyone. It was to be a dinner at the Carlton Club, arranged through Peter Scott's influence with Sir Cyril Hurcomb (later Lord Hurcomb), who had been designated as the first chairman of the British Transport Commission when it came into existence on 1 January 1948. It was a privileged and rare opportunity for such a fledgling organisation to present their case to the man who was going to be at the top of this immense and powerful nationalised industry.

On the night, the dinner at the Carlton Club was not regarded by any of the IWA members as being particularly effective; they recognised that Hurcomb, already in his sixties, would have more than enough problems in becoming familiar with the vast national railway network (not yet shorn of the thousands of miles to be axed by Beeching in the 1960s). Tom held forth in detail about the state of the Llangollen and explained that the abandonment Act created a threat that any local council could erect new bridges or culverts that would prevent navigation. Robert asked Hurcomb why the Derby canal – one of the few not owned by a railway – had not been brought into the nationalised system since it provided a vital link between the Trent and Mersey and the Erewash. 'Ah, that was one I managed to miss,' replied Hurcomb.

As the evening progressed, it became clear that the chairman had little knowledge of or interest in the waterways, and the conversation switched to bird-watching, which Hurcomb pursued enthusiastically around the Grand Union's reservoirs at Marsworth, near Tring.

After the dinner Robert sent Hurcomb a copy of the memorandum already presented to the Minister of Transport, together with a letter stressing the Association's key targets. Firstly, before any large-scale changes, including abandonments, were made to the waterways there should be a completely independent inquiry; secondly, there should be a *national* canal policy so that *all* navigable waterways came under one management, thus encouraging a standard system of tolls and trading practices, instead of the existing chaotic and unco-ordinated situation. So, for the first time, Robert floated the concept of a national and specialist waterways authority which was to become one of the cardinal points of IWA policy in the next decade. Interestingly, the main emphasis of Robert's letter was on developing traffic and improving the plight of the working boatmen (including a reference to their poor diet), since it was far too early for the leisure potential to be taken seriously.

Though the dinner may have seemed unproductive at the time, it had ensured that the Association's views had been heard at the highest level and the message was passed down the line to Sir Reginald Hill (another retired civil servant with little or no knowledge of the waterways), the newly appointed chairman of the Docks and Inland Waterways Executive, BTC's waterways division. A member of the Executive, Robert Davidson, who became something of an ally of the IWA, reported to Robert that Hurcomb had set up a meeting to discuss their proposals.

As the Association approached its second anniversary, all

its activities in every way had increased immensely in response to the demands of a rapidly growing and enthusiastic membership. The *Bulletin* was appearing regularly and increasing in size with each issue, monitoring threats to waterways all over the country: the Derby canal, the Chelmer and Blackwater in Essex, and the Kennet and Avon. A cruise along the Grand Union from Solihull to Kingswood had attracted 130 members; the first of a series of Christmas parties (with a show of amateur films of the waterways) had been attended by 100.

The council had been joined by two members distinguished in their own way: Samuel Barlow of the largest commercial carriers then operating, S. E. Barlow and Company, and Lord Bingham, Colonel of the Coldstream Guards – 'Pat' to his friends. The latter had come into Gower Street one day accompanied by his eldest son 'Lucky' John (the future 7th Earl of Lucan, who mysteriously disappeared after the unsolved murder of his children's nanny, Sandra Rivett, in 1975), then a teenager recently returned from wartime evacuation to an enormously rich American family, and they consulted Elizabeth Jane Howard about routes and conditions for one of the many holidays they were to spend on the narrowboat *Hesperus*.

Taking the chair again at the AGM on 29 May 1948, Peter Scott praised the Association's progress; yet Robert Aickman reported that there had been no improvement in the central organisation. One of the spare rooms in his flat still served as a rent-free office; indeed it had become known as 'the IWA room' and was stacked with files and papers. The work load was becoming very onerous, involving much travelling around the country, and most of it was undertaken without remuneration by Rolt and himself. They again said that they were prepared to continue for one more year – and only for one more year – to allow time for funds to be raised to improve the organisation which was suffering from the lack of labour and resources.

One step aimed at relieving these pressures was to set up a Midlands branch. Birmingham, being at the centre of the

inland waterways, had attracted many members and generated much activity, and there had been a move afoot for
some time to form a local branch. Lord Bingham and Sonia
Smith joined Robert and Tom at a well-attended inaugural
meeting at the Market Hotel in Birmingham which started
with an embarrassing hitch. The man who had taken the
initiative in trying to set up the branch and was regarded as
chairman-designate rose shakily to his feet, 'turned completely and visibly green', and froze into silence. Robert,
who was sitting next to him on the platform and had never
failed to say the right word at the right time, saved the
occasion. In the end, Arthur Goodland, who was general
manager of Birmingham Corporation's Gas Department,
became chairman, and Cyril Taplin treasurer.

The formation of branches – and others were established
in the north-east, the Fenlands and the Kennet and Avon
area within twelve months – was to prove a mixed blessing.
While they relieved the headquarters of the need to meet
popular demand for local social events, Aickman was often
unhappy about their tendency to take an independent line
on waterways issues since he believed fervently that any
overt split in the Association's views would be seized upon
and exploited by the opposition.

'Everything depended on finding the right individuals to
run the branch,' he wrote years later. 'Certainly the branches
added greatly to my knowledge of life in general . . . I
harangued them, I went to their parties, I stayed with their
officers and their families. I never passed a week without
writing them long letters.'

Indeed, Robert's worst fears were confirmed almost
immediately when the brand new Midlands branch showed
greater concern about boating facilities on Earlswood reservoirs (which supplied the canal) than in the Stratford navigation itself, for which the IWA had fought so hard at
Lifford Lane. 'I feel it is very important that you and I take
every opportunity to put down a heresy which, if we fail to
do so, will lead to the Association speaking with completely
disunited voices,' he urged Tom. 'The whole incident does
not encourage the formation of further branches.'

Rolt supported him totally on this issue and drafted a closely argued four-page letter to be sent to the Birmingham officers. Despite this, the affair dragged on for some time, creating additional work and involving both of them in emergency visits to persuade the committee to fall into line.

For Tom this meant further inconvenient interruptions to his year's boating on *Cressy*, which he was taking down the Gloucester and Sharpness. There always seemed to be a pressing need, he complained, to be at a certain place by a certain time, which made him feel anxious if he was not available to pick up post every day or two. It was completely contrary to the way of life that he had chosen to adopt.

'Between us we make, I think, a pretty formidable combination,' he wrote to Robert, 'and if we were to devote ourselves wholly to the IWA I can see no limit to what we might achieve. But is it worth it? Personally, since I have a disposition which dislikes personal publicity and applause and has no desire to be a public figure, I am only interested in results and doubt whether this justifies the sacrifice of a way of life for one that is so alien to my nature.'

Robert, meanwhile, was making plans for a most ambitious, adventurous and lengthy cruise with Elizabeth Jane Howard later in the summer. Over six weeks, starting from Stone in Staffordshire, he intended to undertake a round trip along the Macclesfield and Huddersfield canals to Leeds, returning over the Pennines on the Leeds and Liverpool. Like Llangollen, the Huddersfield Narrow had been abandoned by LMSR under the 1944 Act, so permission had to be obtained to make the passage, which included the longest tunnel ever built in Britain – Standedge, over three miles long.

The route itself – completely unknown to any of the IWA officers – offered unpredictable problems and tough conditions; in addition, the only suitable boat then available from the very limited range of craft offered for hire at that time had a suspect hull. *Ailsa Craig* was rented from R. H. Wyatt, who had just set up the first pleasure-boat business on the northern canals, and it was believed to have been a former ship's lifeboat of unusually slim dimensions on to which a cramped cabin, containing four berths, had been built.

Robert and Jane were planning to undertake the whole trip, for part of which they would be joined by James and Anthea Sutherland, recently married. James was known affectionately by his friends as Teacup, and signed his letters with beautiful illustrations of that object.

The Rolts were also invited, but Tom prudently rejected the idea of joining for the entire six weeks. He felt that it was too long a period for the same group of people to cohabit in very confined quarters and suggested that Robert and Jane 'might prefer to proceed as a duo for a time'. Nevertheless, the prospect of Standedge was too attractive to refuse, so the boat would have six people on board over this period and Robert decided to purchase a tent to provide overflow accommodation.

No doubt feeling that the excursion was in the interests of the waterways campaign, Robert bought the tent as an item of IWA equipment and told Tom that it would be made available to members at a rental of ten shillings a week. He and James were paying this sum for the six weeks; in addition, 'the hon. treasurer has himself purchased two collapsing beds for use in the tent . . . and he asserts that these particular beds are well known to him and the absolute acme of comfort'.

'The treasurer is commended for the purchase of the "collapsing beds",' replied Tom. 'I trust that they do not live up to their title in too literal a manner.' However, he was not so amused at the way in which the tent had been acquired; he did not approve of debiting its cost to the IWA, nor of the ethics of doing so, and suggested that it should be purchased by the group and afterwards advertised for sale. The tent, in fact, was to prove still more unpopular with Tom on the night he came to use it.

Bulletin 15 announced that between 7 August and 25 September, during the absence of the chairman, hon. secretary and hon. treasurer on their 'cruise of inspection' through the northern waterways, the Association's offices would be closed except for the receipt of money, despatch of literature and essential business. The stand-in work was, presumably, to be performed by Ray.

BTC had not only granted permission for the journey but the Executive had also promised, in view of the poor state of the canal, that a gang would be posted at the lowest lock of the Huddersfield Narrow to assist them along this section.

The *Ailsa Craig* party found the approach along the Ashton difficult and slow; they encountered a great deal of underwater debris, and daylight had almost disappeared in a torrential Manchester downpour. They arrived late on a Friday afternoon at the bottom lock, feeling depressed and despondent, and discovered that there was no gang and that the gates were padlocked. Fortunately, a friendly watchman on a nearby mill allowed them to moor in safety on a firm bank until they could continue after the weekend.

It was still raining steadily on Monday morning, but this time the gates stood open and a gang of twelve men were sheltering under a tarpaulin, enjoying a breakfast fry-up. The reason for the Executive's concern became apparent as the boat rose through the first lock and moved into the pound towards the next lock: a strong rope was attached to the bow and the gang physically hauled *Ailsa Craig* over the shallow course, its hull grinding and shuddering on the rough surface.

As the boat rose in the fourth lock, Anthea looked inside the cabin and saw water rising rapidly above the floor; the hull must have been holed while being dragged along the previous section. Everyone dashed on board, seizing their possessions (enough for six weeks' holiday, including books, typewriter and paper), and emptied them on to the lockside while crowds of gaping spectators gathered from the stark granite mills surrounding the canal.

By the time the water had reached the level of the banks, the gang managed to haul the sinking boat out of the lock; closing the gates of the next lock, they raised the bottom paddles and emptied the pound entirely of water, leaving the *Ailsa Craig* forlornly stranded on oozing, slimy mud like a dying seal. Not being flat-bottomed like a narrowboat, it started to heel over and the crew rushed to shore it up with struts and built a rough jetty of flotsam across the mud. The rain was still ceaselessly descending as the group, now totally drenched, looked around and found that they were alone – the gang had vanished and the sightseers drifted away into the curtain of rain.

That afternoon, Robert dashed off a letter to Sir Reginald Hill, and the locals started to re-emerge out of the rain with kind offers of help, including free tickets to the evening's performance at Ashton music hall. The managers of the cotton mills were not so pleased to have a stranded boat as they drew water from the canal (the only reason why it had been kept in water) and production had had to cease. No doubt this explained the exceptionally rapid response to Robert's cry for help; within twenty-four hours Wilf, the foreman in charge of the canal, and two Merseyside ship-wrights arrived. A day later, the boat was refloated and set out again along the Huddersfield, making better progress this time under the watchful eye of Wilf. Even so, it took five days to push and pull through the seventy-four locks on the twenty miles route – and it never stopped raining for long.

At Diggle station, they were joined by the Rolts. Ahead lay Standedge tunnel, one of the great triumphs of the eighteenth-century canal builders – it was driven through hard rock at a greater depth than any of the other major tunnels and is nearly twice as long as Blisworth (the longest now open to traffic). The fact that it took twelve years to build seems a relative success bearing in mind that it had to be excavated entirely by hand, using primitive tools and faint illumination; unlike the construction method used for other long tunnels, it was not possible to drive many shafts from above.

As *Ailsa Craig*, a small craft with an unreliable engine on a rotting and patched hull, approached the black half-circle of the entrance beneath the rising scree of a Pennine hill, the individuals on board must have felt apprehensive at undertaking a passage which had been made only rarely in past years, but if they were frightened no one admitted it – they were more intent on what lay beyond.

Once inside the portal, the boat chugged noisily further and further into the utter blackness, the half circle of daylight behind growing smaller and dimmer, telescoped to a tiny dot and finally extinguished. Ahead, a yellow beam from the headlamp reflected off water as thick and putrid as molten tar and the uneven face of the rock walls cast weird and ghostly shadows. Suddenly a dull pounding noise, like a hammer beating on an anvil, started in the far distance and quickly advanced on the frail boat, echoing along the empty tunnel and growing into a deafening, thunderous roar as the fiery sparks and acrid smoke of a passing train poured through a side passage linking to the adjoining railway tunnel.

The rock walls were jagged and posed a constant hazard to the shaky sides of *Ailsa Craig*. At places the tunnel opened into a wider section more like a natural than a man-made cavern; then in the middle the walls narrowed and the boat became wedged. Tom calmly advised them that they had two choices: either to go back laboriously or to push forward. Fortunately, Jane, who was steering, was able to reverse and free the boat so that someone could crawl along the roof and gradually prise off the rubbing strakes (protective strips of wood) from the rotten hull, thus reducing the width just enough to enable them to continue forward.

After two hours the crew began to discern a faint glimmer of daylight through the swirling sulphurous smoke from the passing steam trains, and the end was in sight. They emerged as blackened as coal miners and, having few washing facilities on board, they took a train to Huddersfield where, at the George Hotel, they wallowed in the best hot baths that anyone could remember.

Trauma was not over for the Rolts, however, who had to spend their first night in the tent. On a bleak piece of land, surrounded by belching mill chimneys, they erected the tent, checking that the field was empty of animals and rejoicing that, at last, the evening had turned fine and sunny.

As they insinuated themselves in to the camp beds within the narrow triangle of canvas, the first light drops started to fall and the wind began to stir. Before long, the rain was lashing down, driven horizontally by a fierce gale; above the sound of the storm, Tom and Angela became aware of the heavy breathing and shifting feet of animals nudging around the guy ropes. With the tent in danger of collapsing over them, Tom stumbled out into the wet and mud, drove away a herd of bullocks and repitched the tent, swearing in no uncertain terms that he would never, ever again sleep in one after this trip was over.

4

Canal Sold to the Highest Bidder

The autumn of 1948 brought a totally new and unexpected problem before the leaders of the still fledgling Association; one that was far removed from the excitement of canal-busting along the Llangollen and the Huddersfield, and from the political manoeuvering at Westminster – the privately owned Basingstoke canal was being put up for sale at an auction.

The canal had been constructed under an Act of 1778 linking Basingstoke with the river Wey (which itself had been navigable since the mid-seventeenth century) and then with the Thames. A plan to carry the route right through to Southampton had foundered and the original company was wound up in 1869, since when there had been a complicated legal situation with the private owners in conflict with Surrey County Council over responsibility for the maintenance of bridges.

The news that the canal was to be auctioned (on the decease of the latest owner, who had been making some efforts to improve conditions and attract more traffic) immediately created widespread public interest which flared up in the national newspapers, largely because of the canal's situation in the prosperous commuter belt and its proximity to London, out of proportion to its importance compared with the potentially more threatening problems elsewhere.

The temptation for the IWA to acquire 'its own canal', and demonstrate how to run it, was great, but the council wisely decided that they were in no position to consider the step. For one thing, the articles of association did not permit them to enter into business; for another, they simply had insufficient funds. It was thought that a price in the region of £6,000–9,000 would be needed for success at the auction scheduled for 1 March 1949, and then it would take substantial capital to make the canal viable again for commercial and pleasure boating.

Given the right level of investment, the Association felt that the canal could be restored successfully as its beautiful route passed through an area of growing prosperity and it would attract traffic from the Thames (especially for the safe flood-free moorings it offered), already established as a pleasure-boating waterway. None other than Kyrle Willans, now a member of the IWA, pressed strongly the case for the Basingstoke's leisure potential and he wrote a feature in *Country Life* on these lines.

Another member, L. A. 'Teddy' Edwards, who lived at Ashtead, Surrey (in later years, he published the most authoritative guide to Britain's waterways), took responsibility for co-ordinating the Association's role. Although individual enthusiasm for saving the canal was widespread, this needed to be organised as official attitudes were opposed to it. Local authorities would have liked to purchase and fill in the canal, perhaps retaining a small part as a boating park. Letters in the local press suggested that it could be turned into a 35-mile-long motorcycling track, free from roads.

A public meeting at Woking, organised by Edwards, was held on a bitterly cold night and the atmosphere was depressing. Local authority representatives ('who, armed with vast folios of documents, assured the meeting that they spoke solely in a personal capacity') tried to distort the main issue by saying that the canal provided a breeding ground for mosquitoes. None of the planners seemed capable of visualising its future as a fine linear park, ideally placed close to London.

At the end of the meeting a Basingstoke Canal Committee was set up with the simple objective of making the canal 'navigable and available for both commercial and pleasure craft'. Edwards was elected secretary and the committee, which included several IWA stalwarts such as Cyril Styring (who promised a donation of £1,000), C. G. B. Poulter and Christopher Grundy, was joined by a new name, Mrs Joan

Marshall of Fleet, Hampshire. Although the Association saw
this body as a way of keeping in touch with the progress of
the sale, there was no formal link or representation.

During the intervening two months before the auction,
press interest remained high, keeping both Aickman and
Edwards busy, and more letters poured into Gower Street
about this than any other current issue. Somewhat to the
council's chagrin, since there had been a poor response to an
appeal for members to convert their subscriptions into tax-
free convenants, donations also flowed in steadily, but there
seemed to be little hope of sufficient funds being raised for
the committee to buy the canal and place it under a
management trust.

On the eve of the auction, Robert was telephoned by the
mysterious Mrs Marshall, of whom little had been heard
since she appeared so enthusiastically at the original meeting;
she asked to see him that evening and arrived at nine o'clock.
She outlined an ambitious plan for restoring the waterway
exactly on the lines envisaged by the IWA, and when Robert
pointed out that they had barely a third of the anticipated
price Mrs Marshall replied, 'I think I can find the balance.'
She announced that she had been empowered to bid at the
auction on behalf of a Purchase Committee formed that day,
implying that it was a subsidiary of the Basingstoke Canal
Committee.

The next day, public interest had been so great that the
auction rooms had to be changed to a different and larger
venue and the town of Aldershot was placarded with signs
pointing the way 'TO THE SALE'. 'It was appropriate that the
sale of the Basingstoke canal should have taken place in the
Traction Hall, even if the comments of some of the drivers
outside, that the canal might well be filled in to make a good
road, were less in keeping,' *The Times* reported tartly.

Inside, canal supporters from all over the Home Counties
jostled for space with an invasion of Fleet Street reporters
on a scale never before seen in connection with the forgotten
waterways, and, once under way, the platform was illuminated with the flashing of photographers' lights.

The actual sale hardly justified all the excitement; it was

soon over, with the only other bidder, a local contractor, dropping out at a comparatively early stage and the hammer falling at £6,000 to Mrs Marshall, who went on to bid a further £3,000 on various ancillary lots, including a lock cottage. Spontaneous applause broke out at the result, most supporters thinking that the canal had been acquired on behalf of the IWA, and the auctioneer made a congratulatory speech on the canal's preservation in safe hands. The outcome was featured right across the nation by BBC News and the national press. Robert was left sceptical about the source of the funding and concerned about the ability of the Canal Committee to meet its undertaking.

The next morning, Mrs Marshall was on the telephone. 'You mustn't think that the Association has bought the canal,' she cautioned. She explained that a majority of the Purchase Committee – those putting up the money – regarded it as an autonomous body and in no way bound to the IWA, whose name had been freely used to gain public support; nevertheless, they had every intention of running the canal along the lines advocated by the IWA. The Basingstoke had been saved from destruction, but its future would not necessarily be guaranteed in the way that Robert and the council had hoped.

In a carefully worded statement in *Bulletin* 19, it was explained that, while the Association continued to support the aims of the new Basingstoke owners, it was in no way responsible for the decisions and actions of the Purchase Committee. For Robert himself, it was a blow to his pride and a first setback, yet it was a lesson he took to heart and benefited from when the opportunities arose in later years for the restoration of the river Avon and the Stratford canal.

A month after the auction there was a last-ditch attempt to bring the two sides together, though Robert refused to attend the meeting. Over a preliminary lunch Teddy Edwards briefed Tom Rolt and gave him the impression that there were grounds for optimism if he took a strong line. 'I hoped for fireworks between him and Mrs Marshall, but in the event she appeared to hypnotise him into silence,' Tom reported. 'Partly as the result of this I formed the opinion that she had out-manoeuvred Edwards throughout the whole of this business.'

Setting the record straight, Robert answered that Edwards (who was not yet a council member) had always argued for the Association to go all-out with an appeal for the Basingstoke and felt that some good had come out of their efforts, if only in acquiring experience for the future.

Worse was to follow – the Basingstoke situation would not lie down and die. A fresh attack on the council's handling of the affair came from inside the Association and from a most unexpected quarter – Kyrle Willans. At the AGM held in May he asked some prickly questions about the constitution, which Tom answered. On this occasion, Robert made his now annual statement about the IWA's continued dependence on the time devoted by Tom and himself, and on the use of his own flat as office. He once again issued an ultimatum that the first priority should be given to finding sufficient income to recruit a full-time organiser whose primary task would be to raise funds.

After the meeting Robert began to receive a number of abusive letters from Willans. At first he kept the matter to himself and tried to defuse the situation. Finally, as the letters continued into July, Robert could stand it no longer and turned to Tom in the hope that his family's relationship with Willans could be of use, although, he added, 'I believe that you are no longer on speaking terms.'

The Rolts had departed after the AGM on their second attack on the Llangollen, where they spent a long golden summer and, in the company of Welsh actor Hugh Griffith and his wife Gunde, finally made the crossing of Pont Cysyllte. On the far side of the great aqueduct they turned *Cressy* and stern-hauled it 200 yards up the canal to the mooring which Tom regarded as most perfect – from the large windows of the cabin they looked across to a park-like landscape of heavy trees on the opposite hillside. They stayed for nearly three months of fine summer weather, and Tom was able to return to another interest that he had stumbled on two years earlier.

From the Llangollen canal, he had travelled in 1947 over

the massive dark mountains of central Wales and descended from Dolgelly to the coast of Cardigan Bay. Here he had found a narrow-gauge railway built in the early nineteenth century that tortuously ascended a mountain pass from Towyn to the old slate quarries at Bryn Eglwys. Quarrying had ceased in 1946, so the railway was only being kept open for summer tourist traffic. In studying the draft Transport Act for its effect on canals, Tom had chanced upon the extraordinary accident that the Talyllyn Railway Company had escaped the notice of the legislators, probably because it was thought to be defunct, so it was one of the few British railways to avoid nationalisation and remained in the private ownership of Sir Hayden Jones, a former Welsh MP. On his first visit in 1947 its remaining diminutive steam engine had failed, and there was a break in service. Now, in 1949, Tom returned, became captivated by travelling the line as a fare-paying passenger, and realised how much work was required if it was to be kept going for much longer.

During his few days' visit to Wales this summer Robert had been asked not to send any correspondence to Tom – Angela pointed out that there had not been more than a day or two since the IWA's founding when they had not had to deal with some matter or other. The latest batch of letters from Willans, however, proved too much for Robert; and with many apologies he forwarded them to Tom, who became involved for the first time.

'There seems to be no doubt whatever that Willans is simply out to injure us and cause as much trouble as possible in every way; an aim deriving no doubt in part from a family feud, and in part from his preposterous quarrel with Edwards,' Robert explained. His immediate reaction was that Willans should be expelled from the Association, adding, 'I feel that we shall be unable to work effectively until we are rid of this trouble.'

Robert's concern was heightened by the news that Willans was taking an active interest in the Kennet and Avon branch, which had been formed in January 1949, and he was afraid that such an aggressive and outspoken critic would create the kind of discord within the movement that would be damaging to its overall objectives. Indeed, there were rumours that he was trying to build personal support within the branch by offering to pay half the subscriptions of new members.

There was light relief from these problems for Tom at the beginning of August when an entertaining party arrived at his mooring on the Llangollen. Roger Calvert, his wife and family were travelling on an unconventional home-made boat pulled by a donkey. After some hesitation it had crossed Chirk aqueduct, but no amount of coaxing would induce it to pass through the tunnel or to cross the much longer aqueduct at Pont Cysyllte; in the end the boat had been manhandled while the donkey was led around these obstacles.

The Rolts joined the Calverts for part of their journey to the top of the canal. 'It is a silent and pleasant method of progression which certainly solved the weed problem,' wrote Tom, 'but the donkey displayed a tendency to wander off into the woods occasionally, with the consequence that the vessel's course would be suddenly deflected in an uncontrollable fashion.' Tom left Calvert repairing a hole in the hull after one of these unpredictable deviations.

While away on a further visit to Talyllyn, Tom reported that he himself was now receiving letters directly from Willans. 'My worthy uncle touches a new "low" in imbecility and pettiness,' he told Robert. He was demanding a written explanation of the Basingstoke affair, which Tom refused to give in view of its complexity; in any case, the council had already offered to hold a meeting with Willans (at which, if it took place, they planned to have two shorthand-writers); he had ignored this offer.

The troublesome business escalated still further when Sonia Smith was shown some of the letters, blackening Tom's character, by the Kennet and Avon branch chairman, John Gould. Hearing about this, Tom was furious and considered that his uncle had put himself in a dangerous position and that 'his mental balance seems to have become very precarious'.

Robert was convinced that the expulsion of Willans was

the only solution to the problem and sought the advice of their solicitor, Sidney Davis. He was not encouraging as there was no rule in the articles of association which covered this action; the alternative would be to hold a Special General Meeting at which, after the council had given an explanation, Willans and any supporters would be called upon to resign.

As the unpleasant affair dragged on, without any obvious solution to it, through the summer and into the autumn, both Tom and Robert were trying to deal with other problems. Tom had returned to Abersoch for a meeting with Sir Hayden Jones, in his spacious office over the post office in Towyn from where he surveyed the little town where he had been such an influential presence throughout his long and busy life. He was a striking white-haired figure, dressed in an old-fashioned fly-away collar, black coat and pin-striped trousers, and he worked between two large desks, each piled high with papers. He agreed to Tom's tentative proposals to launch a public appeal to preserve and improve the Talyllyn railway and gave a guarantee that the railway would not be closed within his own lifetime.

Robert turned to deal with the renewed saga of Lifford Lane bridge on the north Stratford canal. Shortly after *Cressy*'s original successful passage it seemed that the battle had been won when the then Parliamentary Secretary for Transport, G. R. Strauss, had informed Robert in writing that GWR 'have decided to replace the fixed bridge at Lifford by a modern-type movable bridge'.

Over the intervening two years, during which GWR had been nationalised, the fixed bridge had remained and boaters' experiences had varied. Lord Bingham had been refused passage for *Hesperus* on the grounds of water deficiency; and the working boatmen had despaired of the route because it was so unreliable. Eric de Maré, however, had obtained permission to navigate his boat *Pyrrha* on a long-distance voyage from Hampton Court to Llantisilio.

In view of the failure to carry out the pledge given by George Strauss, Robert took up the issue with his successor as Parliamentary Secretary, James Callaghan. His initial reply simply referred the IWA to the British Transport Commission as a matter of day-to-day administration.

Robert seized upon this to raise the important principle of whether or not a minister was still responsible to Parliament for the functioning of a nationalised industry under his care. In particular, he wanted to know the position regarding a nationalised industry which had failed to meet its statutory obligation, in this instance to maintain navigation along a route approved by Act of Parliament. 'Is it the case that the former efficacious procedure of raising alleged grievances against the owners in Parliament is no longer available against the new authority?' he demanded. 'If not, the public is losing a valuable means of expressing its views and protecting its interests.'

It took Callaghan a month to reply as Robert had touched on a question which, in the early days of nationalisation, had not been fully thought out. While maintaining that a minister could not be responsible for day-to-day running, and that it would be wrong to interfere too much in such matters, he agreed that a member of the public was still able to approach the government, though whether the minister would intervene 'would depend on what was involved'.

Reminding Callaghan of the issue at stake, namely the failure to replace the bridge as assured by his Parliamentary predecessor, Robert thundered back: 'In such matters we represent the right of the public that the law be enforced: and the British Transport Commission cannot be entrusted with the task of enforcing the law upon themselves.'

The bridge was still fixed in place when a further passage of the canal was requested – this time by the Association's vice-president, Peter Scott. The Severn Wildfowl Trust was starting to establish its bird sanctuary on the marshy flat grounds of the Severn estuary at Slimbridge (now the world-famous centre for the study of water birds, especially the migration habits of Bewick swans) and, to accommodate visiting ornithologists, it had bought a narrowboat, *Beatrice*.

After the boat had been converted into a floating hostel by a Birmingham yard, supervised by Cyril Taplin, Scott applied to the Docks and Inland Waterways Executive to pass along the north Stratford as the most direct route to the Severn. Their initial reply stated that it would not be possible to remove the obstruction until after the date requested by Scott, and suggested an alternative route of twice the distance. The letters bounced backwards and forwards, including a personal appeal to Peter Scott advising him not to press the issue, until, at long last and with obvious reluctance, permission was granted.

Once more, the bridge was laboriously lifted and *Beatrice*, watched by a large crowd attracted by Peter Scott's popular reputation, passed on its way to the Worcester and Birmingham canal; shortly afterwards, in the middle of West Hill tunnel, 2,726 yards long, it ran out of fuel and had to be pushed by hand to the end. One member of *Beatrice*'s crew on this journey was Philippa Talbot-Ponsonby, then working at Slimbridge, soon to become Peter's second wife.

Lifford Lane bridge had to be raised twice more during the summer – for the return passage of the narrowboats *Cornwall* and *Roseland* from Stourbridge and Bournville to Shirley, where they picked up 100 IWA members for a day's outing to Lapworth. Such a trip would have been impossible before the Association's campaign, Robert pointed out in *Bulletin* 20, and the increased use of the canal was already improving conditions; there was now much less weed and debris than there had been two years earlier.

The Midlands branch was now starting to turn its attention to the southern half of the canal between Kingswood and Stratford-upon-Avon, which was in far worse condition than the section to King's Norton. On the Wilmcote flight of locks, pounds were kept permanently empty, thus destroying the puddle at the bottom of the cut and leaving open the brickwork of the locks to winter frost damage. In Stratford an 'ornamental' bridge had been placed by the council across the bottom of Bancroft basin at a height that totally prevented boats from passing between the canal and the river Avon. The only boat that had managed to navigate the canal in years had been greeted by one of the lock-keepers with the remark that if any more boats came along, he would resign!

'Though this lower part of the canal is heavily locked,' Robert wrote, 'it is obvious that it would none the less carry a considerable pleasure traffic were it permitted to do so.' He urged Midlands boat-owners to insist on their right of passage, so that the Wilmcote pounds would have to be filled, and to display their IWA burgees in the basin opposite the Shakespeare Memorial Theatre.

The river Avon itself, at this time, was only just navigable upstream from Tewkesbury to Pershore, and even this part was deteriorating rapidly. Further east through navigation was no longer possible and the upper section between Evesham and Stratford had been impassable for a century. Over the past two years both Rolt and Aickman had received several approaches from people keen to see the navigation restored. Now Robert made a strong plea in a visionary letter to the *Evesham Journal* that reopening of the route between the Severn and Birmingham should be looked at as a whole, taking the river and the canal together as one system.

'It may well be thought that this particular route should be restored with an especial view to pleasure traffic,' he wrote. 'Waterborne traffic would pour into Stratford by both private and public boat . . . The restoration of the Avon and the reconditioning of the Stratford canal should play a prominent part in any contemplated scheme of expenditure for the advantage of the tourist traffic, home and foreign.'

At Gower Street the postbag continued to swell. As public interest in the Basingstoke declined, a new issue about the canals caught the imagination of the public and media. The Docks and Inland Waterways Executive, driven by a misguided desire to impose a nationwide image on its fleet of hundreds of commercial boats, decided to paint them in a standard livery of blue and yellow. The colour scheme was to be imposed regardless of the style of any particular craft, which meant that the past traditions of narrowboat painting were to be ignored and the fine craftwork of roses and castles obliterated. The story was taken up across the country by the BBC, national and local press, and correspondence flooded into Gower Street, adding fresh work pressures to the emotional disharmony that already existed and creating a tension that had to snap.

Ray was hard-working and loyal, understanding Robert's commitment to the cause and his passion for Jane; she looked after the literary agency, which was not very demanding, and kept house for everyone. Since she recognised that her own marriage had been a contract rather than a love match, she came to terms with Robert's philosophy of free love, but it was not so easy to come to terms with the practical implications of a complex situation. 'It's not so much that I mind them being together, but I do object to taking them breakfast in bed,' she complained to Eric de Maré and other friends. Beneath the surface, jealousy was always liable to break out. Once, during the Huddersfield trip, Tom in a light-hearted and flirtatious mood had plaited a boatman's belt from long grasses which Jane swung provocatively around her hips, infuriating Robert.

At this point Jane decided that she could no longer cope with the work, considering its 'part-time' basis and the emotional circumstances, and she resigned to concentrate on writing. 'I got tired of that job. It used up so much of my energy that I wanted to get out, and he didn't want me to do that, so it wasn't really a very happy situation and I decided that I'd had enough, enough of tantrums and rows and personality clashes. Of course, in doing that I left poor Ray to cope with it,' she said.

Her first full-length novel, *The Beautiful Visit*, had been accepted for publication by Jonathan Cape and appeared in 1950. Its hauntingly sad story of a lonely girl's search for friendship on a visit to her better endowed relatives perhaps reflected Jane's gathered impressions of Robert's own friendless childhood and the occasional warmth that he found in visiting the large family of his father's only close friends, the Haslocks at Broomclose. The book was dedicated to Robert Aickman.

Jane joined the council shortly afterwards, so her close connections with the IWA continued for some years. She had worked 'at our headquarters since the Association was only a few weeks old,' Robert wrote, 'and it would be impossible to estimate how much it owes to her devoted labours and initiative, undertaken much more for our cause than for an increasingly incommensurate salary. To few individuals does the Association's good progress owe more!'

Following the decision at the AGM to give priority to recruiting a full-time organiser, Robert had been searching for a suitable candidate. No one had answered IWA's pleas for members with an interest in the campaign to come forward and in the end the job was given, at the time of Jane's resignation, to an applicant from the London Appointments Board of the Ministry of Labour. Robert's public reference to the matter in the *Bulletin*, 'it must be admitted that the ideal candidate has failed to offer himself', was hardly a warm introduction; privately he was even more damning with faint praise.

Writing to Tom soon afterwards, Robert was most revealing about his own attitudes towards work. 'My father always dinned into me that men of character seldom take jobs at all; they make their own careers from scratch. Many of my father's views were singularly misguided, but my own experience has always confirmed this one.'

Only a few weeks passed before the IWA, which now boasted 800 members, was looking for its *second* general secretary.

As the long dry summer slipped into autumn and the trees in the Dee valley turned to gold, the Rolts left the beautiful mooring in Llangollen, where the summer days had almost been too hot, and made the great cross-country trek from Trevor in Wales to Gayton in Northamptonshire, chosen again as a winter mooring in view of its appropriate location. This time it brought Tom close to Market Harborough and the plans for the next great advance in the campaign.

When Tom was running the Vintage Sports Car Club one of its most successful activities before the Second World War had been a rally of cars to Presteigne in Herefordshire, including prizes for the car coming from the greatest distance, the best turned-out car and similar awards. It had become a popular annual event. During the summer Tom had had the brilliant idea of organising a similar rally of boats for the IWA – it would bring together a variety of different craft owned by members and encourage them to travel along many diverse routes to the meeting point. No other event would be so likely to act as a catalyst for new members to join, and to focus attention upon the state of the waterways.

In taking up the idea enthusiastically, the other council members had agreed at their October meeting that Market Harborough would provide the ideal rallying point – it was in the centre of the country, along a little-used side-arm which meant that the boats would not obstruct commercial traffic, and there was access in one direction (from the Trent) for widebeam craft. An initial approach to the local council had received an encouraging reply.

At the beginning of November no definite plans had been made, although there had already been a preliminary announcement that the rally would be held over the week ending 19 August 1950. Robert urged Tom, after he arrived at Gayton, to join him on a visit to Market Harborough council as 'it is necessary that a fairly detailed announcement should go into the next *Bulletin*, which cannot go out later than the beginning of December'.

Tom replied three days later that he and Angela would be willing to go, but that they would have to make the journey by train – a reminder that petrol was still severely rationed in 1949.

The Aickmans and the Rolts met in Market Harborough – the last time that they were to do so in a thoroughly friendly atmosphere – and received an enthusiastic response from the council beyond their wildest dreams. Full support was promised in making land and facilities available, and council staff were assigned to help with on-the-spot arrangements. The event was to be held in the year preceding the Festival of Britain, and already communities up and down the country were lifting themselves out of postwar despondency and gearing themselves for the nationwide celebration.

The proposed waterways rally, in fact, began to be perceived as a trial curtain-raiser for the 1951 Festival of Britain. During their visit to Market Harborough, Robert told Tom of a discussion that he had had with Leonard Crainford, Secretary General of the national organisation, who had 'professed unexpected interest' and implied that, if it was a success, they would want to repeat it the following year as part of the official programme. 'It is true that Festivals are springing up in the most improbable places,' he added.

Unconsciously, almost imperceptibly, there had been a subtle shift away from Tom's rally of boats to Robert's festival of boats; yet the two were not incompatible. Both accepted that the core of the Market Harborough event was to be a rally aimed at encouraging anyone with a boat to make the journey, however distant and difficult, across the country to the meeting point. Robert simply believed that this did not go far enough, however. As most of the members did not own a boat (indeed, at this early time, few had any real experience of inland boating), he reiterated that the Association could not afford to be seen as an élitist boat club; the event should endorse their role as the body qualified to speak on behalf of waterways nationally.

With his love of theatre and the performing arts, and a latent desire to play a more active part in these fields, Robert plunged with colossal energy into starting to plan a programme of land-based activity – an exhibition, films and perhaps drama. He visualised an opportunity of attracting hordes of August holidaymakers, who probably had never thought about canals, to come to Market Harborough and experience a small slice of the waterways scene that, largely unrecognised, existed in so many other parts of the country. Here was an unequalled chance to preach to a captive audience and send them home better informed about the deplorable state of the nation's waterways.

Robert found himself, once again, at odds with Tom over the manipulation of publicity to achieve their ends, and he recognised that he had to press on urgently if the rally or festival was to be held at all in 1950. He knew that, above all, its success depended on the number of boats attracted to the gathering. Nothing like this had ever been attempted or even thought of before, so no one could forecast the scale of response but, if only a *few* boats turned up, the Association would have placed itself in an irretrievably ignominious position. It was obviously vital that members should be told as much as possible about the event in the *Bulletin*'s December issue as families would be making holiday plans for the next year over the Christmas and New Year break.

Robert rushed into print in *Bulletin* 23 with a hard-selling, action-packed description of the forthcoming Summer Rally of Boats. After an appealing description of the waterways setting and the historic town, he announced plans for 'a variety of indoor attractions, mainly in the evenings; including a dance, a dramatic entertainment, and a small exhibition . . . Fireworks and a Fair are hoped for.' Emphasising the need for every boat-owner to cruise to Market Harborough, he stressed that it was intended to be a 'great demonstration of the potentialities of the waterways; and more harm than good will result if attendance is not good. We are, in fact, risking much on the co-operation of all our boat-owning members.'

With less than eight months in which to set up this first ever national rally of inland boating – with routes to be agreed with BTC, mooring to be laid out, public halls to be booked, films and plays to be selected, speakers to be briefed, publicity to be scheduled, accommodation to be arranged and, in fact, almost everything still to be organised – Tom Rolt sent a letter to Gower Street announcing his resignation as honorary secretary.

Market Harborough Rally and Festival

A few days later Robert travelled out to Gayton by train in the hope of ironing out the differences with Tom and persuading him to withdraw his resignation. The countryside was held in the grip of ice and snow, an overall whiteness blanketing out any features, and creating an eerie atmosphere of stillness and isolation. The only sign of life and motion was the small train and its carriages cutting a dark furrow through the whiteness, winding and weaving on the branch line that criss-crossed Northamptonshire before the Beeching axe fell, the long plume of black smoke rising towards the snow-laden clouds, the silence punctured by the shriek of its whistle, the steady pounding of its wheels.

The day was in stark contrast to the balmy summer's afternoon five years earlier at Tardebigge, when the two men had first met in such a spirit of anticipation and enthusiasm. On board *Cressy* Robert found a fire roaring in the solid fuel stove and the warm air in the comfortable cabin was thick with the pungent smells of wood and coal. Angela's greeting was as affectionate as ever, but there were signs of strain between the two men.

Talk turned first to Market Harborough and the dramatic entertainment that Robert visualised as the centrepiece of the land-based festival. Tom had agreed to this, provided that they could contract a sufficiently reputable company such as the Bristol Young Vic, and he was disappointed to hear from Robert that they would be far too expensive. Instead of hiring an existing company, Robert said that a new scheme had been proposed whereby the Association would mount its own productions of two one-act comedies. He reassured Tom by explaining that they would hire professional actors and actresses, although Elizabeth Jane Howard, who had originally trained in the theatre, was keen to direct one of the plays. As Peter Scott had undertaken to meet any financial loss there would be no risk to the IWA, and the possibility of making some money.

Tom was not convinced about the merit of this proposal and pointed out that the Assembly Rooms in Market Harborough were not really suitable for a theatrical production as there was no proscenium arch. Robert again assured him that this problem would be solved: James Sutherland, a civil engineer, and Mary George, who ran the Electrical Association for Women, had undertaken to construct a stage.

Turning to the more pressing problem of forcing the resignation of Kyrle Willans, Robert explained that he had sought the advice of the Association's solicitor, Sidney Davis, about the existing Rule XX. 'It's even more badly drafted than he had pointed out previously. Not only is the question of calling upon a member to resign inadequate and inconclusive, but there's nothing mentioned about the length of notice to be given if he wishes to appeal,' stated Robert.

Davis had thought that a court of law would regard two weeks as sufficient time to lodge an appeal. The point was, however, that Rule XX would have to be amended – and strengthened – if the Association was to have the power to expel members who disagreed openly with the council's official policy.

The discussion thus reached the key and sensitive issue of Tom's own resignation. The last straw, he explained, was when he discovered that he had been made a member of the rally committee, without being consulted, on top of all his other commitments. There were, after all, another twenty-six people on the committee, including representatives of organisations such as the British Travel Association.

Tom apologised for the consternation that his proposed resignation had caused. He pointed out that he had had no intention of continuing in the role of honorary secretary for ever; on the contrary, he had assumed that he would give up as soon as the Association was firmly established. Robert agreed that their duties were a heavy imposition on their time – he himself had not been able to pursue his writing ambitions. All the same, he felt that they should stay at their posts for another year, until after the rally had been held.

Tom challenged Robert's assumption that they were both in similar situations as he believed that Robert obtained more enjoyment from the public prominence that his role had brought. 'This is perfectly understandable and any satisfaction you get in this way is certainly well deserved,' he said. 'But, you see, it's a position which I strongly dislike. My only satisfaction is in doing and the results achieved.'

Robert stuck to his determination to win Tom's continued support and obtain a retraction of his resignation. As darkness fell over the bleak landscape outside *Cressy*, Tom gave way to the extent that he agreed to postpone any announcement of his resignation for some months, though he refused to withdraw it completely and suggested that, to give him some relief from the work load, a joint honorary secretary should be appointed.

Before leaving to return to London Robert pressed the Rolts to come and stay at Gower Street, or at least to have lunch on the following Friday before their meeting with Lord Lucan (Bingham had become the 6th Earl of Lucan on his father's death), to discuss tactics for the Kennet and Avon branch AGM. His hospitality was rejected – the time had passed for such niceties. Tom and Angela had other arrangements which could mean a late return and 'it would be straining hospitality to park ourselves on you on such occasions as this'.

Later Robert was to regret bitterly that he had won a temporary remission from Tom. He came to realise afterwards that, when someone in a position of value and importance has had a change of heart, it is better for that person to go and to accept their decision. 'I have often since been heard to say,' he wrote in later years, 'that when one is offered a resignation, one should always accept it. Steady increase in experience has confirmed this view.'

If Rolt's resignation had been accepted then, in January 1950, he would have withdrawn honourably, without any overt animosity, and retained a highly valued place in the

Association. As it was, Robert's successful persuasion was to rebound disastrously, creating a rapidly deteriorating personal relationship until the quarrels escalated into a bitter personality clash that was to affect many members of the IWA and fracture the movement from top to bottom.

The patched-up agreement lasted only a few days – until the meeting with Lucan. Since it was decided to confront Willans at the AGM with the damage that his behaviour was inflicting on the IWA, Robert was insistent that Tom should accompany him there so that there could be no doubt about the unanimity of the council.

At first Tom refused. Not only was it an impossibly long and difficult cross-country journey by train from Blisworth to Newbury, but it was also his birthday that day. Angela and he had already made arrangements to meet his mother in Stratford and go to a matinée at the theatre. Robert savagely harangued Tom for placing his own selfish interests before those of the Association, culminating in the acid remark: 'I am afraid you will *have* to come to Newbury on Saturday.'

Tom rose icily and left the meeting without another word, visibly upset at such high-handed treatment, which would not have been justified even if he had been the full-time organiser instead of an unpaid volunteer.

On his return to *Cressy* he wrote to Robert that he had decided to cancel his own personal arrangements, though, he added, 'it will be the last occasion on which I shall disrupt my affairs at your bidding and, moreover, instead of giving way to you as I have always done I intend to handle this matter in my own way'. The condition of his acceptance was that Robert should stay away.

Robert, however, remained adamant that he himself should be present at Newbury and blamed Willans for driving a wedge between himself and Tom. By now he had a further reason for insisting that he should attend – Willans had made a fresh attack on the council for deciding to refund Aickman at the rate of £120 per annum for the use of Gower Street as an office (to cover heat, light, telephone and other costs). Robert, in fact, refrained from drawing this modest sum until the affair had been settled.

Newbury was not the only disagreement to flare up between the two men. Tom was further angered when he received proofs of a printed leaflet giving the entire Market Harborough programme at a time when many of the events such as a fair and fireworks display were only at a provisional stage; in addition, he objected to Robert's persistent plugging of 'celebrities', including Lord Cromwell, the Lord Lieutenant of Leicestershire, who had agreed to be the festival's patron.

'My mind boggles when I think of the amount of organisational and practical work involved in realising the programme to which, as soon as your booklet is printed, we are irrevocably committed,' he complained. Yet Robert, who was just as concerned about the risks they were taking, had shrewdly recognised that the most effective way of ensuring that a voluntary committee carried out their offers of help was by committing them publicly in advance. Everyone who worked with him throughout the years acknowledged that he had an exceptional gift of leadership in terms of enthusing others to put effort into the cause. Moreover, he had a sound, practical reason for producing a comprehensive programme at this stage; printing and distribution costs would be cheaper than producing a promotional flyer followed by a second leaflet.

The row now exploded openly between the couples when Ray decided to complain to Tom about his attitude. 'It had, of course, been obvious to me for a long time how both you and Angela dislike Robert intensely,' she wrote in defence of the implication that Robert was just seeking to be a 'public figure'. She then took a step which, in view of her own shaky marriage, was singularly unwise. 'I do feel that your present state of mind on all subjects is, to be frank once more, much influenced by the fact that you and Angela are patently extremely unhappy – a state of mind that makes the rest of life unbearable.'

Tom was stung into making an instant response: 'I have always noticed that the light of sweet reason and common sense prevails at Gower Street and, so far as I can make out, nowhere else.' He said that if anyone disagreed with Robert, criticised him or his policies, it was never seriously considered that he could be in the wrong; such criticisms were dismissed on the grounds that it was the other person's attitude that must be warped in some way.

Repeating that he had started out with implicit faith and trust in Robert, Tom recalled how he had become disillusioned in 1947 when he believed that he had been misled over Jane's holiday; though, since then, he had tried to sink this and other differences in their common cause of building up the IWA ('which Robert has done with a competence I would be the last person to question').

'It is not my business to enquire into, still less to pass judgement upon, your personal relationship with Robert,' he hit back. 'Similarly, it is not for you to pass judgement on our personal affairs and thereby invent a situation which, you believe, has warped my judgement.'

Angela, who had been away during this exchange of letters, returned a few days later to discover, as she then told Robert, that Tom was 'in what is known as "a state"'. 'What Tom has been writing to you I do not know, but it would appear that the fact that I do not always agree with Tom in his differences with you has given him the idea that you have been influencing me,' she wrote. 'You see, women are not meant to have minds or any ideas of their own.'

The Willans affair – the original source of the trouble between the two men – began to fade into the background when it was found that his membership had lapsed and, just as it seemed that peace was returning to the inner circle, Lucan unexpectedly intervened by urging Aickman in a long letter at the end of March to 'strengthen the council by bringing it up to strength and bringing in the best people we can find among the members'. He proposed two names known to be unacceptable to Robert because of their support for Willans.

The letter arrived on the very morning on which Robert was setting out to join *Beatrice* on a month's promotional cruise of the north-west. He was furious with Lucan for creating a further upset at a time when he could not be available to meet him; in the circumstances he suggested calling a council meeting to ensure that nominations were unanimously agreed.

An extremely arduous and ambitious schedule had been set for the cruise on *Beatrice*, with long distances to be covered each day to arrive at destinations where, almost each night, Peter Scott was to give a lecture about the Slimbridge Wildfowl Trust; this also provided opportunities for Robert to meet many waterways enthusiasts and carry the IWA's message into parts not yet reached. Starting from the Gloucester and Sharpness, they traversed 450 miles and passed through 273 locks on the route that took them up the Severn and the Shropshire Union to Nantwich, thence on to the Trent and Mersey and a great loop around the north-west, encompassing Manchester, Wigan and Liverpool, returning through Stoke-on-Trent and Birmingham. James Sutherland and Lord Geoffrey Percy, younger son of the Duke of Northumberland, were members of the large crew that varied over the course of the journey.

From the outset the schedule proved to have been over ambitious, as the boat's engine immediately began to give trouble on the Severn between Gloucester and Tewkesbury. The conversion of *Beatrice* had been based closely on that of *Cressy*, right down to using a similar Model-T Ford engine, though *Beatrice* had a much smaller propeller. So badly did it perform upstream against the river that a rapid change of engine was made at a Tewkesbury boatyard, but it produced little improvement.

With the need to keep to the strenuous lecture timetable, they were forced to travel at all hours with even Robert (who was not notable as a navigator) steering after dark on the Severn to Stourport; despite their efforts, Peter Scott often had to travel many miles by taxi to keep his appointment. On the high, exposed banks of the Shropshire Union they had to fight gale-force winds by towing the boat with ropes. On occasions, there were ribald shouts from onlookers: 'Is that the boat that took you to the South Pole?'

From Wigan they descended the Leeds and Liverpool

around the famous canal turn alongside the Aintree race-course on their way to the most adventurous sector of the voyage – up the immense tidal Mersey estuary to Weston Point and the Runcorn canal. The night before tackling this they were spotted by Sir Malcom Sargent, who had been an IWA member from early days. He insisted that they accept tickets for a performance the following evening of Beethoven's 'Mass in D' by the Liverpool Philharmonic, even though no one in *Beatrice*'s party thought that there would be any possibility of crossing the Mersey and return-ing in time for the concert.

The omens seemed good the next morning, when for the first time in many days the sun came out from behind the heavy rain-laden cloud that had accompanied their trip. Equipped with new charts, anchor and bilge pump pur-chased at Liverpool docks, and joined by a local IWA member, Martin Grundy, they passed from the safety of the narrow canal out on to the wide expanse of the estuary, then still a busy shipping lane for trans-Atlantic liners and vessels bound for every part of the world. It was the first recorded attempt by a narrowboat to make this passage, even more daring in a craft with a suspect engine. They were carried along fast on an incoming tide, hugging the north shore as far as Hale lighthouse, and the boat, which was not designed for rough water, swung dangerously from side to side in the rolling wash of sea-going ships. However, the fifteen-mile crossing was safely accomplished with only one engine failure and they reached Weston at around 3 p.m.

On the ascent of the Runcorn locks they were held up by a dispute between two lighters and arrived at the mooring too late to catch a train back to Liverpool in time for the start of the concert. Even so, they threw themselves into suits, dashed for the next train and reached the Philharmonic Hall just before the interval.

From Runcorn they continued along the river Weaver to Anderton Lift – one of the most fascinating engineering feats of Britain's canals – where *Beatrice* was lifted fifty feet in one of two water-filled counterbalanced tanks up to the level of the Trent and Mersey. Now, on the homeward-bound route,

Beatrice's high-sided cabin (unlike the tent-shaped covering of a working boat) became firmly wedged in the long, claustrophobic Harecastle tunnel at a point where the roof had subsided. Fortunately, the tunnel was one of few built with a towing-path, so the crew were able to add 200 bricks to the boat's ballast and shave away the corners at the top of the cabin. *Beatrice* was freed and, six and a half hours after entering the pitch-black tunnel, emerged on the far side into an April snowstorm.

'This voyage brought home to me the essential good sense of trying to save our canals and navigable rivers from abandonment and destruction,' wrote Peter Scott. 'For two generations the railway companies had been trying to rid themselves of canal competition . . . Not many people thought that because they did not pay for commercial traffic they should be abandoned and filled in. They had not the vision to see that here was a great new recreation ground for our overcrowded people.'

A navigation which in 1950 had not yet been destroyed, but had simply fallen into utter dereliction, was the river Avon, and there was great excitement at this time as the prospect of its restoration began to seem likely.

The river had been one of the country's oldest navigations. The rights, originally granted in 1636 by Charles I to William Sandys of Fladbury, were acquired a century later by the Perrott family, who were subsequently paid an annual compensation for loss of trade when the Birmingham and Worcester canal was opened.

The river had not come under the nationalisation Act and there had been interest in restoring the navigation as early as 1947, when Tom Rolt dined at Evesham and found great enthusiasm for the idea – but, he told Robert, 'as usual, the present situation is chaotic and everyone waits for someone with the initiative to make the first move'.

That 'someone' turned out to be Douglas Barwell, who lived near Birmingham and worked in his father's steel-tube-making business. Having always been keen on boats and water, in the summer of 1949 he and his wife took *North Star* on to the Avon at Tewkesbury and managed to work the delapidated, dangerous locks as far as Pershore, though fearful all the time that they could be stranded if one of the locks failed completely.

On his return he contacted the IWA and Robert encouraged him to join the Midlands branch committee. The situation came to a head shortly afterwards, when Evesham council threatened to build a solid weir across the river downstream at Chadbury to replace the unsafe, derelict lock upon which depended the town's fine waterfront and wide reach, much used for rowing.

The Midland's branch turned to Robert for advice and, drawing on his disappointing experience with the Basingstoke, he helped in the setting up of a non-profit-making charitable trust, composed mainly of IWA members. Barwell, who became chairman, succeeded in negotiating with the owners for the purchase of the navigation rights for the sum of £1,500 although it was estimated that £20,000 would have to be raised to complete the restoration, even using volunteer labour. Only one year after Basingstoke, the Association had finally found a promising venture, though they realised that restoration between Tewkesbury and Evesham could only be achieved stage by stage over several years.

From the outset, the complete restoration of the Avon was envisaged as the ultimate target. *Evesham Journal*, whose editor Kenneth Gill Smith had enthusiastically supported the plan, wrote:

It would appear that the Inland Waterways Association have visions in the future of progressively restoring the Avon up to Stratford-upon-Avon and even extending the navigation to Warwick. Such a scheme was considered in 1921 when it was estimated, even in those days, to cost a quarter of a million pounds. There is no harm in dreaming dreams and seeing visions. Sometimes dreams come true and visions prove to be prophetic; we hope they may do so in this case.

The first formal announcement of Rolt's intention to give up the honorary secretary's job came at the AGM on 19 May

1950. He explained that the pressure of his own work unfortunately compelled him to put a very early term on his services, which he had given uninterruptedly since the Association's foundation. He himself proposed L. A. Edwards as joint honorary secretary and indicated that he would retire from office when Edwards had completely taken over the role. Both Aickman and Lucan paid tribute to Tom's outstanding contribution.

The council was brought up to full strength with the selection of four new members, including Michael Streat (who started one of the earliest 'hotel boats' and also had a hire boat operation), Barbara Jones (a well-known artist who designed the Market Harborough poster) and A. S. Cavender (who had become chairman of the Fenlands branch in early 1950).

All now seemed to be set for a united and determined run-up to the rally until Cavender dropped a time-bomb on to Robert's desk. 'I have just recollected some correspondence received from Mr Rolt,' he wrote to the Gower Street office in June, forwarding letters he had received in April which implied that, because of a difference of opinion, Aickman had failed to carry out properly the wishes of the council. Cavender had been upset and refused to be drawn into the situation.

'I send you these two letters from Rolt for the express purpose that no one shall imply that I am in league with Mr Rolt,' he told Robert, 'and further that I feel that at this juncture you shall be assured of the absolute confidence of members of the council.'

At the June council meeting, when the matter was brought up for discussion, an unpleasant argument erupted between Tom and Robert which ended in Tom walking out of the room. Aickman was unanimously re-elected as chairman and, after a further exchange of angry letters, Tom finally resigned from the council on 14 July.

Although increasing differences of opinion and method had made it impossible for the two men to work together any longer, Tom wrote years later that he had good reasons for wanting to resign, not least the pressing need to earn

1a and **1b** *Cressy* with Tom Rolt at the helm

1c Robert and Ray Aickman on board *Cressy*

2a A pair of working boats leaving Anderton Lift

2b 'Tom Pudding' boats carrying coal on the Aire and Calder

3a Mr and Mrs John Wilson –
'Number Ones' who owned their own pair of working boats

3b The Skinner family on the Oxford canal

4a
Herbert Tooley
decorating the bow of
a narrowboat in his
yard at Banbury

4b
Sonia Smith on
the Oxford canal

5a An empty, disused pound on the Ashton canal

5b An overgrown flight on the Caldon canal

6a *Ailsa Craig* on the Trent and Mersey

6b Robert Aickman stern-hauling on the Peak Forest

7a Elizabeth Jane Howard with Peter Scott at the helm

7b Angela Rolt setting up
the 1947 waterways exhibition at Heal's

8a
Boats assembled at
Market Harborough
for the 1950 rally

8b
Robert Aickman
bringing a pair
of working boats
to London for the
Festival of Britain,
1951

some money. Unlike Robert, who had a very small private income, Tom was totally dependent on his writing, and his bank balance had dropped from four to two figures since 1946.

'I was discovering that a freelance is always under pressure from others who assume that his time is his own . . . He can easily find himself caught up in a plethora of rewarding – and often thankless – "honorary" tasks,' he wrote. Moreover, he was forfeiting the freedom which he had sought from a life on the canals and was putting at risk the whole concept of his 'design for living'. 'The brutal truth was now becoming only too clear, it [IWA] was becoming a bandwagon . . . We, who had originally sought refuge on the canals to escape from all we disliked in the modern world, deeply resented what we felt to be our exploitation for such purposes by others.'

Tom's last piece of work for the Association was for a part of the waterways scene that had always been closest to his heart – the working boats. In July 1950 Lucan, John Knill, Sonia and Tom published the first report of a sub-committee that had been set up a year earlier to investigate conditions of life on working boats and to endeavour to bring some improvements.

Their first step had been to look into why the existing machinery for the ventilation and redress of grievances was not working, since the boatmen were represented on the national negotiating body by the Transport and General Workers' Union. They had succeeded in arranging for a union official to make two visits to working boats; in the light of his first-hand experience of their poor conditions, he had undertaken to press for better amenities.

The committee had also examined a contentious proposal to set up a boarding school in Birmingham for boat children, the problem being that it had only thirty places and on the Grand Union alone there were known to be 250 children. Sadly, the promising work of this group was aborted by the ensuing row over IWA policy.

Cressy was on the Thames this summer, so that Tom could acquire material for his fifth book, *The Thames from Mouth to Source*. In July they reached the head of navigation, negotiating the last tortuous bends of the now slim river, winding through water meadows below the soaring spire of Lechlade church, and they moored close to the lofty single-span bridge that led into the village of elegant Cotswold stone houses.

From Lechlade he wrote to Teddy Edwards saying that Angela and he had been in two minds after what had occurred about whether to miss the Market Harborough rally, but that various friends, including Holt Abbott (builder of the first purpose-designed canal cruiser), had persuaded them to attend.

By return, Robert pleaded in the most reasonable and balanced way that the Rolts should not come to the rally under such sad circumstances; after a lapse of time, the general atmosphere would become easier and then they would be welcome again.

Tom was outraged. 'As the IWA has grown in stature and prestige so you have grown increasingly arrogant and intolerant of the views of others when they failed to coincide with yours,' he replied. 'That you should dare to request me not to come astonishes me, accustomed though I am by long experience to your ways.' He concluded three pages of deep bitterness by stating that he and Angela had every intention of going to the rally, not for any ulterior reason, simply to meet friends.

Ignoring a further appeal by the council for them not to attend, *Cressy* set out on the long-distance journey from Lechlade to Market Harborough on what was to be the last cruise for Tom and Angela together. From the wide Grand Union at Norton junction they turned up the narrow canal towards Leicester, crossing open rolling uplands, descended the unusual flight at Foxton – two groups of five staircase locks separated by a middle pound – and turned into the short rural arm leading to the little town of Market Harborough.

They glided into an exciting and colourful scene such as had never before been seen on the waterways: the basin packed with craft bedecked with bunting; flags flying from shops and houses in the streets thronged with holiday-makers, the waterfront busy with stalls selling all kinds of items linked with canals, such as Brindley and Telford headscarves, model boats and swans, and replica Buckby cans and dippers; and Frank Jones demonstrating the genuine article in painting traditional patterns on boats. There were displays of Polish dancing, a cricket match, the martial music of a police band and massed singing led by a silver band, a fancy-dress dance for children and the Festival Queen's election accompanied by Scottish pipers. The events of each day were inaugurated at 8 a.m. with the reverberations of a detonated maroon and concluded at night with dancing to the 'Rogues of Rhythm' band around the floodlit narrowboats.

Cressy arrived, officially not invited, and, instead of the place of honour which would have been its right a year earlier, was cold-shouldered to a distant mooring among the 120 boats that had come from all parts of the country. It was an amazing gathering at a time when pleasure-boating on canals was barely recognised, and when there were few privately owned craft and almost none for hire. *Beatrice* had come from the Gloucester and Sharpness, Lucan and his sons had brought *Hesperus*, Sir Reginald Hill, chairman of the Docks and Inland Waterways Executive, arrived on *Kingfisher*, the Executive's launch, and S. V. Offley, in the cabin cruiser *Marbeth* travelled 320 miles from Ellesmere Port, claiming the A. P. Herbert prize for the longest distance. Another thirteen boats had booked in advance, but an unannounced and protracted stoppage of the river Witham had prevented them coming.

The festival attracted over 50,000 visitors during the six days. There were queues to see the waterways exhibition in the mediaeval Grammar School, Peter Scott's own popular paintings of birds in flight, and a collection provided by the Arts Council. The cinema screened a film (which was to become a classic) called *Painted Boats*, enchantingly portraying the life of the working boat people. Tom Rolt had advised the Central Office of Information on its production, for which the poet Louis MacNeice wrote the script with everyday boaters taking part.

The Assembly Rooms, a spacious hall with a large dress circle, had been transformed for the plays by an elaborate proscenium arch and lighting gantries built from scaffolding by James Sutherland. As Robert wished to keep the programme light and amusing to suit the festive atmosphere, he had chosen a double-bill of Benn Levy's farce *Springtime for Henry*, preceded by a curtain-raiser, Alfred Sutro's *A Marriage Has Been Arranged*, directed by Elizabeth Jane Howard. A leading repertory actor, Barry Morse, had been engaged to direct and act in the farce together with two attractive actresses, Carla Lehmann and Nicolette Bernard, and, unexpectedly, Peter Scott had volunteered to play the other male role – though he had never before taken part in a dramatic production, he was an admired home party entertainer.

The productions were lavishly staged with furniture from Heal's and dresses sent by Hardy Amies; Anthony Quayle, then director of the Shakespeare Memorial Theatre, loaned other props. Everyone was roped into making a success of this centre-piece of the festival: Mary George and Ann Pym ran the box office, while Nigel Balchin's daughter Pru was stage manager. On the night the productions were a tremendous hit, notable for the surprisingly rakish performance by Peter Scott, transformed by a thin moustache and trilby hat. On the Thursday Sir Barry Jackson asked if the plays could be transferred to fill a week's gap in the programme at the Birmingham Repertory Theatre (at that time enjoying an outstanding reputation), but the invitation had to be rejected as none of the cast were available.

The last night of the plays had to be on Friday, as on Saturday the Assembly Rooms were stripped of the stage and returned to their normal function for the festival's concluding event, a grand ball, at which a glittering array of trophies was to be awarded, on the lines of the Vintage Sports Car Club, to recognise the boat coming the longest distance, the best turned-out boat and other achievements. A dinner for distinguished guests was to be held beforehand in the town's main hotel.

The Three Swans Hotel had been a haven of *bonhomie* for Robert throughout the week. It was run by a distinguished restaurateur, John Fothergill, now in his seventies, who had tried painting and running an art gallery before turning to the hotel business, originally at the Spead Eagle, Thame, which he made famous with his book *An Innkeeper's Life*. Every night during the festival an exhausted band of workers had collapsed around a large table at 11 p.m., to be revived by one of Fothergill's own meals. On one such occasion, he took Aickman aside, conspiratorially whispering, 'Where did you find *so many* beautiful women? How did you *do* it?' – to which Robert murmured something about the magic of the waterways.

Saturday, the last day, had been incredibly busy and tiring, starting with the arrival of the Lord Lieutenant in full dress uniform escorted by outriders (despite Robert's request for informality), and followed by a lengthy lecture on waterways in the packed Assembly Rooms. Robert drifted wearily back to the hotel to change for the dinner, due to begin at 7.30, and decided to make a last check on the layout. Approaching the room, he was surprised to hear a low buzz of many voices and, pushing open the door, he was stunned to see it packed with a coach party taking high tea. Fothergill had forgotten that there was any change to the usual routine of providing dinner at 11 p.m.

While hotel staff shooed out the disgruntled coach party and set to work in the kitchens, Robert and one of the guests set about clearing and laying the tables, a task just about accomplished as they dashed off to change before the arrival of the first of the official party, including Gerald Barry and Hugh Casson (director general and architect for the Festival of Britain), James Robertson Justice, Michael Ayrton, Cecil Day Lewis and Jill Balcon.

As the festival reached its tumultuous conclusion amid praise for its undoubted success and congratulations to the organisers, few noticed the widening gulf between the two men who had started the waterways campaign – at the final event Robert sat at the top table among distinguished guests while Tom and his friends were at a table in a far corner.

The week had been a triumph, not just in terms of the organisation of a successful event but in immeasurably raising the public's perception of the waterways. The tragedy was that the week passed without any healing of the wounds between the two founders of the movement.

Angela had valiantly tried to bridge the gap with daily visits to the headquarters at Welland House, but the bitterness of the past months prevented a reconciliation between Tom and Robert. The opportunity could have been there, it had passed and now it was too late.

Save Every Single Mile

From the outset, Robert Aickman had believed fervently that the object of the campaign was to save, and eventually restore, every single mile of waterway that remained in existence. He had no other thought from the time when, long before the meeting with Rolt and the setting up of the IWA, he first walked along the canal from Stratford to Wilmcote. It was one of the most derelict and disused sections in the country, yet the prospect of one day opening this waterway had fired his imagination and inspired him to take the first tentative steps towards starting the movement.

He was not, in the true sense, a boater. He had never owned a working craft of his own. He was not influenced by a desire to see one section of canal improved at the expense of another, and was just as concerned about the loss of navigation on the Chelmer and Blackwater in Essex and the northern end of the Lancaster, both isolated and cut off from the main system, as the problems of Kennet and Avon which provided, if maintained, an important through route.

It was not just that he valued every mile of waterway as an amenity, though certainly he considered this aspect to be of great value in a society that seemed bent on concealing more and more open land under motorways, housing estates and industrial parks. Robert's implacable belief in the need to fight for the survival of every mile of navigation had a far more realistic and practical basis – he knew that if one propounded a principle it was absolutely imperative to stand by it and not show any sign of weakness. If one acknowledged that even a small section of canal was not really needed and could not be restored, then the authorities would seize upon this and suggest closing more; also, in practical terms, the routes linking with an abandoned canal were bound to start declining rapidly. Moreover, people who were supporting a national campaign could not be asked to accept that their own local canal was less important than another more distant route.

During the latter part of 1950, it began to emerge that there was another faction within the Association, stemming mainly from the Kennet and Avon branch, which took a contrary view. They felt that it was completely impractical to seek for the survival of every remaining waterway, regardless of its present condition; far better, they argued plausibly, to concentrate IWA's limited resources on ensuring that the best routes survived and were improved.

It was obvious that the campaign would be seriously undermined if it became generally known that there was a policy split, and the authorities would not take notice of a body that spoke with a divided voice. At the November council meeting the issue was debated and the Association's role was clarified as being 'to advocate the restoration to good order, and maintenance in good order, of every navigable waterway; the fullest use of every navigable waterway by both commercial and pleasure traffic'. Lord Lucan resigned from the council in protest and a Special General Meeting was called to resolve the issue, as well as to change the rules of association to provide powers (lacking at the time of the Willans affair) to request the resignation of members who disagreed with any fundamental aspect of policy.

Meanwhile, Tom Rolt on *Cressy* had returned from Market Harborough to Banbury, where he was spending, on his own admission, the most unhappy winter of his life, partly due to the deteriorating state of his marriage with Angela and partly to the horrifying discovery that the hull of his beloved boat was rotten, probably beyond repair. In converting the boat twenty years earlier, the fatal error had been made of not allowing sufficient ventilation between the floorboards and the hull, and the boards had been laid in such a way as to make it impossible to lift them and inspect the bilges underneath. While the outside looked in good condition, the hull on which everything rested had been steadily rotting away for many years.

He was suffering from this mood of deep depression when Rendel Wyatt from Stone called on him one dark winter night 'like some gunpowder-plot conspirator' and obtained his signature to a memorandum (later known as the 'Black Memorandum') to be circulated to all IWA members, calling for the Association to campaign more vigorously for the working boats and the improvement specifically of the canals still in commercial use. Afterwards, Tom wondered if he had been right to put his name to the statement, thus encouraging members to see him as a figurehead of the dissident faction; whereas in fact, by this time, given all the circumstances he was no longer in the mood to take part in any further power struggle.

The Special General Meeting was held at the Kingsway Hall, Wigmore Street on 30 December 1950 and attended by 70 members. The atmosphere was tense and nervous, and the proceedings opened in general confusion when it was announced that 200 proxy votes had been collected and no one was certain whether they could be used. A vote was taken and the members present agreed by a majority of 24 to authorise the use of proxies.

Next on the agenda was the vital question of whether the IWA would support *all* waterways as against the concept of priorities. This was approved, proxies being cast, by an overwhelming 233 for and 26 against.

After this rout of the minority group, John Knill questioned the competence of the meeting and the subsequent debate about the rule changes broke into violent argument, with some members shouting abuse so loudly and personally that no serious discussion could take place. It was finally agreed to adjourn the meeting until 3 February, giving the whole membership time to consider the issues and an opportunity for a larger number to attend and vote.

In the intervening weeks, tension mounted. It was an inflammatory situation; one group believed that there had been a deliberate, provocative attempt to alter policy, whereas the other side felt that the original ideals were being reaffirmed. Members previously unaware of the dispute, and concerned about the state of morale in the Association, wrote to Robert seeking clarification about what was happening. To one of them, he replied: 'You are right in supposing that the trouble in the Association is not based on any real difference in principle or policy. Such a difference exists . . . but its present exploitation is in my view merely a cover for or rationalisation of differences which are truly personal and also (on one side) commercial.

'One of my difficulties is that I have a number of other interests in life, at least as strong as the waterways,' he continued, 'so that after a year of subjection to bitter attacks and determined efforts to frustrate everything one does, it is difficult not to give the whole thing up and turn to something possibly more agreeable.'

As the date of the resumed meeting approached, each side sought to ensure that there would be a good turn-out. Eric de Maré, a respected and knowledgeable member who was not involved in the politics, was offered a lift to Birmingham by 'one of the Kennet and Avon gang', who told him that they would set up an independent Thames Valley branch if the voting went 'the wrong way'. Robert urged the distant Fenlands and North-West branches to organise coach parties to bring in their members.

Over a hundred members attended the Special General Meeting which was held, ironically, at the Friends Meeting House, Bull Street, Birmingham. It was another stormy occasion, with each amendment to the rules being loudly opposed and repeated shouts for the chairman to 'sit down'. Finally, in an effort to maintain order, Aickman, in the chair, specifically invited the meeting to move a resolution of 'no confidence' in him, but the challenge was not taken up. All changes to the rules were approved by 92 out of the 117 members present.

'I supported Robert because he was quite right: one joined the movement because of its purpose and that was clearly stated,' Eric de Maré recalled. 'Why should these people take over and change its purpose? They should start their own movement. So I was morally on the side of Robert – but one felt this terrible tension and personal animosities, which were unpleasant.'

Two weeks later Knill, Sonia Smith and J. C. Lester (Kennet and Avon branch chairman) failed to turn up for the council meeting, sending letters of apology that only arrived that morning. In their absence, the members present decided to ask Edwards, the honorary secretary, to write to them – and to Wyatt and Angela Rolt who had failed to acknowledge the meeting – and request either their resignation or 'recantation'.

As the internecine squabble deepened, plans for a second Market Harborough boat rally and festival had to be abandoned. In January Robert had carried out a survey which showed that 105 members, including 73 who would travel by boat, favoured a repeat of the full festival, compared with 24 desiring a boat rally only. News of the internal row, however, had reached the Market Harborough officials and local support was on the wane. Even such dedicated members as Cyril Taplin refused to take on the organisation of the event for fear of the likely unpleasantness.

In an atmosphere more reminiscent of the Civil War than twentieth-century Britain, a kind of Star Chamber 'expulsion' committee was formed comprising A. S. Cavender (chairman), Eric de Maré and Teddy Edwards. The signatories of the so-called Black Memorandum circulated by Wyatt received the following communication:

In view of the fundamental difference between the policy advocated for the Association by the minority and that approved by the majority, our council had been expecting from the signatories, in accordance with the usual practice, either intimations of their desire to resign from membership or expressions of recantation or regret. As your resignation has not been offered, our council assume that you are prepared wholeheartedly to follow the policy adopted by the majority; to support the present council in carrying out that policy; and (while constructive criticism is always welcomed) to refrain from aspersions upon that council's conduct of affairs.

Recipients of the letter were asked to give within two weeks their 'express assurances' in writing that they accepted council policy. Needless to say, none of them was willing to take this action.

At this time, part of the 'evidence' of disloyalty was lost in a bizarre accident. A set of Rolt's letters – regarded by the council as inciting discontent – in a package was dropped in a Birmingham street and immediately set upon and torn to pieces by a dog. 'Much of my evidence against Rolt has therefore been eaten,' Robert related jokingly to Cavender.

Robert's health was being seriously affected by the long-drawn-out bitterness of the affair. 'It has become apparent to me that the majority of our members neither grasp nor care about the issues involved; and, even more to the point, belong just to that section of the population which has brought the waterways to their present condition,' he complained to Edwards. 'I always regarded the only hope for the waterways to lie in interesting entirely new types of people in the subject. My consistent efforts to do this have been systematically frustrated by stupidity, envy and malice.'

At his own suggestion an informal meeting of the council was convened, which Robert did not attend. At this Eric de Maré proposed that the pressure should be taken off Aickman by electing him vice-president, so that in future he could spend as little or as much time on IWA business as he could spare; in his place a new chairman would be elected on an annual basis. Unfortunately, the meeting ended without any clear decision, so Robert had to continue in the front line for some further months.

In May the 'expulsion' committee decided to bring the issue to a head by confronting the dissidents with termination of their membership, under the new rules, within twenty-eight days unless they appealed. Pat Lucan took the sensible course of submitting his resignation, although his sons retained their membership. None of the rest bothered to reply, so the day was reached on which, automatically, the membership was terminated of Tom and Angela Rolt, Charles Hadfield (who was away in South Africa and did not know what was happening), Sonia Smith, John Knill, and twenty-five others. As already threatened, the Kennet and

Avon branch was disbanded and a new independent association was formed.

Tom Rolt had far too many other problems to tackle to be
much concerned about this final break with the organisation
that he had helped to found. In June, Robert told Cavender
that there was a rumour that Angela had left her husband,
though 'perhaps not formally'.

'All the time I knew her, she was in the habit of stating
her intention of joining a circus (with or without her
husband's approval),' he explained. He also understood that
Cressy was on offer for £1,000.

Both rumours proved to be true. As it became apparent
that *Cressy* was finished, Angela and Tom flatly disagreed
about the way in which they wanted to spend the rest of
their lives. Angela wanted to buy a larger vessel, perhaps a
converted sailing barge, so that they could cross the Channel
and explore the continental waterways. Tom felt that there
was still enough for him to discover about Britain.

In the spring, Angela spent £10 on an ancient Morris
Oxford two-seater coupé which Tom worked on and turned
into reasonable shape. One day, she stowed her belongings
in the dickey and drove away from Banbury, unable to resist
the strong pull of wanderlust. Tom and she later divorced
and were not to meet again for twenty years; she joined Billy
Smart's circus as the assistant to a ringmaster and clown, Joe
Isaac from Hereford, with whom she fell in love. Together
they travelled the country for many years, until Angela came
into a bequest large enough to enable them to travel the
world, eventually settling in the Dordogne. Until her death
in 1984, Angela took some interest in leisure-boating on the
French canals.

After twelve years of living together on *Cressy*, Angela's
departure was the final blow to Tom's chosen way of life. He
set out on one last sad journey to Stone, as there was a
possibility of Wyatt selling the boat, but when he got there
the survey showed that the timbers below the waterline were
beyond repair and the sale fell through. Tom miserably
cleared out his possessions, took a final look at the rose-and-
castle decorations, and shut the cabin doors behind him. He

recorded in the log that since 1939 he had covered 2,318 miles and passed through 1664 locks. Two years later, *Cressy* was broken up, but Tom salvaged the famous Ford Model-T engine to power a track-inspection vehicle on the Talyllyn railway.

Turning his back on the waterways that had meant so much to him, Tom drove once more over the mountainous ridge of central Wales and down to the coast at Abersoch to pursue his other great enthusiasm in life – steam engines. The situation had totally changed since his meeting in the autumn of 1949 with the railway's sole owner – the following summer Sir Henry Hayden Jones had died. Although the executors were prepared to allow the service to continue to the end of September, it was thought that they wished to close it in the autumn and raise whatever funds were possible by selling it for scrap.

Tom threw himself with great zeal and energy into the task of saving what he believed to be the oldest surviving steam-hauled narrow-gauge railway in the world. With a close friend from Banbury, Bill Trinder, who had worked for the old GWR, they called a meeting at the Imperial Hotel, Birmingham on 11 October 1950 which was attended by some seventy enthusiasts.

'It was Tom Rolt who led with his chin,' reported one of those attending. 'He said he hoped that the meeting would result in the formation of a strong working committee to investigate the possible acquisition of the railway and the formation of a supporting society which would keep the line running.'

A Talyllyn Railway Preservation Society was set up and – five days after the IWA's fiery meeting in Birmingham – Tom went to Machynlleth on 8 February 1951 to negotiate with the executors' solicitors, who proved to be unexpectedly generous. Agreement was reached that the railway would be transferred to a holding company jointly owned by the original railway company and the Society, which would be responsible for improving and running the service; in the event of it failing to operate the value of the railway would be returned to Sir Henry's widow.

Tom Rolt took on the demanding role of general manager and, now free of domestic ties and the waterways commitment, he threw himself into the daunting task of reviving its fortunes and carrying out the first ever railway restoration scheme. By the time the fateful letter terminating his IWA membership arrived he was already busy issuing and stamping passengers' tickets from the little station at Towyn. With very limited funds, and a great deal of hard work, they tackled the problems of relaying track and completely rebuilding the engines. They were hit desperately hard by unforeseen difficulties in the first operating year, yet Tom in his usual determined way fought to keep the line working and saw the number of passengers rising rapidly. Before he left to concentrate for the rest of his life on writing books and playing a leading role in the preservation of historic industrial artefacts he had laid the foundations for one of the most commercially successful vintage railways in the country.

The internal conflicts of the Association did not end with the departure of the dissident group. As the troubled year of 1951 passed from summer through to autumn, Robert found himself under a fresh attack from no less a person than A. S. Cavender, who had been such an ardent supporter previously. The issue now concerned the IWA's finances, which had been much depleted by the withdrawal of members and the lack of fund-raising activity.

At this time, despite Robert's heartfelt pleas at each AGM over the past five years, most of the correspondence and organisation was still handled at Gower Street by Robert and Ray; indeed, the burden had increased considerably as the IWA became more widely known and no one had replaced the hard-working Elizabeth Jane Howard. There had been a suggestion that Teddy Edwards's wife, Patricia, could carry out some duties from their home in Ashtead, but nothing had been arranged. At the council meeting in October it was agreed to recognise these services with the payment of £5 a week to Ray and a further £5 a week to cover the actual costs of the office.

Cyril Taplin, without warning, then threw a firecracker into the discussion by demanding an immediate rise in the capitation fee paid by the IWA to the Midlands branch of three shillings per member – a threefold increase. He suggested that it should be funded by raising the annual subscription which had remained unchanged at one guinea since the start. Since the matter had not been on the agenda, there was general uncertainty about the effects of his proposal and the subscription increase was violently opposed by Edwards, who threatened to resign if it was carried out.

The day after the meeting, Cavender circulated a memorandum to the president, vice-president and council members implying that the finances were being poorly managed and querying the desirability of paying Mr and Mrs Aickman for rent and services.

Robert, who had been ill in bed for some days before the meeting, was utterly weary of this endless trouble. 'My health has been deteriorating over a considerable period,' he stated in reply. 'It is clear that the continuous strain of running this extraordinarily disloyal and ungrateful organisation is detrimental.'

He was fearful that the next AGM would not be the right time to raise subscriptions as they still had to face criticism from some members over the handling of the split. Although he suggested to Taplin and Cavender that extra capitation could be found for the branches by reducing headquarters' expenditure, they still implied that there was some suspicion about the Association's financial position.

'My wife and I are weary of this almost incredibly unpleasant and malicious organisation,' he wrote on 26 October. 'I hereby state that I am resigning the chairmanship upon the date of this notice, together, of course, with all responsibility for day-to-day conduct of the Association's business, and my wife that she is resigning what may for convenience be termed the acting general secretaryship.' He requested the removal of the Association's property from Gower Street at the earliest possible date, reminding the council that he had only received payment for the past twelve months; until then, no charge had been made for the accommodation and facilities.

'I can really see no future in this body along the lines one had in mind at the outset; nor I imagine can you,' he wrote to Peter Scott. 'The vast majority of members want only a boating club, or rather a collection of boating clubs; and most of the council members are out, odd though it seems, for their own self-advancement.'

The year in which the Association had been driven to its nadir and Robert to the very brink of leaving it, had been marked by one success in the other sphere in which for so long he had cherished an unfulfilled ambition.

We are for the Dark, a collection of ghost stories, had been published by Jonathan Cape and well received by the reviewers. Three of the stories were written by Elizabeth Jane Howard, and three by Aickman, but since they were not separately identified in the contents there was an air of mystery about the book itself, and it was thought at the time that it could have been written jointly. They were Robert's first stories published in book format, and the beginning (though there was to be a long gap before it developed further) of a highly successful career as an author of tales of the unexpected.

Both writers had drawn to an extent on material observed during their experiences on and around the waterways. Jane must have recollected her trip up the Huddersfield in her spine-chilling, superbly crafted 'Three Miles Up' – the tale of a boat that turned up a canal not marked on the map, pressed along a thickly reeded section and arrived into a dark lagoon that seemed to have no entrance and no exit.

Robert's sinister, creepy story 'The Trains' (about stranded walkers who shelter in a remote guest-house built beside a railway along which trains pass unceasingly, yet with no apparent destination) was based on an incident related to him by a railwayman while he waited for the Rolts to arrive at a station near Standedge.

In the first ghost story that he wrote, 'The View', the location was clearly based on the Isle of Man and the influence of the gods was acknowledged. More significantly, its mood reflected the emotional and sexual trauma that he had been experiencing over recent years. He wrote: 'Men are divided into those who know they find women too attractive for their peace of mind or happiness to be long continued; and those who know they would be happier if only they could come to some sort of terms with the intransigent and rather trivial opposite sex.'

'Cut out the Dead Wood'

In the shock waves caused by Aickman's resignation, the other members of the council buried their differences and rallied together in an effort to set the Association on a more formal and professional footing. There were already signs that the need had become pressing to have an efficient organisation ready to campaign more vigorously for the waterways.

During the early years of the British Transport Commission, in the immediate post-war period, there had been little change in the policy of keeping open the navigable waterways, even though their condition was poor and lacking proper maintenance. The first warning that a tougher approach was being considered came in the Minister for Transport's reply to a Parliamentary question on 12 March 1952:

> . . . a number of canals (accounting for approximately one-third of the total mileage transferred to the Commission) were little or not at all used commercially and had already become derelict, and the Commission are satisfied that many are no longer required as a means of transport. It may be decided that some should be abandoned as no longer needed.

By now, the IWA had elected a new chairman in place of Aickman – Captain R. M. Bilton, RN, DSO, MSc. It had been decided that the position would be put up for re-election annually to avoid the accusation that, in the past, it had been dominated by one personality.

A salaried general secretary, R. J. Evans, was appointed and the offices moved out of Gower Street and into rented accommodation at 14 Great James Street, still in Bloomsbury. For the first time in six years the Aickmans' relatively small flat was no longer the target for all correspondence, and tributes were paid to the sterling work that had been performed, almost unrewarded, by Robert and Ray.

Teddy Edwards was persuaded to continue as honorary secretary, though the task would be eased with the help of Evans, and Captain Vivian Bulkeley-Johnson, a senior member of Rothschild's merchant bank, was brought in as honorary treasurer, a move that was to bring considerable benefits in the future. Together, these two members were to provide a reliable foundation for the Association's work for several years.

Meanwhile, Robert accepted the compromise position of 'founder and vice-president' (as he wrote pedantically and crossly to Edwards some years later, vice-president is spelt with a hyphen!) which the council believed would enable him to withdraw from day-to-day responsibilities, allowing him to concentrate on the main issues.

The quiet, mundane sanity of the opening months of 1952, devoted to routine reorganisation, was in stark contrast to the bitter personality clashes of the previous two years. Little seemed to be going on. There may have been office procedures to be sorted out, but of the campaigning for the waterways there was little sign.

To a member, S. T. Wilcox, who wrote to Gower Street enquiring what the Association was doing, Ray replied: 'The position is that for the last six months or so there have been no activities in the field in which my husband founded this Association to operate! Latterly squabbles among members, the rights of members, etc., etc., have been the sole topic. Finally despairing of an alteration in this situation my husband resigned the chairmanship last autumn and, with it, the general administration of the Association and editorship and production of the *Bulletin*.'

She added that, as the new chairman lived in Yorkshire, he could not undertake the day-to-day business as her husband had done, voluntarily, since the IWA came into existence.

Freedom from routine organisation allowed Robert to take a more personal interest in various individual waterways activities. One that particularly appealed to him was D. and T. Whitley's attempt to run a pair of narrowboats – a motor towing a butty – as 'hotel boats' carrying tourists around the country. Not only did this mean that business on the canals was being generated, but it also provided the immense advantage of introducing people to the pleasures of inland boating.

Waterborne Tours were courageous in pioneering this kind of holiday (which thirty years later had become a flourishing industry, attracting thousands of tourists each year from all over the world), in view of the unreliable conditions of the canal. Whitley reported to Robert around Easter 1952 that the Docks and Inland Waterways Executive had not warned them about the state of the river Soar in Leicestershire, even though officials knew that they were starting their tour programme from there on 3 May.

'It doesn't appear that we shall get to Loughborough before Whitsun at the earliest as a large chunk seems to have fallen out of Thrumpton Weir, practically drying out the entrance to the Soar,' he complained. 'The poor old Trent and Mersey is in a shocking state from Burton down – very bad pounds and one or two locks with top gate paddles jammed open about four notches, which makes taking a pair down them a damp and hazardous proceeding . . . Trade, of course, is completely non-existent, and I don't wonder, considering the state of the cut . . . Oh, well, we shall at least improve the channel a bit by the end of the season, I suppose!' (Meaning that his boats would dredge a passage through it.)

Throughout the next few years, Whitley made a practice of keeping Aickman informed of the conditions of the waterways that he travelled; each time, Robert took up his complaints with the Executive and received a series of officially sympathetic, bureaucratic replies, though there was little news of any action being taken.

About the middle of 1952, a canal which had always meant more to Robert than any other came into focus – the south

Stratford, providing a link between the Grand Union at Kingswood and the Avon at Stratford. A Birmingham member, D. E. R. Hughes, complained to Robert that the Midlands branch showed little interest in the dreadful state of this southern section, preferring to concentrate on improvements to the (less attractive) northern link between Kingswood and King's Norton.

Robert believed that the branch committee had acquiesced, at least to a degree, in an understanding with the Executive that if the north Stratford was kept open in good condition they would not press for the restoration of the southern section.

'This represents very customary procedure on the part of the waterways authorities,' he wrote, making a comparison with a similar situation on the Rochdale. 'At the time of the controversy in the Association about a year and a half ago an overwhelming majority of members voted in favour of our agitating for the retention and use of *all* waterways: and it was, in fact, to forward that policy that the Association was founded! The other policy is the one which has brought the waterways to their present condition.'

The Stratford canal was placed on the agenda of the next council meeting and – in the absence of the two Midlands representatives – Robert obtained unanimous backing to seek the reopening of the southern part. 'It is very important that we produce evidence of the extensive demand to navigate this waterway,' he stressed.

To support this aim, Robert pushed for the idea of a rally of boats at Stratford – an extraordinary idea at that time as the canal was virtually impassable, especially at the Wilmcote flight, and the river Avon above Evesham had been out of use for a hundred years. For anyone else, the odds would have been so high against achieving this objective that they would not have tried. Robert, perhaps because he was such an impractical man in many ways, perceived no such obstacle to his dream.

He addressed T. E. Lowth, Stratford's Town Clerk, on the subject, pointing out the financial advantages of attracting another group of tourists. 'If both the river and the canal were again fully navigable, Stratford would immediately become the boating centre of the Midlands. I hope that you will keep this aspiration before your Council.'

Turning to a feature that could be changed more easily, he complained to Lowth that it was incorrect and improper for the canal to be shown on maps as 'disused' as the right of navigation existed until abolished by Parliament. 'There is no question of any part of the Stratford canal being abandoned,' he insisted. This was a small, yet significant issue that he won, extracting a promise from Ordnance Survey that in future all legal navigations would be marked on their maps.

Robert had an additional incentive in campaigning for the Stratford canal as work was now proceeding at a steady pace on the lower Avon under Douglas Barwell. Restoration of Chadbury lock had been the first urgent task because it helped to maintain the level of the fine reach of river passing through Evesham. Early on, Barwell had had an extremely fortunate break when the army offered to make an engineering unit available on a more or less full-time basis.

The opportunity, however, produced a fresh problem in that they would require a large quantity of materials far more quickly than anticipated; while labour was free, the materials had to be bought. On checking with the bank, Barwell discovered that the Lower Avon Navigation Trust had a balance of precisely £58. An appeal was immediately launched for £4,000 and the sum was raised. However, before the work could be completed, first floods and then the Korean war interrupted the army's commitment to the project.

Robert's own travels around the waterways during this period were mostly in the company of a new friend, Kenneth McConnan, who had undertaken the editing of the *Bulletin*. Sadly, Peter Scott's *Beatrice* had been put up for sale at Slimbridge. Throughout the summer, Robert joined Kenneth on his boat *Croxley* for a variety of weekends and longer trips, bringing with him an assortment of companions, including Lady Cynthia Asquith, editorial director of Fontana Books, and Lord Geoffrey Percy. Accommodation, as on *Ailsa Craig*, was restricted, so the tent and primus stoves were restored to active use.

These were hard-working cruises. Over one weekend in August *Croxley* travelled from Stoke Bruerne to Market Harborough, some forty miles and twenty-four locks – no mean feat, as Robert warned in advance. From there Kenneth McConnan, sometimes accompanied by Robert, moved on and explored the less frequented waterways around the northern circumference of Birmingham, including a sortie down the Wyrley and Essington which was still, at this time, directly linked with the Trent and Mersey – they found it a 'forlorn and inexcusable sight'.

Robert brought a new companion on this week's holiday, an Australian pianist, Elspeth Lesslie. She was prepared to do the cooking throughout the trip, Robert told Kenneth, but warned that she was penniless – 'only the very rich and the very poor are free.' 'We shall have to divide her expenses between us,' he explained. 'I am not sure that it is a brilliant proposition! But time is short and the free are few. I think she is a nice girl.'

Robert's withdrawal from direct involvement in the day-to-day running of the Association came to an end after six months when Captain Bilton was forced to resign from the chairmanship. Peter Scott had discovered that he was not and never had been a Royal Naval captain and that he had no right to the decorations he claimed.

Reliance on the services of a salaried general secretary proved to be equally illusory. After a few months Evans, who had a history of mental problems, retreated for a long absence to a sanatorium. Although he returned to his post, he was often absent during the following years for periods of treatment, and there can be little doubt that the pressure of working under someone of Aickman's drive and intellectual intolerance was hardly a suitable position for a person of nervous disposition.

By the beginning of 1953, with Evans still on long-term sick leave and the chairmanship vacant, the council became very concerned about the state of the organisation. There was renewed discussion about the possibility of Teddy

Edwards's wife standing in for Evans, but it came to nothing. Finally, only some twelve months after his withdrawal from day-to-day work, Robert resumed most of his previous responsibilities and the organisation once again revolved around his direction.

It was decided, at last, to put the role on a proper basis by paying him £600 for the initial six months; in return, he undertook to give most, though not all, of his time to the campaign. An appeal was to be launched to raise funds; in the meantime the gap was bridged by a private charity known by the appropriately innocuous title of the Mrs Smith Trust – it was, in fact, run by Bulkeley-Johnson's American heiress wife.

Robert's resumption of such an active and demanding role proved to be the breaking point in his relationship with Ray, who had felt increasingly distanced from him, unloved and unwanted. Her friends sang her praises for being an exceedingly capable woman – a good cook, competent typist and efficient organiser. While Robert threw himself with unstinting energy and commitment into the causes that attracted him – theatre, music and, above all, the waterways – Ray quietly and calmly kept his work in order and ran a good home for both of them. She was just the kind of companion that Robert, who never even bothered to boil a kettle for himself, needed, and originally his dependence on her was sufficient reward; but his undisguised interest in other women had driven an insuperable wedge between them.

Robert claimed that female company – and he did not necessarily mean in a sexual way – was essential to him as a writer, and Ray had tried to come to terms with this. He flourished in the presence of women, whereas he felt constricted and uneasy with other men. Women were generally more attracted to him by the fascination, almost hypnotic, of his personality rather than by his physical appearance, so he was completely thrown off balance by his relationship with someone as young, brilliantly attractive and universally appealing as Jane. Ray never really recovered from the intensity of this affair.

Ray was the kind of person who needed to dedicate herself to somebody, and Robert did not need or desire this kind of dedication. Frustrated and unhappy at his cavalier and inconsiderate treatment of her, Ray was desperate to keep her own personality intact and decided to move out of Gower Street into a flat in Oxford Mews, Bayswater lent to her by the husband of Audrey Bowley (née Linley). She had a short-lived relationship with a well-known artist. For a period she and Robert continued to work together and to meet socially from time to time, and they did not obtain a formal divorce until 1957.

The real parting came when Ray suprised nearly all her friends (who had thought that she was an atheist) by entering a High Anglican convent in Hertfordshire; unknown to them, she had had a 'religious experience' while visiting a church and had felt called to the service of God. This was reinforced when she came under the influence of a proselytising priest. Wearing formal habit, she was known as Sister Benedicta and, as a novice, led a very constricted life, only allowed to see certain friends and, of the newspapers, to read *The Times*.

She stayed with the order for the remaining years of her life and earned an admired reputation for her fine work among 'fallen women' at their mission in Soho. She died at the Convent of All Saints, Oxford in 1983.

Before moving out of Gower Street, it was typically in character for Ray to ensure that Robert should be as well looked-after as possible. She had kept in touch with a former schoolfriend from Bournemouth – now married and living in Radlett, Hertfordshire – Barbara Balch. 'I seem to remember some time ago you saying you would like something to do, and that you could type.' Ray wrote to her. 'Things have been happening in this Association which now makes it necessary for us to find someone to implement with part-time work the part-time work that I do.'

No shorthand would be required because of Robert's idiosyncratic manner of dealing with correspondence – standing over his secretary and dictating directly on to the typewriter. 'This is far less formidable than it sounds, and is much easier than taking letters down in shorthand as the person dictating just waits until you have come to an end of the bit you are typing, instead of dashing on not knowing where you are,' Ray explained. 'Anyone who can type can get this kind of typing going – given the will – in a week.'

Barbara was engaged to work on Monday afternoon, Tuesday morning and Thursday morning for about three to four hours each day, and she was paid £1 for each half day. Ray calculated, rather imaginatively, that this was equivalent to £14 a week, then a good rate for a typist, but she also admitted that the journey would make a large hole in the earnings. It was the start of a loyal and close working relationship between Robert and Barbara that was to last for twenty years.

When Barbara arrived for her regular schedule at Gower Street, where Robert continued to work, he would merely say 'Hello' and precede her into the study. Without further conversation of any kind he would dictate perfect prose, with immaculate punctuation, for three hours or more, without break or pause of any kind. She was expected to type without error or spelling mistakes, even though she never saw the correspondence to which they were replying. At about five in the afternoon Robert would utter the single word, 'Tea', and Barbara would go upstairs to prepare a tray of tea. In the winter the office was so cold – Robert never felt the cold – that she would delay the tea-making and huddle over the gas stove. She carried the tray down nineteen steps, then they would sit and relax in conversation – the only stimulating part of an otherwise tedious day – until it was time to go home.

Barbara was immediately impressed with him, even a little over-awed. 'I found his intellect prodigious: he was tremendously well-read and well-informed and could talk with erudition and authority on any subject, literature, theatre, music or art. I had never met anyone like him, and do not suppose I ever shall.'

In reality, he was a shy man and did not appear best in company. He had few social graces and was not prepared to indulge in small talk. Barbara admitted to being somewhat afraid of his quirkish sense of humour. On one occasion, when they were discussing their mutual interest in writing, Barbara proudly told him that she had had a short story accepted by *Tatler* magazine. '*Tatler* doesn't publish anything of merit any more – only trivia by Mrs Perkins of Peckham!' he retorted.

The Association had only just put its house in order in time as rumours were steadily mounting that the British Transport Commission was seriously examining the policy of shedding responsibility for hundreds of miles of waterways. In its annual report for 1952, it was stated that out of 1,751 miles open to traffic, about 747 were narrow canals of a largely uneconomic character. 'These uneconomic canals are no longer required for transport purposes, and the chief need is for greater expedition in the proceedings involved in formal abandonment and in transfer, where appropriate, to other authorities interested in them for various purposes (e.g. land drainage).' Over this year, the deficit incurred by these uneconomic routes was a mere £100,000 out of revenue of more than £45 million.

The theme was developed by Sir Reginald Hill, the Executive's chairman, in *Public Service* journal. 'If this industry is rationalised by the shedding of responsibility for the maintaining of hundreds of miles of unused canals, it should continue to play a useful if minor role in the national transport system.'

Proposing that waterways no longer required for navigation could be converted to other uses, Sir Reginald took a side swipe at the IWA (though not by name). 'This desirable objective is not, however, to be assisted by indiscriminate demands for retention, at great expense and to little or no purpose, of every bit of so-called canal.'

The Executive rejected the Association's request for a list of endangered waterways. The Kennet and Avon was obviously one of them, as Sir Reginald said on another occasion that 'it was not going to receive any more maintenance and was finished, as there were no large towns on the route'.

It was clear that the ultimate battle would have to be

fought at Westminster – even though campaigning in the country had its part in influencing electors to put pressure on their representatives – as the operation of waterways could only be altered by changing the statutes under which they had been established.

Aickman circulated all Members of Parliament with a leaflet entitled *Our Case*, setting out the IWA's policies, in particular urging the need for a National Waterways Commission: this would not necessarily own or manage all the waterways, but would have powers to ensure that they were all maintained to the statutory standard. It would clear up the existing chaotic position where, for instance, responsibility for the river Great Ouse was split between three ministries – Transport, Agriculture and Health.

Some forty Members responded to the leaflet by sending letters of support and they were spread fairly evenly between Conservative and Labour parties. Robert shrewdly recognised the necessity of keeping the waterways from becoming a party political issue, especially since Sir Winston Churchill's administration had an overall majority of less than twenty seats. His instinct for the ways and means of lobbying Westminster was, in fact, years ahead of its time and he used techniques which have only become recognised practice over the past decade.

In April 1953 he approached Brigadier Ralph Rayner, MP, to convene an informal group of members of all parties and both Houses. 'We feel that it would greatly assist our cause – which, of course, we consider to be very much more than ours only – if this interest could be given some organised expression.'

More than two months passed before Rayner replied, blaming an extremely busy session for the delay, and cautiously proposing that Aickman should address one of the regular meetings of the Conservative Transport Committee before any decision was taken about setting up a special group.

This suggestion was not to Robert's liking, even though he did not reject an opportunity to talk to MPs. Reminding Rayner of the indications of substantial support from Labour members, he replied: 'It would be disastrous if we came to be regarded by any considerable number of people as particularly attached to one political party. Although I fear that there are few votes in our subject, so that in the present state of Parliament there may be limits to the amount of enthusiasm it can arouse, I still think that our ultimate aim should be a Parliamentary committee representing all parties.'

Before any arrangements could be made, a new and serious threat appeared on the horizon. Chuter Ede, CH, MP, the former Home Secretary in the Labour government and now a valued opposition front-bencher, was asked by the chairman of BTC for his reaction to a proposal that BTC should be relieved of its responsibility to maintain the Kennet and Avon in navigable condition. He wanted to include this measure in the Commission's annual Parliamentary bill, and proposed that there should be an inquiry into waterways generally.

'I said that I could only speak for myself,' Ede told Aickman. 'The proposal for an independent inquiry might give satisfaction to some people – the extent would depend on the personnel and terms of reference. As far as the K. and A. was concerned, I didn't like the suggestion.'

Instead, he recommended that BTC should, for a period of five years (in order to await the outcome of the inquiry), be relieved of its liability to keep the Kennet and Avon open for navigation *provided that* there was no further deterioration in its condition. As a seasoned tactician, his advice to Robert was that any tougher demand would meet Parliamentary resistance; the essential manoeuvre was to keep the canal, one of the country's finest assets, in sufficiently good condition until a new authority could be brought into existence.

Shortly afterwards, Sir Reginald Hill showed his hand in no uncertain terms. In a speech to the Institute of Transport in Liverpool in November 1953, he pointed out that 1,200 miles of BTC's waterways generated 98 per cent of the total traffic compared with only 2 per cent on the remaining 800 miles. Yet these 800 miles still had to be maintained at an average cost of £300–400 per mile. 'Obviously the ship is

waterlogged! If it is to recover buoyancy it has to be relieved
of much of the dead weight that it is carrying,' he pronounced. 'If you want a strong healthy plant,' he added,
'you see that its roots are nourished and the good growths
encouraged, but you cut out the dead wood. So it should be
with the waterways industry – improve and rationalise.'

With pressure mounting month by month for decisions to
be taken on the future of the waterways, Robert found a new
and energetic ally in John Baird, MP, who welcomed the
idea of forming an All-Party Committee. The foundations
were laid by inviting thirty Members from both sides of the
House to become honorary members of IWA and, at last, in
June 1953 an inaugural meeting was arranged at Westminster
by Baird and Garner Evans (whose constituency included
Llangollen), with backing from Gerald Nabarro, the controversial Member for Kidderminster.

The attendance was good, but, as with all such briefings
at Westminster, constantly changing. Robert thought that it
was like 'addressing the concourse at Paddington station as
the audience was never quite the same from one period of
five minutes to the next'.

One of the MPs who drifted in and out was Jennie Lee.
'She made an ingenious speech,' Robert reported, 'in which
she implied, without actually stating, that my remarks
constituted a nasty political attack on the supreme achievement of Socialist creativeness, the British Transport Commission. (None of the other Socialists present had said a
word; it is thus that the Bevanites make opportunities and
take the lead).' Even so, Miss Lee (Mrs Aneurin Bevan) did
state frequently that she was 'all for canals'.

On the other side, Hugh Molson, Parliamentary Secretary
for Transport, looked blacker and blacker as the meeting
went on and details of BTC's inferior operating methods –
for which the government was answerable – were revealed.
The meeting ended, to Robert's delight, by setting up the
All-Party Committee. Even so, he recognised the delicate
tightrope they were walking, especially in avoiding any
suggestion of being anti-nationalisation. 'There were distinct
signs of party stirrings (for example, Miss Lee's speech

obviously induced several Conservatives to join the Committee who would not otherwise have done so); and politics will always be liable to wreck this otherwise promising venture.'

The briefing given to MPs emphasised the current threat to three canals in particular: the Stroudwater, Wyrley and Essington and Llangollen.

The Stroudwater ran through a picturesque cleft in the Cotswolds and formed, with the Thames and Severn, part of the original through route from Lechlade to the Gloucester and Sharpness ship canal and the river Severn. It had remained under the control of a private company, avoiding nationalisation as it was not owned by a railway. By this stage, a Bill to relieve the company of its navigation obligations was already passing through the House of Lords.

A fierce local fight to save the canal was being waged, led by an enthusiastic Mrs Airey who had been given a great deal of advice and support by Aickman, both in correspondence and in frequent visits. The aim was to acquire the company and establish a non-profit-making trust modelled on the Lower Avon Navigation Trust; their efforts were totally frustrated by the impossibility of ever finding a shareholder willing to sell – even though the price was purely nominal, they were holding on for development value once the responsibility for navigation had been removed.

The Wyrley and Essington made an important northern connection between the Birmingham network and the Coventry canal near Lichfield. A proposal to abandon it, along with several lesser known routes, had been slipped unobtrusively into BTC's annual Parliamentary bill and in this way, year by year, minor sections were being lost even before any inquiry had been held.

The Llangollen was in a curious situation. Although LMSR had abandoned navigation under the 1944 Act, the right to sell water had been retained for a period of ten years, during which period the consumers were supposed to make alternative arrangements. As they had failed to do so, BTC was compelled to apply to Parliament for an extension of this facility (thus, one of the most popular cruising routes was saved by a technicality).

In the meantime, following Tom Rolt's pioneering assaults, a number of pleasure boats were now using the Llangollen and a strong local committee, led by Trevor Williams, clerk of Wrexham Rural District Council, was fighting for the reopening of navigation. For the first time this campaign had attracted wide official backing with more than thirty organisations involved, including British Travel and Holidays Association. Robert had personally devoted much time to this cause by writing and visiting.

Implicit threats to the Oxford canal had, similarly, produced an astonishingly large and prestigious response from the local community. Although people were sitting on the floor and hanging from the walls, not everyone could get into the public meeting addressed by Sir Maurice Bowra, then Vice Chancellor of the University. The distinguished historian, Lionel Curtis, CH, urged that the inland waterways should, if necessary, be a charge on the Exchequer.

When the IWA entered into the new arrangement with Aickman, he had undertaken to give the 'greater part' of his time to the movement. It is impossible to imagine what he had left for his other interests. In the summer of 1953 he told Teddy Edwards that 'I am unlikely to be much in evidence [in London] during the next few days.' His schedule was Stoke on Wednesday, Evesham on Thursday and York on Saturday; Norwich on 28 and 29 July, Pershore on 1 and 2 August, at Bulkeley-Johnson's house near Oxford on 3 and 4 August; and on a week's 'canal-busting' from 5 August, including a visit to the Macclesfield rally.

Later, at the beginning of November, he had to turn down an invitation to visit Llangollen because he had an engagement in London on Sunday and the AGM of the River Great Ouse Restoration Society (founded by Peter Scott and Aickman in 1951) on Tuesday, followed by lectures on four consecutive days in different places.

Robert's 'canal-busting' travels at this time were on *Canada Goose*, an unconverted working narrowboat acquired by Lord Geoffrey Percy with the object of starting a carrying business. As it had only a boatman's stern cabin, Robert retrieved the two Hounsfield collapsible beds made famous on the Huddersfield trip. In 1953 the two of them made a circular journey from the Trent and Mersey on to the river Weaver and Manchester Ship Canal, thence along the Ashton to Macclesfield.

The following year in *Canada Goose* they covered a truly amazing distance (bearing in mind the poor condition of the canals) in three weeks. Starting from the Weaver, they travelled from one end of the Trent and Mersey to the other, then turned down the river Soar and Leicester arm, continuing along the Grand Union to Gayton and finally down the entire length of the river Nene and out into the Wash.

It seems hardly surprising that, at this point, the engine gave up. They were on tidal waters near Sutton Bridge, with dusk falling rapidly, and the tide turned before they could drift to a landing point. In treacherous waters and darkness, and with no knowledge of local conditions, it was a highly dangerous situation. They managed to beach the boat and Geoffrey struggled across mud flats to the nearest riverside village.

During the night he returned aboard a very small cockle-fishing craft with a crew of three. Although the master said that his engine was nearly fifty years old, he succeeded in towing the heavy narrowboat against the tide to a dilapidated landing-stage where it lay, until repairs had been carried out, for four days, going up and down twenty-five feet with the tides.

On his return to London, Robert received a letter from the calmer, safer waters of the Thames of great potential interest. Captain Lionel Munk, joint proprietor of Maid Line Cruisers of Long Ditton, near Kingston-on-Thames, was enquiring about the feasibility of using his hire fleet of river boats on the Basingstoke and other canals. Munk, who had originally worked in the Stock Exchange and rented out, as a part-time interest, friends' boats, had spotted the growing potential of the leisure market and laid the foundations of a successful business. In 1954 he launched *Maid Maryrose*, a narrowbeam cruiser designed for travelling along any canal, and for three weeks it was featured in a *Daily Herald* strip cartoon about Bill and Sue's holiday trip from Oxford to Birmingham.

As the Norfolk Broads had been the only well-known area for boating holidays, the Maid Line sales leaflet had to explain (in a style which, by today's glossy standards, seems almost more designed to put off customers than attract them) the nature of a canal holiday:

> Inexperienced hirers who have only cruised on waterways uninterrupted by locks sometimes imagine that locks are a nuisance to the cruising party and a material disadvantage. They might be a drawback to the man who is completely unable to master the simple handling of a boat. To everyone else, they are an asset, enabling the cruising enthusiast to exchange flat uninteresting country of marsh and fen, for example, for the beautiful scenic wonders of the Thames and the Chiltern Hills.

Back in Westminster, the interest in waterways stimulated by the All-Party Committee meeting was, at last, starting to register with senior politicians. Although the Stroudwater fight was lost when the Bill received the Royal Assent, the remarkable number of 112 MPs voted against it, whereas a year or two earlier it would probably have been passed unopposed, regarded as a purely local matter.

The most significant breakthrough occurred, however, when the decision to set up an inquiry, as previously forecast by Chuter Ede, was announced by Alan Lennox-Boyd, Minister of Transport (who, fortunately, was a vice-president of the River Great Ouse Restoration Society). 'There has been lately a good deal of renewed discussion about the proper use of our canal system in the United Kingdom,' he said. 'I myself have shared – though I have had to disguise it from time to time – some of the sympathy felt by Hon. Members on both sides of the House towards the need for a new examination.'

The Minister said that a member of the Transport Commission, together with someone outside it who had 'wide

experience of transport methods and practices', would carry
out the inquiry, which had the support of the Chairman, Sir
Brian Robertson. The general terms of reference would be
to inquire into the waterways usage and, in particular,
whether all possible steps were being taken to obtain maximum economic advantage.

Chuter Ede, in giving a cautious reception to the idea of
an inquiry, had pointed out that its success would depend
on the calibre of its members and the terms of reference.
Following the announcement, Robert drew attention to the
inherent flaws in the proposal: the poor record of BTC and
its stated wish to rid itself of a large part of the system.

He wrote to the Minister pleading for an independent
inquiry, including an expert who really knew something
about inland waterways. The Commission should be
requested to justify 'their unsatisfactory canal policy before
a disinterested tribunal . . . It is inconceivable that an
enquiry sponsored by BTC will lead to anything more than,
at the very best, minor and local improvements.'

His views were, of course, ignored and the Board of
Survey was composed of Lord Rusholme, most of whose
career had been with the Co-operative Movement; Sir Rex
Hodges, former general manager of Mersey Docks and
Harbour Board; and R. D. Brown, former Chief Engineer
of the Manchester Ship Canal. Even the original terms of
reference had been changed by adding a second – and far
more sinister – one: 'the steps to be taken in regard to such
of the Commission's inland waterways as can no longer be
put to economic commercial use'.

In due course an IWA deputation was invited to meet the
Board. 'We were very courteously received, and Lord Rusholme made particularly graceful speeches of welcome and
farewell,' Robert reported.

Sidestepping the limited terms of reference, the IWA
representatives pressed the case for a National Waterways
Commission. They also urged an end to the existing tiresome
system of tolls by introducing annual boat licensing; they
pointed to the unfairness of private commercial craft having
to compete with the nationalised fleet, the lack of good

canalside loading facilities, the dispirited attitude of maintenance workers who had no modern equipment, the lack of promotion for waterways, and the indefensible neglect and abandonment cycle applied to many canals.

The Board seemed surprised when the delegation quoted examples of poor maintenance on such an important route as the Grand Union. 'Even on the Main Line?' they queried – and Robert was pleased to see that the point had been noted.

Carve up the Waterways

When the report of the Board of Survey, chaired by Lord Rusholme, was published on Wednesday, 13 April 1955 it was revealed that, 'after careful consideration', the British waterways had been carved up into three categories for the first time in their history. The good news was that the first group was classified as 'waterways to be developed'. The bad news was that this amounted to only 336 miles and was composed of the broad navigable rivers and ship canals, providing direct connections with docks.

The rest of the nation's inland waterways owned by BTC, totalling 1,765 miles and comprising the entire cross-country network, had been offered either no future at all or survival as navigations on a weak and tentative basis. They had been divided into two further categories: 'waterways to be retained' (994 miles) and 'waterways having insufficient commercial prospects to justify their retention for navigation' (771 miles). (See Appendix B.)

The sting in the tail was that no apparent enthusiasm and no positive backing was given even to those canals to be retained which included all the major routes still carrying commercial traffic, such as the whole of the Leeds and Liverpool, Trent and Mersey, and Shropshire Union. Even the Grand Union did not escape, having been cut up for some inexplicable reason with only the lowest section from Brentford to Berkhampsted recommended for 'development', all the rest of the main line to Birmingham being dumped into the next group.

The report said of category two:

> They should be retained for the present to an adequate standard of efficiency. Every encouragement should be given

to the development of traffic. If, however, it becomes apparent in the light of further experience and after consultation with the appropriate Transport Users' Consultative Committee that the retention for transport purposes of any of these waterways is no longer justified, they should be transferred to the next category.

The third category comprised waterways either identified as disused (including the Huddersfield and Llangollen) or carrying insufficient traffic to justify their retention as commercial navigations. The latter group included canals which were essential to the preservation of through routes such as the Ashton, Peak Forest, Macclesfield, Witham, and Forth and Clyde. None of the more isolated canals were to survive, such as the Lancaster, Chesterfield, Monmouth and Brecon, Ripon, Swansea, and Grand Western.

For good measure, the Board threw in 'certain arms and branches' of canals in higher categories which 'serve little or no useful transport use', including the Rufford branch of the Leeds and Liverpool and the Aylesbury arm of the Grand Union.

The Board had no compunction in arbitrarily slicing historic routes into two halves so that they could be placed in separate categories. Only the northern sections of the Oxford and Stratford canals were to be retained for the present, the southern were to go immediately. The Staffordshire and Worcestershire was cut in two at Wolverhampton, leaving the Board with an insoluble problem over the southern half. They were unable to decide between retaining this section (linking the Shropshire Union with the Severn at the height of navigation at Stourport) or the Worcester and Birmingham (a direct connection from the heart of Birmingham to the terminal at Worcester for the largest ships on the Severn), but one of them was to be closed.

The Caledonian and Crinan canals, at one time valued as two of the greatest engineering feats in the world, were dismissed by the Board in high-handed fashion. They had been state-run for the previous century before being transferred to BTC and, despite 'small but seriously inadequate commercial traffic', they had produced a consistent loss (£43,000 in 1953). These, the Board assigned with the Forth and Clyde, Monkland and Union – which were of 'no real value' – to the Secretary of State for Scotland to sort out the problems.

Since rumours had been rife over the past twelve or so months that the British Transport Commission intended to abandon some 800 miles of waterways, confirmation of the plan in the Board of Survey's report was not altogether surprising; but the stark and uncompromising manner in which it was presented caused outrage throughout the country.

From the headquarters of this extremely powerful state corporation at 222 Marylebone Road, London NW1, the Commission's press office released a statement, the day *before* the report was published officially, giving both the salient recommendations and BTC's reaction to them. The Board of Survey's total lack of independence and its domination by the Commission that it was intended to investigate could not have been underlined more clearly than by this extraordinarily brash use of power.

The concept of the Board of Survey had arisen from mounting unease about the Commission's attitude towards the nation's waterways heritage and it had been set up in response to a request of the then Minister of Transport, Alan Lennox-Boyd, to meet the demand from many MPs on both sides of the House that there should be an overall, independent inquiry. Yet before any of the elected representatives (to which the Commission was answerable), let alone members of the public, had had the chance to study and discuss the report, BTC pre-empted all debate by stating that certain recommendations had already been adopted, the rest were accepted and would be carried out in due course.

No wonder the Commission had been so well satisfied with the report. The Board 'found that many of the criticisms which had been made of the present administration were unjustified' and praised the Executive for its work since 1948, which had 'accomplished much which should be of lasting value'. During its first five years, BTC had spent

more than £1.5 million on making good arrears of maintenance and on new equipment, with a resulting 30 per cent
increase in traffic from 10 million to 13 million tons per
annum, while the reduction in the operating deficit from
nearly £600,000 to about £100,000 was seen as evidence of
improved efficiency. In this context, it was even more
difficult to understand the Board's subsequent recommendation to close the category three waterways, which 'involve
a dead loss of about £200,000'.

The Board's recommendations – and their unqualified
acceptance by the Commission – clearly reflected the original
fears about the composition of its membership. Lord Rusholme was a member of the Commission, while the two so-
called independent advisers came from life-long careers in
the docks and shipping industries, which themselves were
confronted with burgeoning competition from the rapidly
expanding airways. There had been no one on the Board
with any personal knowledge or practical experience of the
entirely different forms of transport offered by the *inland*
waterways. From its conclusions, it was clear that the Board
had only examined the problems from the blinkered view of
canals as transhipment points with the docks and envisaged
a system of mainly estuarial routes concentrated on an
interface service with shipping. There was little doubt in
their minds – and BTC was in total agreement – that the
inland canals, both wide and narrow, had a very short bleak
future.

The report had a bad press, though it was saved by a
London newspaper strike that continued until the first
impact had passed. It was the front-page lead story in the
Manchester Guardian, which commented that it was far from
certain that the disposals would produce the desired economies and actually advocated spending money on restoring
rather than destroying the heritage. The *Yorkshire Gazette*
took up a similar stance: 'The canals should be administered
in the broad interests of the community – surely that is not
impossible?' The *Oxford Mail* warned that: 'The Commission is monopoly-minded, but it must not be allowed to
suppose that the nationalisation of transport was ever

thought of as a prelude to the abandonment of a large section of the inland waterways.'

People up and down the country were shocked by the Board's savage proposals and the Commission's unquestioning acceptance, and letters of protest poured into Gower Street and Great James Street. 'The report would appear to be the greatest challenge that our Association is ever likely to face,' wrote a member from Ashton-under-Lyne, Lancashire.

'The Board's power horrifies me, as I'm sure it must do everyone who has started and established business in both commercial and pleasure fields,' stated Holt Abbott, whose Canal Pleasurecraft Ltd would be affected by the possible closing of part of the Staffordshire and Worcestershire. He could not understand how anyone could contemplate abandoning half of a canal; even though the Worcester and Birmingham was much more heavily locked, he thought that this would be the route chosen from the two alternatives since it started in the centre of Birmingham.

'I feel that we have reached the parting of the ways as far as canals are concerned in that either the canals will disappear altogether or that some scheme such as that advocated by the Association will prevail, in which case everything will get better,' commented Christopher Clifford, who was managing director of Royal Worcester. 'Personally, I fear at the moment that the former is the more likely to happen.'

To this pessimistic attitude, Aickman responded that there were two things to be done: firstly, to clamour in season and out and in unison for a National Waterways Conservancy; and, secondly, to raise more money for the campaign.

Since the Board of Survey itself had classified waterways into three groups, Robert came under renewed pressure from some IWA members to modify his belief in saving every single mile. 'I am as convinced as ever I was that we shall get all the (surviving) waterways or almost none . . . we are *not* laughed at for demanding the lot,' he replied to Holt Abbott. 'There is always a proper place for local pride,' he wrote in the *Bulletin*, 'but the biggest single error our members can make is to be led, as our opponents always try to lead, into arguing that one waterway should be preserved and another scrapped.'

Faced with the apparently insuperable task of forcing a reversal of BTC's policy, Robert was constantly fearful of the Association displaying division in its ranks. He recognised that any sign of weakness would be pounced upon by the authorities, who would attempt to enlarge differences and widen splits. Boat-owners he believed to be a particular threat as they had to live with the existing situation. 'They start as belligerents and end as appeasers,' he remarked.

The Association, Robert claimed, had already been subject to insidious counter-action by the authorities. This started with BTC implying that the Association's real objectives were impractical and unreliable; the next stage was to offer various small concessions to boat-owners, thus creating dissension, with some members beginning to advocate compromise. As the Midlands branch had always caused particular concern in this way, Robert wrote to Holt Abbott and Pat Saunders asking for them to help in strengthening the resolve of members. It was most undesirable and impolitic, he said, to haggle over whether the Staffordshire and Worcestershire or the Worcester and Birmingham should survive; they should stick to the policy of 'all or none.'

The Board's report had already revealed a damaging divergence of opinion between IWA and the National Association of Inland Waterway Carriers in the submission of their evidence. Whereas the former had suggested that 'there was a lack of enterprise amounting to defeatism' in the Commission, the latter (whose members' revenue depended, of course, on this authority's facilities) recognised 'the problems that faced the Commission and felt that they were progressing on the right lines'.

The extent to which the carriers had failed to modernise and move with the times was illustrated by the issue of replacing tolls, as urged by IWA, with an annual licence. Even though the existing system, like the old toll roads, made it virtually impossible to give accurate quotations to potential customers for cross-country deliveries, the carriers were content to keep this archaic practice, partly because they continued to receive a substantial subsidy on the tolls, first started during the war.

The report noted that the difficulty in obtaining quotations for tolls for through transit covering more than one region was a comparatively recent one. 'Sir Reginald informed us that [the demand to abolish tolls] came from certain new concerns who were endeavouring to obtain quotations for traffic to a large number of points to which it had not normally passed – in some cases to points on the waterways which were not open to navigation.' Despite this clear indication of potential new business of a different kind – and how else were waterways to be developed? – the Board rejected the proposal for annual licences.

The carriers themselves went on record as supporting the Commission's view that most potential trade was bound up with import/export on the one hand, and short-haul local traffic and the Warwickshire–London coal trade on the other. Demonstrating their total lack of interest in exploring new business opportunities, it was not surprising that they should urge the case for BTC to be relieved of the unremunerative routes so that resources could be committed to improving a drastically reduced mileage. Indeed, the carriers agreed with the concept that there was no need to retain both Worcestershire canals.

There were conflicting views on another important issue. IWA believed that it would be better for BTC to devote its energies to canal maintenance, leaving the private sector – hopefully with a more entrepreneurial spirit – to look after carrying. The Traders' Co-ordinating Committee thought that the Commission should extend their already extensive fleet.

Robert had no illusions about the carriers, who had been troublesome from the Association's early days. Some years before, he had been wooed over lunch by their leaders who had attempted to persuade him to soften his approach. 'They constitute a very serious problem indeed,' he explained. 'Few of them in fact believe that the industry will survive their own lifetimes; and most of them are satisfactorily sheltered by "conference arrangements" [on transport rates] which are thoughtfully provided by BTC – the payment of compensation is a major activity of British Waterways. They pay quite cheerfully, knowing that soon there will be no navigations upon which the claims can be based.'

The most outspoken backing for Aickman's tough line came from Chuter Ede, now a vice-president of IWA, in his speech at the Association's annual dinner (always a high point of the year's programme, it was held this time at the London Zoo so that it could be followed by a cruise on the Regent's canal). Ede had been appalled during the summer to come across a group of members boating on the Thames at Lechlade who did not believe that IWA was going to win the battle; such defeatism, he stressed, might truly be the one factor that would lose the battle. He forecast, in realistic terms, that there was no call for pessimism – the battle would be won.

The Board of Survey's main recommendation on reorganisation had been that the management of the waterways should be separated from docks, with the exception of those most closely connected: Sharpness, Goole, Weston Point and Regent's canal dock. BTC had, in fact, forestalled the report by setting up on 1 January 1955 the Inland Waterways Board of Management – soon to become known simply as British Waterways – and Major General Sir Reginald Kerr, KBE, had been appointed chairman and general manager.

Although Kerr was a member of IWA and had been very active in promoting the restoration of the lower Avon, Aickman was doubtful whether this change of top management would produce any noticeable benefits. 'I think that there is a real danger that we have exchanged King Log for King Stork, although I myself strongly recommended Kerr for the job about a year ago,' he wrote to a council member. 'In that year, things have further deteriorated in a very serious way; Kerr may, in fact, be called upon to execute the *coup de grâce* – which he would undertake with his habitual efficiency.'

Robert's forebodings were confirmed before long when he had an unrewarding meeting with Kerr, followed by a frosty exchange of letters. They disagreed over IWA's policy of pressing for a National Waterways Conservancy which, unsurprisingly, Kerr rejected as being unnecessary. He believed that the Commission as reorganised was perfectly equipped to run the nation's waterways, the only problem being the lack of funds available to support uneconomic sections: 'No one had the right to expect it to spend considerable amounts of money on maintaining a particular waterway merely in order to keep that stretch of countryside looking pretty.' If the public wanted money to be spent in this way, he argued, then presumably the public would put up the money; many people, however, would consider that the nation could not afford this luxury.

Lionel Munk and Michael Streat – as chairman and honorary secretary of the newly formed Association of Pleasure-Craft Operators (APCO) – had a separate meeting with Kerr and came away equally disillusioned. They pointed out that the Board of Survey had not even considered the potential development of private and commercial leisure traffic, which had just started to grow over the past three years; if it continued to expand, revenue from this source alone would, within ten years, exceed the £200,000 being lost by the condemned canals. 'Sir Reginald was courteous, of course, but could say nothing other than that he would do his best to get things moving again,' reported Streat.

During this post-war decade, when many top jobs in industry were taken by retired senior officers, Kerr was a member of an 'old boy' network whose tentacles reached far and wide. Aickman's sense of humour must have been tested when he received a letter from a well-intentioned, though sadly misinformed, IWA member, Captain John Hutchings, CBE, DSO, RN, who had attended the annual reunion dinner of Operation Pluto, which he had commanded.

'I had an interesting talk with Brigadier Bond at our dinner, about waterways,' he wrote. 'Apparently there is a new man at the head of the Department, General Carr [sic], who had relieved Sir Reginald Hill, and I gather from Bond that Carr is a go-getter and is genuinely keen on waterways.'

As the dinner progressed from the fish to the meat course, Bond and Hutchings had sorted out the problems of the waterways to their own satisfaction. It needed carriers first to come forward with substantial contracts so that, once their requirements were known, those sections of canal heavily used for commercial carrying could be improved, though Hutchings admitted that there seemed to be an element of the cart before the horse in this procedure and he was concerned about the time it would take to achieve.

'Bond remarked to me that you and the Inland Waterways Association were a nuisance,' he continued. 'I laughed and said that possibly a Government department might find them so, but that in fact you and the Association were doing the very thing which the Board wanted, namely re-create a public and commercial interest in the canals.' Adding that his letter could only give a sketch of the many points that they had explored, over port and cigars, Hutchings concluded, 'I think on the whole the climate is favourable' and remarked that Bond was going to try and arrange for him to meet 'Carr'.

'I am becoming bored with being described as a nuisance,' replied Robert. 'Considering how we started, our success had been prodigious – and it would have been quite impossible without a very strong tide of public opinion in our direction.' After pointing out to the naval captain that the name was spelt differently from the way it was pronounced, Robert added, 'I think that Kerr personally is quite well-intentioned . . . in other ways he is a prisoner of an impossible and utterly out-of-date system.'

Robert was kept in touch with what was going on at BTC by a 'back-stairs' grapevine. On one occasion he was contacted by a 'mole' within the Ministry of Transport whom he identified as 'an important Civil Servant, not a boy in a pool'.

'Mr Major, whom I know, rang me last week, saying he wanted to see me privately,' Robert reported. 'I asked him to visit me here, but he replied that it was more the sort of thing one talked about over luncheon. There was then a pause. Mr Major gathered himself together, and said, "Well, what about a drink?" I replied that I would consider it, and where should we meet? Mr Major blushed (I could feel the telephone going hot) and, after several false starts, suggested the corner of Bond Street and Conduit Street. Naturally I agreed at once. Unfortunately, however, it has since become clear that I cannot go on Tuesday, the day agreed. And, when I tried to move the date, Mr Major turned quite snappy, and refused to fix another one. All this is absolutely true and omits a great deal of shuffling.'

Aickman's schedule, as usual, was tightly packed. In one particular week he had lunch with Sir Reginald Kerr ('he gave as good a lunch as public money will buy'); dinner on the following day with General Latter, chairman of the North-East branch, who was a leading proponent of the selective canal policy; and a council meeting on the next day followed by lunch with Christopher Clifford.

Widespread interest in the waterways campaign had helped to lift membership to over 2,000, and among people enquiring about the Association's work were Dorothy Tutin, David Dunhill (the BBC announcer 'Dunners' on Jimmy Edwards's comedy show *Take it From Here*) and a young Birmingham-trained architect, David Hutchings, who was working in Coventry and living on a converted narrowboat *Fatateeta*, named after Cleopatra's handmaiden.

Hutchings's letter was so lengthy and effusive, written rapidly in an angular sprawling hand across both sides of several sheets of paper, that, for once, Robert was defeated and failed to reply as promptly as normal. 'Mr Hutchings's letter strikes me as being almost impossible to answer . . . to deal with it adequately would mean dealing with little else.'

Shortly afterwards David joined IWA and met Robert, who immediately picked him out, not only for co-option to the Midlands committee, but as a potential council member and officer.

Within a few weeks of joining, as the campaign against BTC's plans intensified, Hutchings took a lead in producing a series of brightly coloured, waterproof posters, available throughout the country, which could be adapted to local circumstances. 'SAVE THE WATERWAYS! YOUR CANAL WATERS ARE IN CRITICAL AND IMMEDIATE DANGER!' they screamed with headings, varied according to need, addressed to boat-owners, ramblers, or anglers. While Aickman, unusually, dithered cautiously about the law of fly-posting, Hutchings – who was to become known for his hard-driving tactics – ensured that the Midlands, at least, were plastered with the posters.

David also urged the Association to organise a national petition against the threatened wholesale closures, but it had neither the financial nor manpower resources to tackle this. Instead, Robert seized the opportunity provided by the General Election in June, called by Sir Anthony Eden after taking over as Prime Minister from Sir Winston Churchill, to send letters to all Parliamentary candidates asking for their commitment to a National Waterways Conservancy; each IWA member was given advice on approaching their local candidates. After the election, in which the Conservatives won a 67-seat majority over Labour, it was found that 96 government supporters and 81 opposition MPs had replied favourably to Robert's letter.

Although BTC's proposals had thrown the waterways issue into the national arena, threats to individual canals continued to arise from local sources. The south Stratford became endangered when Warwickshire County Council opened negotiations to take over the road bridge at Wilmcote with the intention of demolishing it and piping the canal water. This, if it happened, would effectively close the navigation.

The threat prompted Christopher Clifford to step up the efforts that he had been making already to persuade BTC to give him permission to take a small boat along the waterway to Stratford. The divisional engineer, in the most courteous, though bureaucratic manner, rejected each of his requests on the grounds of expense as it would mean filling pounds that had been empty of water for years and it was likely that there would be many leaks. Finally, Clifford tried a direct appeal to the Commission's Secretary, W. L. Ives, offering to look after the water levels himself.

When this was again refused, Clifford briefly contemplated the subterfuge of filling pounds with water at night;

in the end, deciding that he qualified for 'a special award for perseverance', he settled for making a survey on foot. He found that the canal was unnavigable by any craft, and that unless action was taken soon it would be lost for ever.

'The condition of this canal is so appalling that even with voluntary labour and all the goodwill in the world, I cannot see it being put in order without expenditure of some tens of thousands of pounds,' he wrote to Aickman. 'It seems to me that the only hope of saving this canal would be by acquiring it from the BTC and setting up some form of Navigation Trust.'

This prospect was not encouraged when the parish council at Lapworth, situated at the junction of the Stratford and Grand Union canals, sent a resolution to the county planning committee in favour of filling in the waterway – 'the council have voted that the earth is flat', remarked Aickman, acidly.

The need to keep the Stratford canal intact had become pressing as, further down the Avon valley, work on restoring the navigation had been proceeding steadily after LANT had achieved the first target of reopening Chadbury lock in 1953. Now efforts were being concentrated on the curious diamond-shaped, shallow lock at Wyre, and fund-raising for this project had been undertaken by the local community at Pershore.

A fresh impetus came from the visit to the river of the Bulkeley-Johnsons, who travelled in their narrowbeam cruiser *Willow Wren* from Oxford to Tewkesbury, where Robert met them and introduced them to Douglas Barwell and his exciting plans for the lower Avon. Barwell, who had been tipped off by Robert that the IWA's treasurer had philanthropic leanings to the waterways, made certain that they were well looked after during their visit.

It proved to be very beneficial to LANT, which had not enjoyed any substantial donations, depending on small subscriptions and collections. The 'Mrs Smith Trust' made a series of gifts, totalling £4,500, which enabled LANT to press on with the restoration of Fladbury lock, a particularly complex situation. Here, the mill was still being supplied by a grain barge, *Pisgah*, which had to use the ancient 'flash' lock, enabling the level of the river to be raised slowly above a single gate. With the new funding, this obstacle could be removed and a new lock built of sufficient depth to allow the trade to continue.

The *Birmingham Post* was intrigued by the mysterious 'Mrs Smith', but Douglas Barwell maintained that he had no knowledge of who she was. 'He understood that the trustees made occasional grants to charities, but quietly so as to avoid begging-letters.'

As the year worked its way through to the grey days of late autumn, tension was running high among the waterways campaigners as BTC's annual bill was scheduled to be placed before Parliament in November. No one doubted that it would seek approval for the Commission to abandon around 800 miles of navigation, as recommended by the Board of Survey and endorsed by BTC.

There had been no signs of retraction, not even of modifying the scale of closure. Indeed, as late as 2 November, Brigadier H. E. Hopthrow replied on behalf of the chairman to E. S. T. Johnson, MP, confirming that 'the policy of the Commission with regard to their canals is based on the Report of the Board of Survey . . . the Board concluded that the Commission should concentrate on those activities which were of real value to the national transport system and be relieved of the remainder'.

Setting out the three categories of navigation precisely in the terms published in the Board of Survey report, Hopthrow explained of category three: 'These waterways are either disused or carry insufficient trade to justify their retention as commercial navigations. Some 260 miles have already been closed to traffic or abandoned, and much of the remainder could not again be made navigable except by heavy and unremunerative expenditure.'

Before the end of the month, however, two events occurred that changed the scenario dramatically. Sir Brian Robertson, chairman of BTC, addressing a meeting of MPs, confessed that he had been new to his job at the time of setting up the Board of Survey and he now regretted that it had not had a more independent basis. This, clearly, was tantamount to the chairman no longer accepting the Board's report.

Then on 28 November, the Commission's annual Parliamentary Bill was published, and much to everyone's surprise it did not include a measure for abandoning the 771 miles covered in category three of the Board's report. Instead, only 90 miles were listed, mainly consisting of the Kennet and Avon.

'It is the most important and promising development in the British inland waterways scene for at least a hundred years,' Aickman greeted the news in the *Bulletin*. 'It represents a major triumph for our Association and also for public opinion and an imaginative outlook over interests that are self-seeking, bureaucratic and, above all, rooted in the past.'

He warned, however, that the final achievement lay some way ahead; the fight would now be concentrated on saving the Kennet and Avon, while he understood that the government planned to set up a further, hopefully more independent, inquiry.

For the first time in ten years there was a sudden change in the type of letters being delivered to the IWA. Congratulations poured in from Holt Abbott, General Latter, B. C. Baker (chairman of Lancaster boat club), Lionel Munk, Geoffrey Percy and many other members.

C. F. Clements, chairman of the West of England branch, reported that the decision seemed to have shattered Sir Reginald Kerr as his secretary had written to Clements on the day of the announcement to say that he was ill and would have to postpone a tour of the West Country canals.

'Even though it is over a week since the news broke, I still find it difficult to believe that the Bill has been stopped in its tracks,' wrote Clements to Aickman. 'If we have, indeed, won such a glorious victory, I hope that the part you played in it all will, in the fullness of time, come to be appreciated by the country as a whole.'

The Bowes Committee of Inquiry

As the new year came in, the campaign to save the Kennet and Avon roared into action. By early January, 22,000 signatures had been collected and bound into volumes for a petition to the Queen. The volumes were put on board a cabin cruiser at Bristol and set out on a two-week voyage right through to Westminster – a convincing demonstration of the importance of the linking route from the Severn to the Thames.

At Bath the volumes had to be transferred into a canoe because of the state of the canal, and Commander Wray-Bliss paddled along the canal's semi-derelict section to Reading where the petition was transferred to the greater protection of one of the Maid Line cruisers. The canoe was also loaded on board for the rest of the journey down the Thames.

The cruiser reached Westminster Pier on 28 January 1956, where despite steadily falling rain it was welcomed by a large crowd. A procession, escorted by Metropolitan police, with scores of flags, banners and placards, passed along White-hall, headed by the canoe – looking not unlike the coffin at the head of a funeral cortège.

On arrival at the Ministry of Transport's offices in Berkeley Square, the cortège surged in, deposited the canoe on the floor of the grand entrance hall, and adorned the building with banners and slogans. A deputation of eleven bore the petition to the Minister, who gave the customary assurances that it would be passed on to the Queen. In the ITN news of the event that evening Major Edward Falconer gave a solo performance of the 'Kennet and Avon Battle Song' which he had written (copies were on sale at 2d each).

Meanwhile, an altogether different kind of petition – a petition to Parliament – had been drawn up by IWA's legal advisers and signed by Sir Alan Herbert and Robert Aickman. They had taken this step with some apprehension over the possible consequences as, if Parliament called for detailed examination of the petition, it would have required representation by a barrister, costing at least £3,000, an amount which the Association could not have found.

The Royal Yacht Association threw its prestigious backing behind the Parliamentary petition at first, then withdrew under vague and disconcerting circumstances. Aickman, firmly believing that they had been nobbled at high level, appealed to Peter Scott to use his personal influence and, shortly after, the RYA renewed its commitment.

Lionel Munk, who had considerable vested interest in reviving the Kennet and Avon as it was easily accessible from his Maid Line base at Thames Ditton, started to play an active role in the campaign. He put plans in hand for an 'Operation Kennet' over an April weekend when a fleet of fifteen cruisers would make an assault on the canal from Reading to the furthest navigable point.

He confessed to Aickman, however, that he was concerned about the poor organisation of the Kennet and Avon Canal Association which had not held a General Meeting for eighteen months. As the committee was run by the people with whom Robert had clashed five years earlier before they broke away from IWA, Robert was even more outspoken: 'The Newbury organisation stinks. There is nothing to be said for it whatsoever.'

Munk did not waste any time in sorting out the situation. Within a month, he had become chairman of the Canal Association and pressed Aickman to accept the position of vice-president as a gesture of conciliation between the two bodies. Robert agreed only on condition that John Brodie, who had organised the petition, took on the honorary secretary's job and the two appointments were confirmed at the AGM shortly afterwards.

The British Transport Commission's 1955 Bill had provided for 'the extinguishment of rights to navigate the

Kennet waterways or any part thereof' and gave the Commission five years in which to work out a scheme for disposing of the 'corpse'. The Bill had duly passed its second reading in the House of Commons, but on reaching the Select Committee a motion to delete the first clause was moved by Wing Commander Grant Ferris, MP for Nantwich in Cheshire (now Lord Harvington), who had become chairman of the Conservative canal committee and the IWA's most effective Parliamentary adviser.

Affirming that it was a non-party issue, the motion was seconded by James Harrison, a Labour MP, who referred to the large sums being spent on destroying the canal in his Nottingham constituency. 'Anyone who had smelt those other canals on a summer's day would understand why I, living nowhere near to the Kennet and Avon, come here to second a motion to prevent the closing of this beautiful waterway.'

Anthony Hurd, the Newbury MP, claimed that the canal had declined because traffic had actually been discouraged; he knew that firms who had sought to use it for transport had been advised by BTC against doing so and recommended instead to use road or rail.

On 13 March 1956, the House of Commons unanimously agreed that the Select Committee be instructed to delete from the Bill the offending clause seeking to extinguish navigation. It was a shattering victory: no abandonment proposal of comparative magnitude had ever before been successfully resisted. The BTC was left with the second part of the clause, requiring them to produce a plan for the canal within five years. In the ensuing weeks, during protracted negotiations with the various waterways associations, further concessions were wrung from the Commission concerning rights of navigation over the interim period.

Some weeks earlier, a stay of execution had been granted to all other waterways threatened with abandonment by the Board of Survey. Harold Watkinson, who had become Minister of Transport in a pre-Christmas cabinet reshuffle, announced the setting up of 'a further inquiry on a broader basis than that carried out in 1954'. It was to become known as the Bowes Report after the name of the chairman, Leslie Bowes, CBE, managing director of Pacific Steam Navigation Company.

The terms of reference were:

1. To consider and report on the future of the country's system of inland waterways and to make proposals for any measures to achieve:
   i the maximum economic use of the system;
   ii the future administration of and financial arrangements for such inland waterways as cannot be maintained economically for transport, having regard in particular to the requirements of public health and safety and to the facilities which these waterways can provide for purposes other than transport, such as recreation, water supply, land drainage and disposal of effluents;
   iii the conversion of canal sites to other purposes when this is considered desirable and practical.
2. To consider the present law relating to the closing of waterways to navigation and to make recommendations.

The terms of reference had moved a long way from the intentions expressed in a resolution adopted at a Parliamentary meeting in November 1955 which called for a public inquiry into the best means of administering the waterways on the assumption that they were to be retained, restored and developed. Nor was the composition of the new committee found to be any more encouraging. It comprised: John Corbett, partner, Peat, Marwick, Mitchell, chartered accountants; G. C. Godber, clerk, Shropshire County Council; H. E. Hopthrow, assistant secretary, ICI; W. A. Muddell, chairman, Land Drainage Committee, River Boards Association; Francis Ritchie, National Parks Commission; Michael Rowe, QC; John Wilson, general manager, Clyde Navigation Trust.

Robert was not impressed. 'In all departments of activity, the waterways are overwhelmingly the province of the small man; and he is quite unrepresented,' he commented. 'Despite their great qualities, it is hard to believe that these are the people to assist with such problems as getting trade back on the Oxford canal, or to be responsive to the innumerable small improvements which could transform the waterways situation without heavy cost to the taxpayer.'

His view was shared by someone from an unexpected quarter, Mrs Joan Marshall, now described as General Manager, The New Basingstoke Canal Co. Ltd. Since the auction, there had been reports filtering through about the state of the canal, varying from isolated efforts to improve the navigation to depressing news of its continuing decline and the company's commercial interest in simply selling water supplies to a local army depot. Now Robert found that he had a new ally over the Bowes Committee.

'I must say that I too have not much faith in these inquiries,' she wrote. 'It seems to me that a change of heart and mind is what is needed, that is to say the fors and againsts using the waterways should be thoroughly assessed, not in a superficial way, as has been done up to now, but as an all-embracing, long-sighted perception of what the roads are going to be like in a few years; what the demand for water is going to be; the general appearance of the country and amenities.'

At this point, Vivian Bulkeley-Johnson wrote from his home in Oxfordshire to place a steadying hand on Aickman's impetuous reaction. 'As the appointments, for good or ill, have been made and are almost certainly irrevocable, I can see no point in antagonising the committee before it has even started its deliberations. Surely,' he urged, 'we should exert all our energies to presenting our case as perfectly, unemotionally and factually as possible.'

Robert was suffering from bitter personal disappointment. He admitted to Ted Fowler, a solicitor and council member who was advising on the Parliamentary petition, that he thought that the IWA should have been represented on the Bowes inquiry by Leslie Morton of Willow Wren (by then the largest commercial carriers) and himself. He was right, of course, to believe that they could have contributed the in-depth knowledge of the waterways that the Committee undoubtedly lacked, but he showed a degree of political naivety and misjudgement in ever imagining that the IWA – perceived by the authorities as an aggressive campaigning body – could have been represented directly on a government committee.

Circumstances had cast Robert in a different role: he had to maintain public pressure to save the waterways, a task which brought few thanks and no official rewards, and he would have been completely unsuited to a position which meant compromising with government and nationalised industry. Once over his initial frustration, Robert regained his stride and sense of purpose. 'The independent inquiry will probably be useless in itself,' he told an IWA member, 'but it is likely to give us two years or so in which to develop activities on the waterways and further influence public and official opinion.'

For the first time in ten years since the Association's founding, the setting up of the Bowes Committee did at least ensure that the day-to-day pressure would be lifted. It was unlikely that any sizeable closure of canals would be permitted during the course of the inquiry and no dramatic changes of policy were to be expected until the Committee reported back. In the fiftieth edition of the *Bulletin*, Robert Aickman wrote:

> From the start it has been a race against time, and a continuous battle. It is generally considered that at the best it takes a generation (twenty years) to change the prevailing opinions on any subject; and we have had to work against the background of an endless series of emergencies and disappointments, from nationalisation to the Board of Survey. For this reason we have been unable to accumulate any financial reserves, or to relax for a moment. But many people have done all that we have done, and found that in the end they had hardly advanced at all. All things considered, the return for our efforts has been remarkable . . . There is no doubt that we have effected a transformation in public opinion on the subject of navigable waterways.

Congratulations on the tenth anniversary of the IWA came from a surprising source: Dr R. K. Kirkland had been one of the original small group who attended the foundation meeting at 11 Gower Street but he later allowed his membership to lapse. Now, applying for reinstatement, he remarked: 'You must be well pleased with the strength of the organisation, which seems to have made itself felt in official quarters to good effect. One detects quite a different tone in present-day press references to canals, while even BTC has to adopt a defensive tone while trying to do its worst.'

The strategy of playing for time became even more imperative when the IWA received their official invitation to make representation to the Committee of Inquiry into the Inland Waterways. The letter, dated 13 March 1956, asked for submissions to be sent not later than 1 May. Fears about this inquiry's lack of independence were fuelled by the opening remarks which stated that the Committee (housed in the Ministry of Transport) would have access, 'by courtesy of the British Transport Commission', to the evidence submitted by the IWA to the Board of Survey.

The secretary, Mr G. G. D. Hill, added:

> It would be of much interest to the Committee if, in amplifying their general views, the Association would care to provide specific information about the routes on which they consider that extensive development and improvement would be desirable and feasible; the expenditure which they estimate the recommended improvements would be likely to involve; the means by which they should be financed; the kinds of traffic which they suggest could be attracted by the provision of better facilities; the volume and revenue which such increased traffic might be expected to attain; and the receipts which might be looked for from sources other than commercial navigation.

Attached to the letter was a list of forty-seven canals (virtually all of those placed in categories two and three by the Board of Survey). The instructions continued: 'Whilst not suggesting that the Association should by any means confine their views to these waterways, the Committee would be interested if the Association, in developing the points mentioned above, would care to comment upon the prospects for any of these waterways.' In addition, the Association was asked to comment on whether any of these waterways provided facilities for purposes other than commercial transport.

All of this was to be completed within six weeks, which included the Easter holiday. The new government inquiry was beginning to take on the farcical characteristics of a Gilbert and Sullivan opera, with bureaucracy expecting to be provided with all the answers about all the waterways by a totally under-funded and under-staffed voluntary society. The reaction of some IWA council members was to suggest boycotting the inquiry and setting up one of their own.

If the Association was to make any kind of serious presentation of its case, even though there was no way in which it could attempt to meet the Committee's extraordinary demands, it was accepted that it would need a year in which to prepare a really formidable volume of evidence and to brief a barrister on the complex legal issues at stake. Robert confided to his solicitor, S. W. Pollard of Stallabrass, Bueselinck and Martin, that he would be glad to opt out of the inquiry, leaving it to the paid organiser that IWA was now seeking to find. He himself could spend his time more fruitfully in developing the Association's campaign.

Robert returned to the attack on the Committee's composition when he sought the help of C. Arnold-Baker, secretary of the National Association of Parish Councils, who had organised a meeting at Westminster in support of the waterways, attended by sixty MPs. 'It is neither a committee of experts, nor, on the other hand, composed of persons without preconceptions (like a jury), but an exceedingly unhappy compromise between the two,' he said.

Like it or loathe it, the Bowes Committee nevertheless provided the main channel for the time being for promoting IWA's views. A barrister, Anthony Allen, was engaged and the tremendous task of assembling the submission was started. The backing of other organisations, such as the Rural District Councils Association, was sought, and an IWA member in Cheshire believed that none other than the

Talyllyn Railway Preservation Society was willing to throw their weight behind the cause.

Although the Committee extended the time limit for the submission to 1 August, Robert still insisted that 'it is absolutely and entirely impossible for anyone – let alone an organisation with limited resources – to make a proper job of it'. His repeated appeals for another IWA officer to take on the task were ignored by everyone except Pat Saunders, Midlands branch chairman, who expressed willingness, though he could not be available until mid-summer.

Robert had decided to adopt a fairly relaxed and detached personal attitude to the Bowes submission – they would do what they could to meet the requirements and no more than was possible – and, with other pressures reduced, he found time once again to devote to the regeneration of his social life. During this year, he went to a variety of events, frequently in the company of different attractive women. In April Eric de Maré remarked, 'It was nice to see you and your fair companion last night – a touch of magnificence, elegance and charm in an otherwise depressing evening.'

One of Robert's ghost stories, 'Ringing the Changes', had been included in a collection entitled *The Third Ghost Book* (published by James Barrie in 1955), and its editor, Lady Cynthia Asquith, took a party of contributors, including Elizabeth Bowen, L. P. Hartley and Lord Dunsany, to the first night of Richard Burton's *Othello* at the Old Vic.

The verse-speaking was not to Robert's liking on this occasion, nor did he think that it reached the standard to be expected from the embryo National Theatre. Cynthia Asquith told him afterwards that the second night of Burton's *Othello* 'was even worse, but the S. Times doesn't agree with you'. 'How I *wish* we *could* start a Theatre together,' she added. 'The ASKMAN or the AIKSQUITH Theatre?'

At the end of April Robert had undertaken to join Lionel Munk's assault on the Kennet and Avon as far as they could travel from Reading with a flotilla of fifteen Maid Line cruisers. Although he was offered the use of the largest boat, *Maid Marletta*, for the weekend, other commitments in London prevented him from staying overnight. Instead,

Munk had to run a shuttle service to meet trains at Reading and Newbury. Robert arrived on the 7.30 a.m. from Paddington on Saturday, returned late that evening after a meeting of the canal association, and came back on another early-morning train on Sunday, this time accompanied by 'three young women (whom I have instructed to bring their own caviare sandwiches)'.

In May, one of the sunniest and driest of the century, Robert was struggling to find the means of keeping alive, in a nominal way, the London Opera Society, of which he was chairman. After putting on a number of productions on a union-breaking basis, he now claimed that the society was being forced out of business by the 'poisonous Musicians' Union' and he felt that the best tactic was for the LOS to remain in existence as a registered company until such time as it could become active again.

In June Robert gave a party to return past entertainment, mainly for people who were living on boats in Paddington basin, and they went to see *Hotel Paradiso* at the Winter Garden theatre – afterwards eating and drinking, with musical interludes, on the roof over the Gower Street flat.

In July the IWA's annual dinner, held again at London Zoological Gardens, was a complete sell-out with 150 guests. Before the event, such was his incredible attention to detail in ensuring the success of any function he organised, Robert made a special plea to Geoffrey Percy to ask that one of his guests did not give a repeat performance ('he did it as an aria') of the previous year, when he had explained in a loud voice to all and sundry that narrowboat carrying could never be made to pay. On this occasion Margaret Rawlings, the actress wife of Sir Robert Barlow, chairman of Metal Box, made an extempore speech. She recalled enthusiastically how as a child she had helped clear a course along the river Avon at Welford and 'her deep and moonlight voice set the right mood for the trip along the Regents Canal', one of the guests commented.

Cynthia Asquith sent an SOS – literally written in large letters on heavily embossed notepaper – to Robert to rescue her from the horrors of a debutante country-house party at

Stanway in the Cotswolds. '*Do* come to this. I need someone to talk to,' she gushed. 'And it *is* a lovely house which will be floodlit. No need to dance if you don't wish and you can leave as soon as you like.' She added that she had already booked a room at the Lygon Arms, Broadway.

No wonder that she had to plead so strongly with Robert – such functions were anathema to him. He once said that he disliked some social events so much that he would never attend them. 'Dinner dances: either one should eat or one should dance, if one can do the latter adequately, one had done the former inadequately.'

In August, planning to travel in Pat Saunders's boat along the rivers Trent and Witham to the North-East branch rally at Lincoln, he told Mary Percy, Geoffrey's wife, that the two friends he had invited had gone instead to St Tropez. 'This often happens when beautiful girls are faced with a nationalised waterway. I can never understand it. (They are thinking of turning up for The Wash, being full of death wish as well as beauty.) I have, however, enticed an almost equally alluring substitute (one), subject to her bringing two twelve-year-old girls.'

This was Audrey Bowley (née Linley) with her daughter and a friend. 'The arrangements are easy-going in the extreme, and I have participated in a number of these voyages,' he told her. 'On the one hand, if you do not like it, you may depart at any time without umbrage being taken; on the other, you will be welcome to stay as long as you like.'

She seems to have enjoyed this first experience as in October she joined a demonstration cruise on the rivers Lee and Stort in Hertfordshire, starting from Waltham Abbey and arranged by Lionel Munk. Robert also asked her to go with him to Oxford in November where he was trying to organise an historical water pageant, a son-et-lumière performance, alongside the Thames on Port Meadow.

On another visit to Oxford, Robert stayed with the Bulkeley-Johnsons, remarking to Geoffrey Percy that he had spent 'two liquor-filled days at the Mount'. His insatiable desire for company even took him to a meeting of the

People's League at the Empress Hall with Mary George (now on the IWA council) and Ann Pym – though none of them particularly supported this right-wing organisation.

In response to a letter out of the blue that autumn from a G. W. Noakes, Robert journeyed to Southend and spent one of the most remarkable evenings of his life watching a fascinating Victorian magic lantern show. The Noakesoscope was no ordinary machine: invented by Noakes's father and demonstrated at the Paris Exposition, it was years in advance of its time. The projector had four lenses, so a skilled operator could allow images to dissolve into one another and produce elaborate illusions of motion.

Noakes, who was the projectionist at the Royal Albert Hall, possessed a collection of hundreds of glass plates, mounted in mahogany frames, 2½ inches square, and hand-painted with fantastic delicacy and rich beauty. A series of 200 slides depicted the exquisite memories of a summer voyage in a little boat along the English canals and rivers in 1900. An unforgettable sequence showed a sunny day on the canal at Leighton Buzzard dissolving into dusk and the emerging lights of Japanese lanterns at a night carnival. Noakes himself was ill after suffering a bad accident and, since there was a risk of the whole set being dispersed or lost, Robert brought John Betjeman and others together to form a trust to preserve the collection in working order.

Over the course of the year R. J. Evans, the general secretary, was again absent for prolonged periods of illness, so that it fell to Robert to reply to most of the Association's voluminous day-to-day correspondence. From branches up and down the country there was a succession of reports of threats to the local waterways – the Bridgwater and Taunton, Rochdale, Derwent, Ripon, Lancaster, and Well Creek in the Fens – and, in addition to advising the members, he wrote campaigning letters in abundance to newspapers and periodicals. He gave information to people who made general enquiries about buying or hiring boats, and to David Hutchings who, sadly was intending to sell *Fatateeta*. He answered queries about waterways from multifarious organisations like the Women's Institutes; he dealt with frequent requests to provide speakers; he sorted out a mass of problems about the trophies to be awarded at the Lincoln rally; and he kept in regular touch with Teddy Edwards about production of the *Bulletin*.

To Wing-Commander Grant Ferris he apologised, on being chided by the MP's secretary, for the delay in advising him on the content of his speech to the North-West branch annual dinner and pleaded that, as he himself had spoken at each of the six branch annual dinners for many years, it was difficult to think up new themes. He urged the MP to follow Chuter Ede's line of stressing to members that the cause was not, as some of them were prone to think, hopeless, but on the contrary, doing rather well.

Even Sir Reginald Kerr found time to share his frustrations with Aickman. After British Waterways had announced that they were to spend over £5 million on improved maintenance, John Miller, formerly managing director of the Grand Union Canal Carrying Company, wrote to *Lloyds List* suggesting that the money would be better spent on turning the canals into roads. 'If we don't spend money on the waterways of course we are wrong,' complained Sir Reginald. 'If we do we are equally wrong. It is hard to please everybody, isn't it! What a hard life!'

Robert knew only too well what he meant. He had just experienced a fresh rebuff for an action that had been well-intentioned and caused a lot of hard work. It concerned Lionel Munk and prima ballerina Dame Margot Fonteyn.

After sorting out the problems of the Kennet and Avon Canal Association, Munk had rapidly moved into setting up a new London and Home Counties branch with John Betjeman as patron. This went side by side with the expansion of his hire fleet on the Thames, and he planned to unveil the latest craft at the National Boat Show, Olympia in January 1957. He asked Aickman if he could use his influence with Dame Margot, who had already shown interest in the waterways movement, to perform the ceremony.

Robert was doubtful if she would undertake it; since her marriage the previous year to Roberto Arias, the Panamanian ambassador in London, she had been less willing to undertake such engagements. Nevertheless, she agreed both to the ceremony of naming the cruiser *Dame Margot*, and to becoming a patron of the London and Home Counties branch.

The ceremony at Olympia was carried out successfully and achieved the desired media attention. Robert also seized on the event to present Dame Margot with the Association's honorary membership. The London and Home Counties branch officers pettily accused Aickman of stealing their thunder, while conveniently forgetting that it was entirely owing to him that the guest of honour had accepted. For months afterwards the ill-tempered affair rumbled on, with petulant exchanges about whether John Betjeman should be ranked higher on the notepaper than Dame Margot or vice versa. Teddy Edwards was forced to comment, 'This is quite scandalous . . . How much publicity would he [Munk] have got if it had been left to him?'

The kitchen-drama traumas of the London and Home Counties branch were soon overtaken by a much more serious situation at IWA's headquarters. R. J. Evans, who had been augmenting his small salary with a disability pension, was finally forced to give up work. He died, aged forty-nine, two years later in King Edward's sanatorium, Midhurst, after spending a total of eight out of the last twelve years of his life in hospital.

The few months' respite from intense pressure of the waterway campaign was over and the problems were multiplying. The Association's submission was sent to the Bowes Committee, though against Robert's wishes – he frequently told people how insufficient and inadequate it was, and believed that they should have held out for a longer period.

There were no permanent staff at all in the IWA's offices – and new premises had to be found as the lease was coming to an end. The branch rally at Lincoln had created a backwash of more complaints than compliments, while the proposed 1957 rally at Stourport looked set to be heading for a similar failure.

The mood of the nation was deeply depressed after the disastrous international crisis over the world's most famous canal – Suez. As the year drifted towards its end, with the people suffering a reaction after the brief surge of jingoism, the waterways campaign also seemed to be flowing sluggishly without any sense of direction. The euphoria that followed the government's decision to hold an independent inquiry, thus suspending the abandonment of many hundreds of miles, had faded as it was realised that nothing had been decided and the day of decision had been merely postponed. The gap left in head-office administration by the loss of Evans was filled temporarily by sub-contracting for six months at a rate of £475 to a firm, Waterways Projects, of which Pat Saunders and Aickman were co-directors. Saunders, chairman of the Midlands branch, and Aickman had been friends of several years and together they had been on campaign boating cruises. Another active IWA member, Mrs Betty Bancroft, was assigned to look after the day-to-day office work.

It was an unsatisfactory way to run an organisation that was now endeavouring to influence a major government inquiry and receiving constant demands from specialists and lay public alike, who sought advice and information from the only body entirely devoted to the revival of the waterways. Yet, to Robert, who was feeling increasingly isolated and already burdened with running the campaign, any help was welcome. 'Running the Association has always been like walking a tightrope,' he said.

He was seriously concerned about the IWA's financial instability. Although subscriptions had at last been raised from the original one guinea, the Association could not have survived without the generosity of two anonymous donors who between them gave over £2,000.

The two gifts eased the immediate pressure, but their benefit had been largely offset by a considerable increase in work costs caused by the Bowes Report and the Parliamentary campaign. The barrister's fee was around £500; the solicitors, who until now had given their advice as their contribution to the cause, were making noises that they should receive at least minimal recompense. The *Bulletin*, though mostly written by Aickman, was produced by Teddy

Edwards, who had upgraded its appearance – published quarterly, it had grown steadily in size and number of illustrations, all adding to the expense.

Then, as problem piled on top of problem, Edwards himself fell out of favour with Lionel Munk, now a key council member – there were misunderstandings over his hiring one of the Maid Line cruisers and these were inflamed by loose talk overheard at an evening function. Betty Bancroft, moreover, was complaining that she could not work with Edwards and there was a move to ease him out of his post as honorary secretary on the grounds that such an appointment was no longer needed.

At a council meeting, Edwards agreed to the proposal to abolish the position if it proved to be the general wish, yet the final decision was not taken. At the end of the meeting, Edwards remarked that they would be foolish to dispense with his voluntary services.

Two weeks later he was proved right. As the stop-gap arrangement with Saunders came to an end it became apparent that routine office administration, including the processing of subscriptions and the provision of stationery and other supplies, was in a muddle. Robert devoted a whole weekend to trying to sort out the mess and a chaotic scene began to emerge. He appealed for help to Betty Bancroft who, as long planned, was working the horse boat *Margaret* to Llangollen with a brief pause at Braunston, but she was incapacitated and under hospital care after the horse had trodden on her foot.

After spending another eight hours in the office the following Saturday, Robert told Fowler that 'I can find little to say in defence of what I found . . . Very large sums of money seem to have been spent without any record being kept, so that the Association is hopelessly insolvent; and the records are in confusion. It is all a very sad story of confidence betrayed, especially mine.'

Pat Saunders offered to resign as chairman of the Midlands branch. Vivian Bulkeley-Johnson, as honorary treasurer the person most directly concerned, had gone on holiday to Italy for many weeks without leaving a forwarding address.

Robert was compelled to cancel his own planned three weeks' holiday in Europe, hire two temporary secretaries, bring in a firm of chartered accountants, and start looking for a new permanent administrator.

W. B. Keen and Co., the accountants, brought some order to the past financial transactions, though reporting that few records had been kept. They found that no entries had been made in the cash book for six months, and they had been able to find only a few invoices and statements in support of payments. Since a number of cheques had been drawn for 'cash' or 'bearer', there was unidentified expenditure of more than £350. There were no details of wages paid, income tax deductions or national insurance contributions.

As the administration plunged from inefficiency to dire trouble, the Association somehow managed to put together an oral submission to the Bowes Committee when they were asked to appear before it in March 1957. In contrast to his open disappointment with their written document, Robert was inordinately proud of the performance of the seven-man delegation – no doubt in part because he himself was unfailingly such a fluent and convincing speaker, also because Christopher Clifford had put together a thoroughly researched and apposite scheme which provided the core of the IWA's presentation.

Clifford, who was a Justice of the Peace, brought exceptional clarity to the issues that others found so complex. He laid down three principles:

1. A national waterways conservancy would be set up and embrace all interested parties, i.e. commercial, angling, pleasure boating, water supplies and land drainage.
2. At the top, it would be run by a managing director and executives with not only experience of business but also a faith in the heritage and a determination to operate the canals on entrepreneurial lines.
3. There must be co-operation from government in providing some capital and a reasonable degree of commercial support from other nationalised industries such as coal.

Clifford gave pages of detailed information about the way in which the capital would be allocated to waterways improvements, and he calculated the revenue to be generated by an efficiently run and well-promoted fleet of 400 narrow-boats. The introduction of licensing and a sales force were other prerequisites for the achievement of his bottom-line figures: an estimated annual profit of £345,000, after paying interest and eliminating the current loss of £200,000. The plan, of course, was qualified by the fact that IWA had not had access to British Waterways accounts.

Afterwards, Clifford said that he felt throughout that he had been addressing a hostile audience, typified by the way in which each member of the Bowes Committee had a copy of the Board of Survey's 1955 report, to which they referred constantly when asking questions. The chairman had been inflexible in his attitude: 'A lot of witnesses have told us that the canals could take traffic off the roads, but we cannot find any evidence for it.'

'I thought that our team did very well indeed. I find it hard to think of any way in which any representatives of the Association could have made better use of the time and circumstances,' Robert reported to Bulkeley-Johnson. 'And this is sincere, not conventional: never before on such an occasion have I felt so pleased with our showing.'

The delegates went straight to a Bloomsbury hotel and a press conference, so that their case could reach a far wider audience. It was very well attended by forty journalists and – very surprisingly and uninvited – by W. L. Ives, the Secretary of British Waterways. Ives repeatedly interrupted and contradicted speakers until Ernest Partridge, MP (who was campaigning for the retention of the Ashby canal), advised that he should be ruled out of order and the press agreed unanimously that he should be silenced.

In a year in which disaster often seemed to be just around the corner, another potential crisis was avoided by the timely and energetic action of David Hutchings. The rally, which had originally been proposed for Stourport, had been trans-ferred to Coventry, scheduled for August; some seven weeks only before it was due to start, Pat Saunders resigned from the committee chairmanship, leaving a situation in which little had been organised. Among the omissions was the failure to produce a printed programme for which good advertising revenue had already been promised.

With no previous experience of organising such an event, David Hutchings leapt into the breach. He was very fortunate in winning the wholehearted support of a rare and inspiring local government leader, Pearl Hyde, reputedly a former music-hall singer, who was the current Lord Mayor of Coventry. Although she had had no previous involvement with waterways, she quickly grasped their potential to the city and threw herself into the event with such enthusiasm that she joined David on his boat *Fatateeta* and sailed on it from the Ashby canal right into the heart of the city to the cheers of thousands of people lining the towing-path – an unusual experience for a civic leader, but Pearl Hyde's infectious personality captivated everyone.

She formally opened the rally – and she formally closed it; she presented prizes, she attended a film show packed to capacity; she gave a lunch in the ancient St Mary's Hall so that canal enthusiasts could meet people from other walks of life, one of whom was Harry Secombe, then appearing at the local theatre; she spoke at the rally dinner and then danced until 2 a.m. After the rally closed, she remained actively interested in waterways, her portrait was drawn by Peter Scott, and she was one of the first civic leaders to inspire the building of a narrowboat specially designed for the elderly and handicapped. Tragically, she died in a car crash at Easter 1963.

'David Hutchings succeeded in keeping matters of policy to the fore, and distinct from social and aquatic trivialities, in a degree unequalled since the Market Harborough festival,' Robert told Bulkeley-Johnson. 'On the other side, David has worked from first to last against internal obstructionism and jealousy. It would be impossible for me to praise too highly Hutchings's refusal to be discouraged (including by me).'

Back in London, Sir Geoffrey Lowles, a new council

member, had set up a committee of inquiry into the Saunders-Bancroft affair while Robert was still driving himself too hard in trying to find some firmer and more effective way of running the Association in future. A new administrator was selected – Jean Gorrie – and it was very much Robert's choice to have a woman (rather cynically, because she would be less expensive). The Mrs Smith Trust came up with yet another donation of £300 to cover her salary for six months.

Turning back to a proposal made at the very first council meeting in May 1946, Robert won the support of a cabal of members – Damerham, Fowler, Munk and Offley – that the Association should seek incorporation as a company limited by guarantee. He envisaged a radical reorganisation in which the financial management and campaign planning would be in the hands of a small board of directors (still known as the council) who would draw advice from quarterly meetings with a larger, representative advisory committee.

The proposal was to run into enormous opposition and many technical difficulties, but, before any progress could be made, Robert was forced to withdraw from all activity and take a total rest for three months. His doctor diagnosed that he was suffering from acute blood poisoning, no doubt brought on by worry and overwork. The council members were free to make any decisions about the future conduct of the Association without involving him.

'I am quite certain that this unfortunate circumstance will at least have the virtue of underlining the void which will quickly make itself apparent in your absence,' Lionel Munk wrote to Aickman.

Enter the National Trust

Lionel Munk's forecast was proved to be completely accurate. Ted Fowler assumed the role of chairman in the autumn of 1957 – unoccupied since Bilton's resignation five years earlier – with the aim of steering through the desperately needed reorganisation of the Association. His proposals were defeated at a council meeting by thirteen votes to eight and he promptly resigned. 'I have made clear that I cease to be chairman, and I am not going to stand for re-election to the council,' he told Aickman. 'I would certainly not remain as chairman trying to run something which, in its present state, is unworkable. I have come to the conclusion that all that is left is a council with a majority which represents in effect a few boat-owners. I do believe the Association has no effective future whatsoever.'

The situation deteriorated still further when Vivian Bulkeley-Johnson – who had provided such solid and loyal support as honorary treasurer since 1952 – decided to follow in Fowler's footsteps and resign his office. Both of them felt that their time would be better employed by putting it all behind their efforts as directors of Willow Wren, the last major commercial carriers, which had been formed in 1953 through Bulkeley-Johnson's investment and the management of Leslie Morton, who had run the successful pre-war operations of the Grand Union Canal Carrying Company. The company's name had been adopted from Mr and Mrs Bulkeley-Johnson's twenty-six-foot cabin cruiser, in which the couple had extensively explored the waterways.

The other proponents of the plan to incorporate the Association were in disarray after the council's vote and the two key resignations. Munk thought about setting up a breakaway organisation called the Canals Action Group, while Christopher Clifford's sage advice about their opponents was: 'Keep them guessing.'

The IWA now had no chairman or treasurer, a paid administrator who had little experience, and a policy in tatters, just at the time when the waterways movement was waiting anxiously for the publication of the Bowes Committee's findings. It was inevitable, since there was no one else sufficiently qualified, that Robert became drawn back into the web of intrigue and conflict; but he only took up the leadership again with great reluctance.

'As you can imagine, I feel the greatest hesitation about even attempting to re-enter a sphere of activity which had already seriously upset my health, and which must surely produce more than the normal proportion of objectionable people,' he explained to Clifford. He felt, nevertheless, that he owed a duty to the majority of ordinary members, who still had no idea of the crisis, to set out the position and allow them to make the final decision on the future organisation.

After the initial rejection Robert recognised that there was no point in trying to win approval from the council – he was convinced that the only course was to take a referendum of the entire membership. Within days he made a vital visit to Slimbridge to ensure Peter Scott's influential backing and won a reprieve from Bulkeley-Johnson, who agreed to withhold his resignation until the next AGM. With active and enthusiastic support from Munk and Clifford, Aickman was back in charge.

The referendum approach ran into a serious problem: the solicitors advised that there was no legal provision for this in the rules of association. They would first have to gain the council's support and then go through the tricky formalities of changing the rules before the membership could be consulted.

Leading the opposition to the proposed reform was Sir Geoffrey Lowles, chairman of the North-East branch, who had been on the council for only a year. He produced a report drawn up by the sub-committee, comprising Brodie and Edwards, that he had chaired into the Association's financial failure. One significant conclusion was that 'no dishonesty can be attributed to those in charge of the office'.

Robert felt that the report had whitewashed and thereby implicitly blamed him for maladministration. He complained bitterly that he had not even given evidence to the Committee, though the report stated incorrectly that he had. 'The only evidence taken from me consisted in general remarks over dinner with Lowles (alone) where I was host at my club,' he told Pollard. 'I had absolutely no idea I was giving "evidence".'

Robert, in fact, was displaying one of the worst flaws of his character – his over-sensitivity to personal criticism, which at times of great pressure he would take so intensely to heart that he became almost paranoid in the violence of his reaction. Lowles had not in any way blamed Aickman; he blamed the Association for allowing a situation to develop in which there had been no control as it had neither a chairman nor vice-chairman. He felt that Pat Saunders had been placed in an impossible position caused by the state of muddle after Evans's constant bouts of ill-health.

The Midlands branch, yet again, showed lukewarm support for the proposed reorganisation. Douglas Barwell, though backing Aickman personally, questioned the concept of turning the Association into a 'private limited company' – he was concerned about 'the amount of drawings of directors of such a company, in proportion to the total income received, by way of salary, commission and expenses'.

Robert patiently explained that it was this kind of misunderstanding about the proposal that had been causing so much discord: they were not planning a *private* limited company, but a non-profit distributing company limited by guarantee. He pointed out that, under the present constitution, every member was liable for any debts incurred, and the administration had suffered from chronic instability.

Captain Christopher 'Crick' Grundy, who had returned from the Korean war after being awarded the MC, gave Robert judicious help in wording the resolution to be put, firstly, to council and then, if agreed, to the AGM. In contrast to Robert's habitual inclination to challenge the opposition, his ingenious draft was tactically and diplomatically worded in such a way that opponents would be embarrassed. Moreover, Crick sensibly volunteered to propose the resolution as, he felt, 'I am probably not regarded as such a double-eyed scoundrel as is, for instance, Capt. Munk.'

The rules were to be changed to enable the engagements and possessions of the Association to be transferred to another body, provided that it had the same principal objectives, subject to a majority vote at an AGM or a two-thirds majority by postal referendum.

On 11 January 1958 the resolution was approved by 12 votes to 2 at the council meeting, and subsequently by 400 members attending the AGM with only 11 dissidents; in fact, an amendment moved from the floor made a straight majority by postal referendum acceptable. A great deal of credit for the successful conduct of the meeting was given to the erudite and good-humoured chairmanship of Sir Alan Herbert, who excelled himself in this role, kept to the point and avoided all conflict.

A rather large and untidy man in flannels and tweed jacket sitting in the front row, who offered to act as teller for the 'Ayes', told Aickman: 'I was delighted that the council had shown sufficient statesmanship to produce this last-minute resolution to avoid splitting the Association.'

Less than three weeks after returning to the fray Robert, this time aided by strong and clever supporters, had achieved the turnaround in the IWA's affairs that had been sought for months. 'The ovation that you received at the end demonstrates that whatever some members may think, you still command the confidence and admiration of the vast majority,' Arthur Goodland assured him.

A further three months elapsed before all the necessary arrangements could be made for conducting the postal referendum. It was not until the end of April that the convincing result was known: 699 for, and 336 against, out of a poll in which about half the members voted. The council was now empowered to start the complex and laborious process of incorporation, which was delayed while the position of covenanted subscriptions, subject to charity laws, was sorted out.

During this period, while the Association was effectively in a state of suspension, the Great James Street lease expired and Robert, as there was no one else to take on the negotiations, found and acquired alternative premises in Emerald Street. When the landlords discovered the precarious position of their prospective tenants, they insisted on a surety of £900 (three years' rent) being put up by three members of council. Robert thought that this was an appropriate way in which to involve Sir Geoffrey Lowles, who declined, leaving the hardcore of Munk, Clifford and Aickman to fund it from their own pockets.

Robert also invited – as an olive branch, though much against his inclinations – Sir Geoffrey and three of his supporters to join the new council after incorporation had taken place. Again Sir Geoffrey rejected this. In the end the signatories to the articles of incorporation were Robert Aickman, Christopher Clifford, David Hutchings, Lionel Munk, Stan Offley (branch chairman), Ray Slack (branch chairman) and Michael Streat, together with John Betjeman, Sir Alan Herbert, Peter Scott and Stanford Robinson (the orchestral conductor and IWA member).

As at the time of the first 'civil war' in 1951, there was a backlash of dissension from the losers. Cyril Jewkes and Bayley Manion, chairman and joint honorary secretary respectively of the Midlands branch, resigned on the grounds that they could not operate within the new framework, and David Hutchings, as leader of the rump of a previously large group, was left with the task of rebuilding it.

The Fenlands branch (which in 1951 under Arthur Cavender had given sterling support) decided to terminate its own existence at a meeting which Robert described as 'just about the most unpleasant that I have ever attended (which, unfortunately, is to say something)'. Years later, he still cited this as the most abusive meeting out of his long experience – he was blamed personally for head-office muddle over lost membership records and subscriptions.

Finally, news seeped through the grapevine that a breakaway organisation, the Inland Waterways Protection Society, had been formed in the North-East with Sir Geoffrey Lowles as president (though he had not yet resigned from the IWA council) and Teddy Edwards as honorary waterways consultant. Robert accused Mrs Bessie Bunker, formerly honorary secretary of the North-East branch and a lady given to voluminous, gossipy correspondence, of being the 'founder'. This, according to him, was her reaction: '"Please sir, it wasn't me!" she chortled. "Or at least it was not my original *idea*, although perhaps I should admit (as an Offering to Truth) that quite likely the Society would not have materialised had it *not* been for me."'

Lionel Munk put this minor episode in perspective for Robert, who was again upset by such disloyalty, by pointing out that Lowles and Bunker were only doing what they themselves would have done if the vote had gone against them.

While the IWA council members had been preoccupied with their own internal squabbles at the beginning of the year, two incidents – each one completely separate – had occurred which were destined to coalesce into the most far-reaching development for the waterways so far. Firstly, Warwickshire County Council announced that they were asking the Minister of Transport to issue an abandonment warrant for the south Stratford canal; secondly, a man called John Smith wrote to Aickman.

The county council had decided to seek the closure order so that, instead of rebuilding the weak bridge at Wilmcote, they could raise an embankment over the canal and pipe the water.

'We claim that in no other country would a waterway of this character be closed simply by reason of one defective bridge. Even the comparison of a steam hammer cracking a nut is inadequate,' Robert railed in the *Bulletin*, again reminding readers of the enormous potential for tourism in reopening the Stratford canal and river Avon link.

Christopher Clifford managed to extract vital information

from a meeting with officials of the borough and county councils. The surveyor's estimate for reconstructing the bridge without affecting navigation was £10,000 compared with £4,000 for the plan of building over the canal. 'BTC have informed the authorities that they do not want the canal and they do not ever anticipate restoring it to a navigable condition,' he reported. 'Under these circumstances the county council rather naturally want to go for the cheapest job. As far as they are concerned they would not be destroying the navigation as to all intents and purposes it is non-existent.'

He discovered also that the authorities were considering two other projects: straightening a minor road by eliminating the lock at Preston Baggot, which would precisely cut the canal into two halves, and removing the fine Victorian aqueduct that carried the water in an iron trough over the Birmingham Road at Wootton Wawen.

The John Smith who wrote to Robert Aickman on 29 January 1958 had been a subscribing member of IWA from the start, yet so far had played no part in its activities. An Old Etonian, he was exceedingly wealthy and well connected, a member of the founding family of the National Provincial Bank, a director of Coutts and Company, the select private bank, and of Rolls Royce. More importantly he was also the honorary assistant treasurer of the National Trust, and a man who had taken a profound interest in environmental causes and who liked to be able to influence the course of events.

Michael Streat, who first met him some months later, described him as 'extremely confident but, I think, also extremely shrewd. Demonstrably he is also astonishingly generous and possessed of a very high degree of sensibility and the literary skills to express it. A most unusual character.'

His approach to Robert could hardly have struck a more relevant chord. 'I am convinced that the problem of canals can only be dealt with at the centre – for example, by building up a pressure group of Members of both Houses of Parliament.' He suggested that it would be to their mutual benefit to meet and exchange lists of Parliamentarians of value to both IWA and the National Trust.

Within a month of this initial contact, the dialogue had already progressed to the point at which John Smith had proposed to Aickman that the National Trust could perhaps provide an interim solution by looking after unwanted waterways while the internal wrangles of IWA were sorted out and until such time as the National Waterways Conservancy, or whatever it would be known as, (which was obviously the correct long-term solution) came into existence. Meanwhile, there was a real threat that delay in the government decision-making process would cause the loss of important canals as they deteriorated still further through neglect and individual abandonment orders.

Smith drew a parallel with the existing practice of the National Land Fund, which bought property and gave it to the National Trust to manage, and the position if the Bowes Committee recommended closing any waterways: if the National Trust took over in this situation, it would act only as a caretaker and transfer the canal to a Conservancy when it was established.

'I think my suggestion has two additional merits,' he added, 'one is that it will take the British Transport Commission by surprise; the other is that by implicating the National Trust – which, as you said, is more or less non-controversial and unassailable – it will reduce argument and increase the chances of success.'

Robert responded by inviting Smith to join him on a visit to Stratford-upon-Avon the following Sunday, when they would meet at the Shakespeare Hotel Grant Ferris, Christopher Clifford (who was keen to lead the canal rescue operation) and David Hutchings. 'It should be quite a significant occasion, and, I hope, a productive one,' he added – and, for once, it was nearly an understatement.

John Smith drove Robert out to Stratford on the Sunday and the group looked at the threatened bridge at Wilmcote. Over lunch in the half-timbered dining-room of the sixteenth-century hotel, Grant Ferris told them that he had written to the Minister asking him to withhold any action at least until the Bowes Committee had reported, though this was expected to gain 'only a few weeks" grace.

Grant Ferris also explained that he had dealt with one particular nicety of Parliamentary behaviour in clearing with John Profumo, then Stratford's MP, his own involvement with the campaign. Since Profumo was a member of the government neither he nor his wife, the actress Valerie Hobson, could become publicly associated with the campaign. On a former occasion, when visiting the Dearne and Dove canal, Grant Ferris had failed to notify the local Labour member, Roy Mason, who had been upset by his intrusion and, on being interviewed by the media, said, 'I do not even know of a single canal in this constituency. I only know that the sooner we get rid of them all, the better.'

Faced with an imminent threat to the canal's future, the group decided to hold a public protest meeting at the Stratford town hall within a month, followed by what Hutchings described as a 'disturbance' – a rally of boats at Wootton Wawen, one of the few sections in water – and the formation of a trust to take over the waterway, if the public's response was sufficiently strong to encourage this course.

'I only hope this damn silly controversy over the IWA constitution does not interfere with the progress of the Stratford campaign,' Hutchings remarked. 'This could be the best thing we have yet done, it will be so extremely rewarding in lots of ways. God! what could be done with the energy being wasted in the present dispute.'

John Smith did not waste any time when he had decided on a target. The following evening, after Robert returned from a meeting of the London and Home Counties branch, John came round to Gower Street at 11 p.m. Before leaving Stratford, he reported, he had walked the entire length of the canal from Lapworth to the Avon, thirteen miles and thirty-five locks, and he saw no problem about the National Trust assuming responsibility for it, provided that funds were available. At this stage, the Trust had not been approached officially, though he did know that David Bowes-Lyon, the Queen Mother's brother, was concerned about the state of the waterways, and he was seriously

planning to propose to the Trust that it should look after all
navigations not wanted by BTC. The meeting broke up at
1.15 a.m.

Five days later, Smith put his ideas to the top people in
the National Trust: Lord Crawford and Balcarres, the
chairman, and his deputy, Lord Bridges, formerly permanent secretary at the Treasury and chairman of the Royal
Fine Arts Commission. The atmosphere from the start of
the meeting was encouraging. Bridges, while doodling pictures of narrowboats on his blotter, explained that his father
Robert Bridges, the Poet Laureate, had taken him on canal
holidays, and Lord Crawford recalled how he once lived
close to the Leeds and Liverpool. Smith was asked to present
his case for the National Trust's involvement with canals
generally and to seek the Trust's authority for him to
approach BTC.

Explaining afterwards to Clifford how he had obtained
two 'spectacular recruits', Smith warned that the National
Trust could take fright easily as they had burned their
fingers in the past. Chiefly, they would look for reassurance
over funding so that there was no possible danger that the
Trust's resources could be drawn into financing a single
project. Smith asked whether it would be possible to com-
mence restoration at a less than perfect standard, for instance
using softwood lock gates.

His other concern was that the Trust could be dissuaded
by any sign of lack of local government support for the
scheme. 'Instead of mere apathy, it appears that some
Stratford councillors have a positive wish to close the canal –
I gather in order to extend the bus station,' he commented.
He proposed that restoration should start between Stratford
and Wilmcote so that cleaning and improving the surroundings could become quickly visible to the town, and he was
willing to concede a diversion of the canal to avoid the bus
station and Bancroft Gardens. 'Personally, I think the garden
is terrible, and boats would help a lot, but if that view is
strongly held, then the cut must be made,' he insisted.

In contrast, David Hutchings, ignorant of John Smith's
counsels of caution, was gearing up a dazzling publicity

campaign to arouse maximum local awareness. Looking for any gimmicks, he asked Aickman about the latest pop idol. 'Don't you know Yana? She might pose in a bikini or two?' He planned to plaster the pubs with posters, feed news to the BBC and newspapers, fill Bancroft Basin with protesting boats, and charter coaches to bring in the waverers.

'I have had thoughts about the character of the opening skirmish of this campaign,' he continued. 'I am of the opinion that the first meeting should explode absolutely at top level. I think that all our talent, Scott, MPs, Dorothy Tutin, Sir Whatsisname Flower, Morton, you, every possible body should be there . . . I think we should gamble all on this. After all, what have we to lose? Only the canal.'

In the three weeks leading up to the public meeting on 26 April, Robert made frequent sorties to Stratford and Coventry, where Hutchings lived and worked, dashing back at one point to London to spend three days attending the Transport Tribunal, where the IWA was appealing against increased tolls which were virtually bound to finish the remaining commercial traffic. There was a brisk exchange between the Association's barrister and BTC over their extraordinary claim that there was no right of navigation on the waterways, certainly none for pleasure craft, and the Association succeeded in having the statement struck from the record.

In the five days preceding the meeting, Robert squeezed in a visit to *Twelfth Night* on Tuesday, staying in Stratford at the Swan's Nest, and moving on the next night to *Fatateeta*, where he asked David to keep the catering simple – at night he liked hot milk and plain bread and butter, though a kipper was 'often agreeable'. On Thursday he lunched with Geoffrey Percy at Teddington as he was trying to arrange the sale ('a transaction which, for obvious reasons, I regard as very helpful to the future of the waterways – as well, no doubt, to the Percy finances') of *Canada Goose* to John Smith; then, the same evening, he returned by train to join Hutchings and Smith at the Mulberry Tree restaurant in Stratford for a final tactical session. On Friday morning, he was back at the IWA office in London.

On Saturday he was driven back to Stratford by R. R.

'Ran' Meinertzhagen (whom he had been helping to realise
his idea of setting up a canal-boat company in Aylesbury).
They made a detour around the Warwickshire villages, 'a
slightly nerve-racking journey', to see Hutchings's posters
gleaming with fluorescent print like glowworms from every
available spot. The town hall was thronged with a capacity
attendance of more than 400 people, some of them standing
in the aisles; enthusiasm for the canal was high, and a
resolution condemning the proposed abandonment was
passed unanimously. Sharing the platform with three MPs,
John Smith declared the National Trust's interest in helping
to save the Stratford canal.

On his return to London, Smith drafted a carefully
reasoned and lucid document, setting out the rationale for
the National Trust to take over the 'amenity' canals. He
argued that the BTC was specifically a transport undertaking
whose staff and organisation had been set up to run the
commercial waterways. They had no obligation to cater for
'leisure amenity' nor were they particularly qualified to do
so. On the other hand, the National Trust existed to preserve
things of 'historic interest and natural beauty', it was keen
to help, it was experienced in the transfer of property, and it
had very low administrative overheads.

On the crucial issues of funding, Smith said that it was
extremely expensive to 'eliminate' a canal in a safe and tidy
way, and in many cases the water course had to be kept open
for supply and drainage. It was estimated, for instance, that
it would cost £120,000 to close the south Stratford. On that
basis, it was reasonable to expect the Transport Commission
either to hand over an equivalent sum or to provide an
annual grant equal to the interest of such a capital sum. This
way, the call on taxpayers' funds would be limited, while
expenditure over and above this amount would have to be
found by the Trust.

The Trust endorsed the policy of preserving British
waterways and its willingness to act as a holding body for
them. The scheme was presented to the Minister of Transport. Before there had been any opportunity for discussion,
the Bowes Report was published on Monday 29 July.

'Just had the Bowes Report read to me over the telephone by the *Birmingham Post*. It sounds constructive and optimistic,' David Hutchings rushed to tell Robert. 'Obviously, it does not go all the way, but if it is adopted it will clearly do much for the system. I pointed out that many of *our* recommendations are suggested . . . I cannot see how in all conscience BTC can reject the report, which is backed by the Ministry of Transport. However, we shall see.'

The report retained broadly the same classification of waterways as the Board of Survey, though terming them Class A and Class B, totalling 1,315 miles. The former, the profitable routes, were to be run on a self-financing basis with surplus profits ploughed back into development. The major recommendation of the Bowes Committee, in contrast to the Board, was that Class B waterways were to be put into good working order within five years and maintained to prescribed standards for a period of not less than twenty-five years so that private investment could be encouraged. The cost of these improvements was to be carried by the Treasury, and a licensing system introduced for craft to replace the existing tolls.

Although a considerable change of attitude was apparent in the Committee's claim that they envisaged 'an integrated and efficient system of inland navigation', the remaining 800 miles of waterways were still left with an uncertain future. The axe was still suspended over the Ashton, Peak Forest, Macclesfield, Staffordshire and Worcestershire, the south Stratford, Llangollen and many other superb canals. This time, however, there was to be a right of appeal against the death sentence.

'We do not recommend wholesale abandonment of those waterways which no longer pay their way as commercial navigations,' the report stated. 'There are various reasons why many of them should continue to exist as water channels.' Their future was to be examined under three headings: potential revival of commercial traffic, other economic uses such as drainage, and – at last officially recognised – the social values of recreation.

In the changed climate of public opinion the concept of

abandonment was becoming unacceptable, so – using a tried and tested political sleight-of-hand – a new term was introduced in order to confuse and defuse opposition; the new term was 're-development'. A Waterways Redevelopment Board was to be constituted 'for the purpose of preparing, or securing the preparation of, schemes for re-development or elimination of waterways'. BTC would have the right to request this new Board to assess the future of any of the canals not included in the 'prescribed navigable system'.

The tragedy of the Bowes Report was that the Committee had been split in exactly half over the key question of organisation. While the chairman and three others wished to leave BTC in charge of the nationalised waterways, though recommending a further management shake-up, four other members published a separate view that the whole undertaking should be vested in an Inland Waterways Corporation. It was recommended that the Corporation would be responsible for all nationalised waterways, so the system would be treated as a whole and the Corporation itself would have to deal with redevelopment issues. Before the Corporation could be relieved of a waterway, it would have to apply to the Minister for a Redevelopment Review Order under which a separate authority would be set up for each canal, fully representative of local interests and knowledgeable about social, recreational and scenic matters. Further, the Corporation would start life with a clean sheet, no capital debt was to be transferred to it, and it should be run 'as a public service, substantially at the public expense' (the point at which the minority report clearly overshot the mark, and lost credibility and any chance of approval).

The IWA's initial reaction was that the Bowes Report represented a major triumph for their campaign as it endorsed a number of issues for which they had been pressing and it offered a real hope for the future of most of the waterways. A more carefully considered study, however, showed that its main recommendations had only moved marginally from the Board of Survey's position in that they still centred on the existing commercial routes around the docks, and that much of the rest of the report was imprecise.

R. S. W. Pollard, the Association's solicitor, interpreted the findings as strongly favouring BTC and making their continuing position as the responsible authority even more entrenched. The opportunity to set up a new organisation had been lost in the Committee's failure to reach a unanimous recommendation. 'This in my judgement weighs the report in favour of BTC and makes it more likely that the government will back the less revolutionary proposal,' he said.

As Parliament rose for the long summer recess, Harold Watkinson, the Minister of Transport and Civil Aviation, told the House that consideration of the report, and decision on it, would be 'part of my holiday homework, and I hope that I shall do it properly'.

Among the waterways supporters, however, there was a nagging fear that the greatest danger now lay in lack of action over the report. One of the trade magazines headlined its story: 'GOVERNMENT WILL DO NOTHING ON CANALS REPORT FOR LONG TIME'.

Robert Aickman summed up the situation in the *Bulletin*. 'The first need is to see that action is taken at all. The second and later need is to secure the establishment of the independent authority . . . It is vital that the whole topic be kept outside the world of party politics'.

Abandonment out, Redevelopment in

When, after six months' clampdown of information and activity, a White Paper appeared in February 1959, it was greeted with widespread dismay for its vapid and watery contents – the government had totally failed to tackle the more radical measures proposed by the Bowes Report.

The government, led now by Harold Macmillan, who had taken over as prime minister from an ailing Anthony Eden, was grappling with massive problems left in the wake of the Suez war disaster. Increasing demand for self-rule from Rhodesia, Nyasaland and countries along the South African border forced his 'Wind of Change' speech, and there was a deepening economic depression in Britain which produced a 'credit squeeze' that, among other restrictive measures, put a tight limit on holidays abroad. Meanwhile, within the newly formed European Economic Community, Charles de Gaulle had become President of France and, unofficially, leader of the post-war reconstruction of continental Europe.

The Queen's speech, the first to be televised, had set out the government's legislative programme for the next session of Parliament without referring to waterways, and John Smith discovered from inside sources that the Ministry of Transport was finding the issue 'formidably complicated'. Then the White Paper, setting out future policy, was published, stating bluntly that the government considered that the Bowes Report was of 'a very complicated nature and some of it debatable'. They seized on the fatal division within the Bowes Committee to postpone action on any of the major points.

The establishment of an Inland Waterways Corporation,

which would require legislation and place charges on public
funds, was referred for 'further consideration'. The improvement of Class B canals, providing a twenty-five year guarantee of intent, was a subject on which 'the balance of national
advantage is arguable', though the Ministry added, weakly,
that 'every effort will be made to preserve the system so far
as it is practically possible'. The unanimous view of the
Bowes Committee that tolls should be replaced by licences
was ignored.

The one pragmatic option open to the government was
taken: 'the new concept of redevelopment is common ground
to both sections of the Committee and is fundamental to any
forward-looking solution'. An Inland Waterways Redevelopment Advisory Committee was to be set up immediately:
to promote schemes for redevelopment, to consider schemes
when they had been formulated, and to make recommendations as well as giving 'general advice' to the Minister. The
Committee was to consist of people knowledgeable about the
various interests involved, including local authorities, boat-
users and operators, industry, land and drainage and water
supply.

This was an interim solution, the government admitted
frankly, which would last for perhaps two years 'designed to
enable action to be taken in urgent cases, to try out experi-
mentally the approach recommended in certain directions,
and so to gain experience in the light of which permanent
legislation can be framed'. With regard to finance, the
government expected that redevelopment schemes would be
funded by those who would benefit, with an emphasis on
local authorities, but it allowed a chink of comfort by stating
that, in principle, it would bridge small gaps with special *ad
hoc* grants.

The White Paper was more notable for its omissions than
its inclusions: by implication, BTC was confirmed, as Pollard
had feared, with renewed authority for the entire nationalised waterways. The Commission remained all-powerful in
choosing which canals would be assessed by the Redevelopment Committee and the latter – since it had no responsibilities – was not empowered to take initiative in its own right

and was effectively no more than a satellite. The nature of redevelopment procedure meant that routes would have to be examined singly and in isolation, without positive reference to their place in the system, and naturally those in poorest condition, regardless of other pertinent issues (such as environmental attractions), would be top of the list.

'We deprecate the re-appearance in an official publication of the suggestion that individual waterways should, or can, be expected to be "financially self-supporting" on their own,' Robert Aickman wrote to the *Daily Telegraph*. 'The Waterways, economically as in other respects, stand or fall as a system and not in isolation. If taken as a whole, they can be made not only to pay their way but to prosper. If treated as isolated units, all will fail at an early date!'

John Smith congratulated Robert on his excellent letter which he reported had 'made a most favourable impression at the Ministry of Transport (not, no doubt, that that was your intention)'.

In the *Bulletin*, Robert recognised that the success or failure of yet another government committee would again depend on the quality of the people appointed to it. So he was dismayed to learn that Sir Geoffrey Lowles and Tom Rolt had been nominated to the Redevelopment Committee, and only somewhat reassured by the presence of John Smith and Lionel Munk together with two MPs, Grant Ferris and James Johnson. The chairman was Admiral Sir Frederick Parham – not known to anyone around the waterways.

In a letter to Smith, Robert pressed the view that the very act of setting up the Committee had seriously undermined the case for an Inland Waterways Conservancy. 'The Conservancy proposal implies equal consideration for all the waterways; the Committee is established on the premise that many of the waterways are inferior to the rest, and some of them fitted only for filling in.' He complained about the appointments of Lowles, Rolt and Munk.

Smith did not bother to make a formal reply; he sent Aickman's letter back, by messenger, with his own exasperated observation: 'For heaven's sake, Munk is on that committee for *one reason only* – namely because when I was shown the list for my comment and I saw Lowles and Rolt's names, I said Munk *must* be on it to redress the balance: that is the *only* reason.' He added, 'It's not often one can trace things back to a single cause. In this case, one can.'

John also defended Goodison, the senior civil servant involved, from Aickman's criticisms. He had written the White Paper, and when Kerr and he were together it was obvious who was the boss. He was an intelligent and nice man who would come round in the end to the right way of thinking. 'I am working on the cabinet: as I told you, I happened to sit next to Macmillan in an aeroplane and filled his ear,' he added.

Robert was not, however, to be quickly comforted, still swallowing the acid pill of Tom Rolt's presence on the new Committee. 'Sorry to be ruthless, but if Goodison wrote that tepid and subtly diversionary White Paper, I find it difficult to regard him with much enthusiasm,' he replied. In fact, it made no difference, since, in the usual bureaucratic way, five months later, and just as Smith thought that he was coming around to their thinking, Goodison was moved sideways into another post in the civil aviation section of the ministry.

The Committee's composition had effectively gagged the IWA's outspokenness, at least for a time, and split ranks. Whether or not, as Robert kept on arguing, Munk actually represented the Association, there was no question that his loyalites were bound to be divided between his role as IWA chairman and IWRAC member. Equally, Grant Ferris's appointment to the Committee had reduced his independence as an active campaigner in Parliament. In effect, the poachers had been turned into gamekeepers.

The Committee's terms of reference, moreover, were inadequate and irrelevant to the real needs of the situation. From his long and arduous personal experience of committee work, Robert appreciated that the position could be turned around: the Committee itself could alter its direction and extend its range, he advised Munk. At the very least, it could be prevented from doing actual harm.

There was an early opportunity, in August 1959, of meeting the little-known chairman when Parham accepted an invitation for a day's cruising at Buckby on the Grand Union, joining Lionel Munk and Aickman on the first leg of their three-week journey along the northern waterways.

Munk's opinion of the Admiral was that 'he seems terribly scared of saying more than he should do. He is a surprising man in many ways. I like him very much but . . . he seems afraid of putting a foot wrong. Nevertheless, he makes a sound chairman of the Committee and is in general favourable to the cause of the canals.'

After Sir Frederick left them, the party continued along the Leicester arm and the rivers Soar and Trent as far as the Yorkshire Derwent, a total of 674 miles. Robert's companion was Felice Pearson, always known as Felix, whom he had met a few months previously at a party given by James and Anthea Sutherland. Robert was depressed over his divorce finally going through, Felix sad over the death of her father, who owned a fine house and garden in Kensington backing on to the Sutherlands', and Anthea acted as broker for a deep and rewarding friendship that was created that evening and lasted for the rest of Aickman's life. Felix, at the time, knew nothing about the waterways, though subsequently she shared financially with the Bulkeley-Johnsons in their last efforts to keep commercial carrying in business through Willow Wren.

Before Robert and Felix returned to London, the Association had received its first formal request from IWRAC to submit views on the Stratford, Pocklington, and Staffordshire and Worcestershire canals, as well as the Monkland in Scotland. They were asked to bear in mind the terms of reference: 'To assist as necessary in the promotion of schemes for the treatment of inland waterways which cannot economically be maintained for commercial transport, to consider such schemes when formulated, to make recommendations upon such to Ministers concerned; and to advise Ministers upon any general matters connected with the redevelopment of those waterways.' A brief that, at one and the same time, was narrow and vague.

The selection of the Pocklington canal as one of the top priorities for the Committee's attentions was highly significant as BTC had just lost an attempt to force through its closure in Parliament. The nine miles of broad canal between the Derwent navigation and Canal Head, south of Pocklington on the main York–Hull road, once a very prosperous route, had been dreadfully neglected by the railway companies and had fallen into almost total disrepair, yet it still had a good flow of water appreciated by many anglers, and ramblers and nature-lovers enjoyed walking along the towing-paths.

The first that anyone had heard of BTC's proposed plan to fill the canal with sludge and slime from a pipeline filtration plant was when waterside owners received in 1958 a notice calling for their agreement to the abandonment, to be signed within two weeks. IWA had thrown itself into a fierce battle to save the canal, and BTC had reacted by trying to slip the measure through the backdoors of Parliament. The Commission had asked to make an addition to their Bill already before Parliament – an unprecedented move where canals were concerned and rare in any other context. It called for the suspension of Parliamentary Standing Orders.

The Association had employed specialist Parliamentary agents to fight the measure, which involved many hours of detailed legal work. Their opposition was rewarded with success in March 1959 when the Standing Order Committee refused to allow the Pocklington application to be added to the Bill and coupled this with some very acid comments on the performance of BTC's representatives. Having failed in that course of action, the Commission now turned immediately to test the attitude of the new Redevelopment Committee.

The subsequent referrals to the Committee were of a similar nature: a package of some eleven fairly small sections of the Birmingham Canal Navigations which, again, BTC wished to propose for closure in their 1959 Bill. While several of the sections were unused short arms and wharves which were difficult to contest, the list also included the Dudley tunnel, part of the Stourbridge through route.

It was claimed that the roof of the tunnel had fallen in and that it was unsafe, but no one seemed to be able to produce positive evidence of this. Robert, thoroughly suspicious, set out one day with Felix and Crick Grundy to find out for himself. Crick owned a small plastic boat which was called the 'Blue Bath' as it was similar to and little larger than the trendy coloured baths that had recently come on to the market, and it was small and light enough to be carried on a car roofrack. There was so much bravura and so little conscious planning about the expedition that the party arrived at the tunnel's entrance, and lifted the boat off the car and on to the water, before anyone realised that they did not have a front light. It was Wednesday and early-closing locally, but eventually a bicycle shop was found open and an ordinary battery-operated front lamp purchased.

With this equipment they set out to penetrate the tunnel – at 3,154 yards longer than either Blisworth or Netherton – and they came upon an amazing, unexpected sight. The first part of the tunnel, unlike the brick-lined tubes of Braunston and Harecastle, had been carved out of solid rock as part of a mining operation; it led into side passages and a magnificent cavern open to the sky, with cascades of colourful flowers growing from the walls and waterfalls streaming down the sides.

The next part of the tunnel was conventionally lined with brick, shallow and claustrophobic. Felix in the bow was instructed by Crick in army style not to move and to keep the light pointing into the blackness. The boat's outboard had only two speeds – fast ahead and stop. 'Because we were going full tilt into the dark with this pitiful little light we didn't know if we were going to suddenly hit a barrier of bricks, which we might have done – and according to the authorities we should have done,' she recalled. 'Of course you couldn't see through the tunnel – it was absolutely terrifying – but someone remarked that the air was fresh and indeed it didn't smell like a dead end. We were very hopeful when we realised that there was a draught of fresh air. If we had sunk it would have been the end of us as there was no towing-path and no one knew that we were there; eventually, but too late, my car would have been found at the end. It was a bit of an anti-climax in a way when we perceived the faintest glimmer of light at the end, came out into a narrow defile and saw people going about their daily lives. We blinked and felt as though we were troglodytes come from another world.'

Robert went to work and told the authorities that there had been no fall, Dudley tunnel was not blocked and remained a through navigation; he knew – he had been right through it.

Over the months, BTC steadily applied to IWRAC to rid itself of the various canals which had been an irritant for the past years. Next on the hit list was the Lancaster: out of the total length of fifty-four miles, it was proposed to retain the forty-five-mile pound below Tewitfield locks in water for recreation; the flight of locks and the length above were to be 'made available for agriculture, though retaining a water passage for the pound below'.

'It is the part above Tewitfield which is the most beautiful . . . and anyone with the smallest vision should be able to see the boating potentials over, say, the next ten years,' Robert wrote to Munk.

The proposals for abandonment – or redevelopment – were not only for the more remote and distant parts of the system. Before long, BTC became sufficiently emboldened to propose the City Road basin of the Regent's Canal, in the heart of London, one of the prime wharves upon which any revival of commercial traffic would depend. In this case, the secretary of IWRAC was so certain of the outcome that his letter to the IWA, inviting a response, indicated that the Committee felt that there would be little objection to this closure.

Leslie Morton, general manager of Willow Wren, told Robert that the basin had been the key place for loading and unloading the enormous narrowboat traffic between London and Birmingham right up to the failure of the famous fleet of Fellows, Morton and Clayton in 1950. They had run a daily 'fly-boat' service, travelling between the two cities in little more than fifty hours, with at least 200 tons being carried every day. A vast amount of other waterborne trade had operated from the basin, including the important Stewarts and Lloyds steel business. 'All of these activities were stopped upon nationalisation, and 99 per cent of the premises have been leased to firms who have no interests in carriage by water,' he added, pointing out the value of the land in property development potential to BTC.

The Ashton in the heart of Manchester (providing a direct link between the Ship Canal and the inland system along the Peak Forest and Macclesfield canals) the romantically named Dearne and Dove (part of the Sheffield routes), the Buckingham arm of the Grand Union and the St Helens in Lancashire were among many of the canals whose future lives were submitted to IWRAC's grand inquisition. Outside the nationalised sector, Well Creek on the river Great Ouse and the privately owned Derby canal – a superb link into the city from the Trent and Mersey, for which a young student called David Horsfall put up a stern fight – were threatened.

The Kennet and Avon, which otherwise would have been top of the obituary list, had been protected by the tenuous five-year moratorium forced on BTC by the Parliamentary Select Committee in March 1956.

'I believe that at the moment rings are being run around us,' Robert complained to David Hutchings. 'This Redevelopment Committee has very cleverly made ciphers of our two leading Parliamentarians; and it looks like effecting closures that otherwise would have taken years, and probably been frustrated altogether. Also it has placed us in a very difficult position with John Smith and Lionel Munk; they are undoubtedly doing their best, but, in the sheer nature of the case, it is nothing like enough. I see no answer to this problem.'

To Munk he expressed the view that IWA had been placed – as he had foreseen – in an impossible position. It seemed that IWRAC took it for granted that a waterway should be closed unless a precise scheme for its future was submitted by others; yet there was a limit to what the Association could produce within very short time scales, particularly as their policy had in any case always been to argue for the survival of the entire system, not for this or that particular section.

9a Robert Aickman with a group of friends on a
Maid Line cruiser (Lionel Munk is standing, *centre*)

9b The famous 'Blue Bath' which was used to travel
through Dudley Tunnel

10a and **10b**
The American Wind
Symphony Orchestra
on a floating
concert platform,
1961

11a Grant Ferris, MP, speaking at an IWA dinner.
Robert Aickman and Sir Leslie Bowes are sitting on his right

11b Dame Margot Fonteyn and Lionel Munk
at the National Boat Show, 1957

12a, 12b, 12c
Volunteers
rebuilding
locks on the
Stratford canal

13a An army crane lifting a gate on the Stratford canal

13b Volunteers rebuilding lock walls at Lapworth

14a Boats celebrating the reopening of the lower Avon, 1962

14b Douglas Barwell receiving congratulations
for his work in restoring the lower Avon

15a The lock at Wyre on the lower Avon

15b The first working boats to come down the Stratford canal
after its restoration in 1964

16a The Queen Mother, with Robert Aickman and David Hutchings
(*standing left*), at the reopening of the upper Avon in 1974

16b The reopening of the upper Avon was the culmination
of years of campaigning for the waterways

'I asked you several months ago whether you still felt that we should aim to save every mile of canal,' Lionel replied. 'You said that you were now a 90 per cent man. I was very pleased to hear this, as I am myself a 95 per cent man. But the 5 per cent which I feel are hardly worth fighting tooth and nail for include the Dearne and Dove, the Pocklington and the several unimportant lengths of BCN [Birmingham Canal Navigations], and I am not terribly concerned about the Derby . . . On the other hand, let me assure you, the Committee will recommend abandonment of the Staffs and Worcs, the Macclesfield and Ashton or the K. and A., over my dead body.'

Lionel advised Robert that the best way out of the apparent impasse would be to take an oblique turn away from the grinding examinations of IWRAC and return to the Parliamentary scene with renewed pressure for the early creation of an Inland Waterways Conservancy. The general election in October had returned the Conservative government with an increased majority of 100 seats overall, and a new Minister of Transport, Ernest Marples, had been appointed, who acquired a reputation for using his bicycle instead of a car on congested city roads.

The right opportunity to press the case was provided early in December 1959, when an adjournment debate was arranged in the House of Commons – the first general debate on waterways for many years – on the subject of the Bowes Report, urging the government, in view of the continuing rapid deterioration of the canals, to make up its mind soon.

In publicity terms the debate was an enormous success and a boost to the flagging confidence of the IWA lobby. It opened with strong backing from the Association's greatest Parliamentary friends: Grant Ferris, John Wells, Geoffrey de Freitas, Dr Barnet Stross, Sir Spencer Summers and Humphrey Atkins among them. The case for an independent waterways authority was urged by speaker after speaker, and it was not entirely rejected by the Opposition's official spokesman, Robert Mellish, even though he had to pay lip service to the nationalised system. For Aickman, listening in the strangers' gallery, it was an unbelievable advance to find that the concept that he had been advocating for nearly fifteen years now appeared to be accepted almost as a matter of course.

'The principle which I believe the government must face is that, first, the Transport Commission is not the proper body to be responsible for the main length of our canal system,' said Sir Spencer Summers, 'and, secondly, it is desirable that the whole system shall be under one responsibility.'

'I believe that there should be an inland waterways corporation or conservancy controlling all the nationalised waterways,' added Humphrey Atkins. 'What we want today is a decision from my honourable friend on the future of canals and a promise that legislation, if necessary, will be put in hand at once.'

'I should not like the Minister to go away with any idea that those who support this Motion are wild enthusiasts, with duckweed in their hair,' said John Wells. 'We may be enthusiasts, but we are also people who realise that a very substantial business element is building up.'

'I think that the debate really could not have gone better except for John Hay's dusty (watery?) speech,' commented Grant Ferris later, referring to the newly appointed Parliamentary Secretary. 'This of course was purely Ministry stuff and the poor chap could hardly do anything else as he had not had the time to learn yet what a canal is.'

No division vote was called, so when the Speaker put the motion to the House everyone shouted 'Aye', but the motion, as Robert appreciated cynically, had been phrased in such general terms as to make it impossible for anyone not to agree. On the other hand, Grant Ferris pointed out that a tactical advantage had been gained in pressing the government to make a decision and, he told Robert, he had been given a private assurance that this would happen within three months.

Detached from the proceedings and looking down from the gallery into the deep gloomy chamber of dark wood and green upholstered benches, a group of waterways supporters observed MPs saunter in and out, slide along the seats and exchange whispered observations, and pass white slips of paper to the front benches. Robert later described the scene: 'The enthusiasts, having been carefully mobilised, speak first and say all the right things; then come the busybodies who think they have an independent view of the subject, and therefore have not been mobilised by the promoters; then comes the official spokesman for the Opposition, who, being official, must be cautious, and being an Opponent, must make some party points; finally comes the government spokesman, who, as he may have actually to do something and even involve others, is always quite impossible, and mainly preoccupied with proving that what his friends did in the past was unquestionably the best that could possibly be done.'

Meanwhile, the task of proving that threatened routes were navigable continued right through the bitter winter weather. Shortly before the debate, Robert joined David Hutchings on Crick Grundy's boat *Heron* to make a canal-busting attempt on the Stourbridge, starting at the top of the flight of sixteen locks, with an attack being made from the bottom by a converted narrowboat called *Bumblebee*, crewed by the headmaster and some boys from Rowley Regis Grammar School. It so happened that the parties had been independently in contact with British Waterways for some weeks requesting passage of the canal and had received three different reactions. While Grundy had been told that the route was impassable owing to a bridge being rebuilt, this was not mentioned to the headmaster, who was told that the school could make a passage at their own risk (an improper statement under the statutes). Hutchings, on the other hand, had been told by the divisional manager that 'this canal is open and there is nothing to stop anyone using it'.

Heron set out on a late November Saturday, and soon found that this was not the case. On arrival at the top lock, they found it padlocked. When they applied to the resident keeper, he rudely replied, 'You're not going through,' and retired inside his house. They knocked at the door, and his wife told them that her husband was not called upon to work on a Saturday.

A hacksaw, which was then essential boating equipment, was produced and they cut through the chains, but six locks down, at Swan Lane, they discovered that the route was indeed impassable where the local authority repairing the bridge had simply dumped bricks into the cut. It was a typical challenge to David Hutchings, who organised a work force to start clearing the rubble from the freezing water, but the progress was so slow that there was no hope of continuing further and they returned to a mooring at Black Delph. That evening they were visited by a BTC official who said that, in his opinion, the navigation should be closed. *Bumblebee* had also been halted further down the flight.

On returning to London, Aickman wrote directly to Sir Brian Robertson, BTC chairman, reporting the various experiences. In reply, he received assurances that the canal would be cleared and that 'rudeness will not be condoned on the part of our staff'. Over the weekend before Christmas *Heron* returned to the assault; rain driven by a bitterly cold gale reduced visibility to a few yards.

This time, not only was the top lock standing open but there was also a cheerful gang of men ready to help them on the descent. 'As often proves to be the case, the navigation was not really in very bad shape,' Robert reported, 'the main needs are for routine maintenance and for regular traffic.' *Heron* continued through to a winter mooring at Stourton on the Staffordshire and Worcestershire, passing *Bumblebee* on the flight.

Not far away there was more encouraging news of the south Stratford canal. The Ministry of Transport had rejected the county council's application for a warrant of abandonment, based on the claim that it was a 'derelict' canal which had not been used for navigation for at least three years previously. A single scrap of paper, the toll receipt of a passage made by canoe in February 1957, was sufficient to refute the council's case.

Following this decision, BTC at last reached agreement in principle with the National Trust that it could lease the south Stratford for five years with the option at that point of either handing it back or completing the transfer on a permanent basis. Restoration, using largely volunteer labour, was forecast to cost £40,000 compared with an estimated £120,000 for closure. It would take a further year, however, to complete the formalities as the transfer had to be approved by Parliament; in the meantime, the Commission would agree to some work being started.

On the lower Avon a final appeal of £8,000 was launched to enable the last remaining work in reopening the river to be undertaken at Cropthorne, where a derelict flash gate had to be removed. Apart from this half-mile stretch, the river was in use from Tewkesbury to Evesham. The rate of progress had been relatively slow as, apart from some army assistance, it had been undertaken entirely by volunteers limited to weekends and holidays. Douglas Barwell and his chief colleagues had built up a large body of volunteers by some devious tactics. Over a fine weekend they used to close one of the partially rebuilt locks and wait for the first of the pleasure-boaters to arrive. They were told that the lock would be reopened sooner if they would lend a hand with some small tasks. If this test showed that they were either skilled or enthusiastic, they found themselves press-ganged into service; if they proved to be unhelpful or inexperienced, they were soon on their way.

Barwell himself led from the front and achieved fame as an amateur diver. It was found that the cost of hiring a professional diver to descend under water to inspect work on lock chambers was prohibitive, so he decided to tackle the job himself. 'No one's ever dared me to do something without my having a go,' he said. Douglas acquired a full diving suit and, with his wife acting as mate, he practised in his son's swimming pool, graduating from the shallow to the deep end, before attempting the river.

At the LANT annual meeting in 1960 Robert Aickman paid tribute to Barwell as 'a really remarkable man – six men in one: charity organiser, council chairman, deep-sea diver, impresario, administrator and leader.'

With the prospect becoming more certain of renewing the

canal link at Stratford with the Avon, Robert was delighted to learn that exhaustive research by Kenneth Gill Smith of the *Evesham Journal* had established that no one still living owned the title of the upper Avon navigation. It was, therefore, open to anyone to make a claim under the Rail and Canal Traffic Act, 1888, though LANT decided against taking this step until their work on the lower river was finished.

David Hutchings agreed to become the National Trust's manager-designate in charge of the Stratford restoration, and in June 1960 he moved with his wife Joan, two sons and daughter, and the bull-terrier Creosote into the empty lock-keeper's house at Lapworth. Situated prettily on a peninsular between the Grand Union and Stratford canals, it was built in the style traditional and peculiar to this waterway – single-storey with whitewashed walls and barrel roof, it could have been transplanted from an Aegean island. 'The cottage is slowly becoming more civilised, but there is still much to do,' he told Robert. 'Unfortunately, the well has run dry; however, there is always the cut.'

Although he was still employed in the Coventry City architect's department, weekend work parties started to clear the waterway. One weekend in July, more than eighty people turned up, about thirty-five coming from IWA's South-West branch and a similar number from the Territorial Army, some twelve from the Midlands branch and a few from other areas.

They cleared the pounds over three-quarters of a mile to the first winding hole at Dick's Lane, repaired paddle gear and cleared the heads of the five locks. Hutchings believed that the gates on this upper section were sound enough to be repaired, though further down, near Stratford, they would have to be replaced. By August, when the Royal Assent on the bill transferring ownership of the Stratford canal from BTC to the National Trust was expected, David was confident that a boat would be able to pass along the canal as far as Dick's Lane. Despite this excellent progress, he was still not officially contracted to carry out the restoration as the Trust had hit fresh problems in trying to extract one of the special *ad hoc* grants for which the government provided in setting up IWRAC.

Aickman appealed to Humphrey Atkins, secretary of the Conservatives' Waterways Committee, to use his influence in settling the financial issue. 'The Redevelopment Committee have recommended in the strongest terms (and I repeat it is their only recommendation to date) that £25,000 be made available for the restoration, and the government have been refusing for nine months to make any answer one way or another,' he wrote. 'If this small sum is not forthcoming, the Redevelopment Committee have surely been working all this time under false pretences?' Robert added that the band of volunteers was becoming disillusioned with this procrastination and starting to fade away, and that it was too late for the Trust to launch a public appeal

The National Trust's annual report had confirmed its enthusiasm for helping with the survival of the waterways.

> The transfer of canals represents a new departure; it is not to be expected that the legal and financial arrangements will be simple or rapidly completed. But the council are aware of the pleasures – not least an escape from the bedlam of the roads – which can be given to a wide cross-section of the community by the preservation, rather than the destruction, of these long-neglected amenities.

Brave words, but the Trust, as John Smith had warned, could be easily frightened and the top people were already disenchanted by the endless difficulties encountered in negotiating with the authorities for just the one canal.

During this summer Aickman again joined forces with Munk for a lengthy flag-carrying and navigation-proving cruise deep into the Fenlands. Since these waterways were relatively unknown, the pair first went on an overland reconnaissance. Then, in May, they set out from Braunston, Lionel in his latest Maid Line cruiser, Robert and Felix this time in a boat hired from Michael Streat's new Blue Line fleet.

Munk and Aickman left little to chance in planning these

journeys. Since they had a different crew for each of the three weeks they were going to be away, they sent in advance the most incredibly detailed and precise joining instructions, right down to the times of trains from London to St Ives and March, the two changeover points. 'It is customary to have dinner at a moderately expensive restaurant two or three evenings a week,' they warned. 'The climate of the Fens in May can be fresh, but equally we can enjoy a heat wave.'

Each day of the three-week cruise was set out in a timetable with designated distances and locks. On the first Sunday they travelled 17 miles and worked 30 locks to arrive at Northampton, and in total they covered 480 miles and 177 locks, spending four days in each direction along the river Nene between Northampton and Peterborough, and making a round trip of the Middle Level and the rivers Ouse and Cam, reaching the navigation limits at Tempsford and Cambridge.

The only really difficult conditions were found at Welches' Dam, where a long-running contention over responsibility between the river board and the Middle Level Commissioners had resulted in neglect, with heavy weed and a low water level.

Robert liked the vast expanse of flat scenery. 'Much of the countryside is surprisingly attractive, though as always the sun does help, and the feeling of remoteness is as bracing as the salty air,' he wrote. 'The passage of Whitlesey is especially fascinating: the waterway, here very narrow, winds and twists between walls and under bridges, recalling certain minor navigations in Holland.'

The trip was important to Munk and Aickman in helping to re-establish their personal links with waterways enthusiasts in the eastern counties. After the original Fenlands branch had broken up in disarray over the IWA's incorporation issue, the Association had no presence in the region except via a tenuous connection with the Great Ouse Restoration Society, which itself had become moribund. Meanwhile, a breakaway group called the East Anglian Waterways Association had been formed with Teddy Edwards as honorary secretary. Now proposals had been made by Alan

Faulkner, of GORS, to bring together the two bodies. Arthur Cavender, who had been such an enthusiastic IWA supporter in 1952, had dropped out of active involvement as a result of domestic and financial problems, and now he was approached to become chairman of both organisations.

Despite the opposition from some quarters, the Association's restructuring had proved to be very successful. Munk, in his chairman's annual report, stated that the destructive vendettas of the past had been eliminated and that the smaller council of seven members worked smoothly together. The council was advised by a committee of some forty experienced enthusiasts who held many varying points of view. Once a quarter, the two bodies held a joint meeting when discussion was devoted entirely to waterways problems, with no time wasted on internal administration. It operated rather on the lines of a debating group, without a formal agenda, dealing with themes such as: 'Is the Association's campaign succeeding in its aims?' and 'Has there been a decrease in Parliamentary interest?'

Another aspect of the Association's work, the *Bulletin*, received independent praise from a financial journal, sent to Robert by John Smith, which urged students of literature to read it: 'it is entertaining, intelligent and exceedingly well written.'

Robert often explained just how much effort was involved in writing the *Bulletin*. Each quarterly edition contained around 10,000 words, virtually all written by him, so he estimated that every year he wrote the equivalent of half of an average-length novel. It was a *tour de force* between him and his secretary. Over a three-month period he would assemble relevant correspondence and information in a large wicker basket, of the kind used to hold logs for an open fire. At the appropriate time he would spread out the material in little piles across the living-room floor of the Gower Street flat and then walked around for hours on end turning it into editorial copy and dictating it directly on to the typewriter. For two or three days until the task was finished nothing was allowed to interrupt the process, and on the conclusion they would depart for a sustaining meal at one of his favourite restaurants in Soho.

The review in Smith's journal went on satirically to draw comparison between the *Bulletin* and 'the noblest of all literary forms, the epic or saga':

> The central and continuing theme is the struggle of Mr Robert Aickman to rescue the ravished waterways of England from the bestial clutch of the British Transport Commission. As in all epics, there are fabulous digressions, and splendid minor characters who come and go and reappear; but Mr Aickman remains, a combination of Odysseus and Mrs Pankhurst, tenacious, unsquashable and vocal, a figure of heroic stamp. Meanwhile, the heroine, the canal system, still languishes thirteen years older (and minus a limb or two) but more beautiful and desirable than ever, still kept locked up and neglected by the Giant (BTC), who changes his shape, vanishes, prevaricates and is just as rough and uncivilised as he was at the beginning. *Can he save her?*

A few days before Christmas 1960 there was fresh hope that the story had reached a happy ending: the heroine rescued, the giant vanquished. In a White Paper the government announced that British Transport Waterways would be placed under an independent statutory board to be known as the Inland Waterways Authority, which would own and manage the nationalised system. It would be responsible for 'proceeding with the redevelopment or disposal of waterways which no longer have a transport use', and it was recognised that 'special aid may have to be given in the initial years'.

As Robert and Felix made plans to spend Christmas with Peter and Marion Froud on their converted hotel narrowboat, *Saturn*, near Wolverhampton, they knew that another battle had been won, but that the ultimate victory was still a long way off. The new authority (whose proposed name would ludicrously be shortened to IWA!) had been given renewed responsibility for the ominously designated 'redevelopment or disposal' role. In any case, it was understood that legislation to implement the plan could not be introduced for at least another year; meanwhile, BTC's policy remained unchanged. Its latest annual Parliamentary bill called for the closure of the Dearne and Dove, the northern end of the Lancaster, remaining parts of the Manchester, Bolton and Bury, a branch of the Ashton, and five sections of the BCN. Altogether, a greater mileage of statutory navigation was proposed for abandonment than in any other year since the IWA was founded, except only for 1955, when the Kennet and Avon project had been defeated.

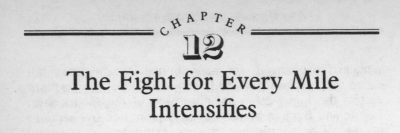
The Fight for Every Mile Intensifies

Early in 1961 British Waterways took the so far unprecedented step of closing the Ashton canal to pleasure boating, even though it was still under active consideration by the Redevelopment Committee. The reason was the poor and, allegedly, dangerous state of the locks; on the other hand, the local authorities had been pressing for some time for its closure and in-filling, save for a few boating lagoons.

This autocratic action was immediately perceived to be the most direct challenge to the campaign to save the waterways since IWA started to fight for the Kennet and Avon ten years earlier. With government policy once again suspended until the new Transport Bill was published, it was apparent that BTC would seize the opportunity provided by the interregnum to seek the closure of as many unwanted canals as possible so that the new authority, when it came into existence, would have fewer miles and fewer problems with which to deal. In closing the Ashton a gauntlet had been thrown down, open warfare had been declared and the fight, once again, was on to save every mile of threatened canal.

The case for keeping the Ashton was completely different from that of other waterways under review by IWRAC since it formed an integral part of an important series of canals. Passing right through the centre of Manchester, within yards of Piccadilly station, it linked directly with the Manchester Ship Canal and the port then ranked fifth in Britain. Eastwards, it joined the Peak Forest canal at Dunkinfield junction, and the waterway continued on a fine aqueduct over the river Goyt and ascended the attractive flight of locks at Marple to the highest point of the English system. Here, in one direction, the canal traversed the side of a deep valley to Whaley Bridge; in the other direction, it descended one of Britain's most scenically beautiful waterways, the Macclesfield, notable for its scores of perfectly proportioned stone bridges.

> From start to finish, the Ashton canal passes through a densely built-up area in which the canal is conspicuous as an avenue of escape from the oppressive townscape that flanks it. Its clear water, its excellent towpath, its functional but dignified bridges and the peace that surrounds it makes it a natural haven for local schoolchildren, anglers, walkers, and idlers, and for anyone who enjoys an environment that is quite separate from and unrelated to his ordinary everyday life. [*Nicholson/Ordnance Survey Guide to the Waterways*, Book 3, North].

Robert Aickman aroused the immediate concern of MPs Grant Ferris, Humphrey Atkins and John Wells, who planned to see for themselves on a fact-finding Easter visit. Lionel Munk envisaged the Ashton providing a linear park through the wastelands at the heart of a great industrial city.

Robert was convinced that Sir Reginald Kerr, who had recently visited the canal, had selected the Ashton for a 'grand showdown'. This theory was corroborated by the behaviour of C. M. Marsh, the divisional manager, who was known to have an equivocal attitude to BTC policy, often privately disclaiming responsibility for their actions. Stan Offley, North-West branch chairman, reported that Marsh, in one of his famous 'frank calls', had told him that British Waterways would take no action against anyone going through the Ashton unless damage was caused – but neither would any help be given.

After putting out diplomatic feelers, Robert obtained significant backing from one of Manchester's most influential figures, Laurence Scott, chairman and managing director of the *Guardian*, and son of the famous C. P. Scott, who had established the newspaper's renowned reputation for editorial independence. Scott agreed to take the chair at a protest meeting at the Albert Hall which, on a typically wet

Monday night in Manchester, attracted 400 people, about ten times more than the audience that night in the Free Trade Hall for R. A. Butler, the Home Secretary.

Another limb of the media, BBC's *Tonight* programme, presented by Fyfe Robertson, caused consternation with John Smith and widespread horror with other IWA members for its one-sided presentation of the story; the Association, given only twenty-four hours' notice, had been unable to field a spokesman in time.

'It was a reflective piece filmed in the area of the canal describing the process by which the canal itself fell into disuse, commenting on the present consequences of its present neglect and mentioning in passing a plan, of which I am sure you are aware, to fill in part of the Ashton canal, leaving lagoons,' defended Alasdair Milne, deputy editor.

'The Ashton has not declined into its present condition by some process of nature or even through social progress,' Robert thundered back. 'It has been fairly systematically wrecked during a period of thirty to forty years at least, originally by the railway company which was unwisely permitted to acquire it, and latterly by the joint activities of the British Transport Commission and the Manchester Corporation, both of whom admit they want to get rid of it.'

As an IWA campaign cruise of the Peak Forest and Ashton canals was being planned for Whitsun, the right of British Waterways to close the section to navigation was challenged in a solicitor's letter to Marsh. It quoted the Regulation of the Railways Act 1873:

> Every railway company owning or having the management of any canal . . . shall *at all times* keep such a canal . . . thoroughly repaired and dredged and in good working condition so that the whole . . . may be *at all times* kept open and navigable for the use of *all* persons desirous to use and navigate the same without any unnecessary hindrance interruption or delay.

This was the unassailable foundation of the concept of the right to navigate which had been the crux of IWA's policy from the outset. Before long, this fundamental tenet was itself to come under threat of abolition.

British Waterways gave way, agreeing to allow the passage of boats, but at their own risk (whatever that may have meant) and without any assistance. About fifteen boats set out from Marple junction and had great difficulty in descending the flight of locks which in previous years had been in a satisfactory state. 'Their condition emphasises our constant contention that the abandonment of one canal soon leads to the abandonment of the next one,' Robert remarked. That the Peak Forest was next on the list was confirmed by odious blue and yellow notices proclaiming that the canal was 'Not Recommended for Pleasure Boating'.

At Dunkinfield, ten boats continued a further three miles along the Ashton to Fairfield, travelling at a very slow pace because of the bad conditions. At the twelfth lock they found that the bottom gates had been destroyed by fire, detached from their bearings and thrown into the waterless chamber. Only one boat was light enough to continue past this hazard: Brian Knight's fibreglass cruiser *Bruce* was lifted around the lock and the crew, working day and night, took another forty-two hours to reach the bottom of the canal, five miles in distance.

'It is my conviction that if the Ashton canal is closed to navigation, our long fight must be regarded as lost in its essential aspects,' wrote Robert. 'From a waterway that has been abandoned, the rot spreads to adjoining waterways, and for reasons that are obvious and logical: the death of the first waterway reduces traffic on the next one; and, even more important, the arguments used to kill the first one can readily be adapted to kill another one.'

In Scotland, the threat to the Forth and Clyde was even more dire. The Association had not established a branch north of the border, nor had any local pressure group sprung up. The course of events demonstrated indubitably how the authorities behaved in the absence of strong and organised opposition. No other incident more clearly showed what would have happened in England and Wales if there had not been a waterways defence campaign.

When the imminent threat to the Forth and Clyde arose, Aickman had appealed in the *Bulletin's* January issue for Scottish members to come forward and form a branch; in the event, the only active opposition was provided by Scottish emigré Michael Macfarlane, Midlands branch chairman. By June, effectively, it was already too late. John Maclay, Secretary of State for Scotland, announced that legislation was to be introduced to extinguish BTC's obligation to keep the canal open for navigation – the first time that a canal abandonment had been declared by direct government intervention. IWRAC declined to give an opinion until they had seen a plan for the waterway's redevelopment which, they were told, would take several years to produce.

The Forth and Clyde was one of Britain's most spectacular shipping canals, exceptionally wide and deep, thirty-five miles long, crossing the waist of Scotland between Edinburgh and Glasgow and the two firths. Far from being derelict, it was regularly used by masted vessels, mainly a fishing fleet of at least 60 vessels which took advantage of seasonal changes to pass from the herring to the white-fish grounds. In 1956, the canal had been used by 139 pleasure boats, 98 fishing vessels and 14 cargo ships.

BTC's annual working deficit for the canal was not particularly great, ranging between £30,000 and £60,000. The decision to close had nothing to do with its use as a navigation but was based entirely on the cost of renewing some of the fifty bridges that crossed the canal. It was brought to a head by the claim that £100,000 would be saved in constructing a fixed, in place of a lifting, bridge on the new Denny by-pass of Glasgow. Purely for the sake of road transport, the interests of fishermen, whose livelihood had depended for a hundred years on their annual transits of the canal, were arbitrarily swept aside, though government spokesmen went through routine motions of grief.

'I am, of course, conscious of their problem – and, indeed, the fact that I am Ministerially responsible for Scottish fisheries as well as Scottish roads has ensured that the difficulties involved have been brought before me,' stated

Lord Craighton in a letter to Macfarlane. 'But, having given the fishermen a full opportunity to state their case, I have concluded that the balance of advantage lies in saving public money on road bridges rather than continuing what the Bowes Committee called a "disguised subsidy" to a small section of the Scottish fishing industry.'

The Bowes Committee had, additionally, stated that the closure of the canal would 'undoubtedly be a blow' to the fishing industry and 'its impact would be likely to be severe'.

Grant Ferris, Munk and Macfarlane had meetings with both Lord Craighton and John Maclay, but their arguments were overwhelmed by a battery of cost-saving figures in favour of roads. The growing use being made by the burgeoning leisure activities, particularly yachtsmen crossing between the two seas, was ignored. By the autumn, a special 'hybrid' Bill had been placed before Parliament and the case for the canal had been lost. Hugh McKnight in *The Shell Book of Inland Waterways* described 'this incredibly stupid and short-sighted move' as 'perhaps the greatest post-war scandal on our waterways'.

In England, rumour flourished in advance of the annual BTC Bill that the government would try to press through considerable reductions in the new authority's commitments, in cases totally ignoring IWRAC's recommendations, by seeking wholesale closures of waterways which had been the subject of debate for many years.

'It is very important to stop the large-scale abandonments which, even in prospect have already caused much bitterness and indignation, especially in the cases of the Dudley tunnel (a trumped-up piece of spite, if ever there was one), the upper Erewash (an entirely unnecessary proposal) and the Chesterfield canal (wrecking on a very grand scale),' Robert wrote to Grant Ferris. 'The newest equivocation is, I gather, that, according to the officials, abandonment, i.e. withdrawal of status as a statutory navigation, need not imply actual closure; but that is certainly sheer humbug in all the present cases.'

Robert was referring to bland assurances being handed out by the Parliamentary Secretary, John Hay, who told

Brian Batsford, MP, that 'loss of navigation rights does not necessarily bring an end to the recreational uses of canals such as boating and fishing', while to Sir Cyril Black, MP, he wrote: 'There is a distinction between redevelopment and abandonment. "Abandonment" means simply leaving a closed canal to decay with no further maintenance . . . "Redevelopment" means positive action to put a canal which is of no further use for commercial navigation to some other useful purpose, e.g. as a channel for water supply.'

Despite the gathering storm clouds and ominous threats, the Association's chief officers remained sanguine that the future would improve when the new authority came into existence. It was recognised that everything would depend on the choices of chairman and board members. Aickman, Munk and others spent many happy hours concocting their own ideal version of an entirely new body which would break completely away from the past. They visualised Munk as chairman and Crick Grundy as general manager.

As the day of decision came closer and the reality of the situation clearer, they began to appreciate that, in the best traditions of bureaucratic evolution, the new authority would largely be carved out of the existing BTC set-up with only the names at the top changed. John Smith, neverthless, encouraged the view that they should prepare a short-list of about six people whom they wished to see on the board – if they provided a longer list, the Ministry would be able to pick and choose.

He thought that the Association had a faint chance of having its nominees selected. 'It is dreadful the way such appointments are almost always done on the "old boy" basis,' he added. 'The Association starts at a disadvantage through having agitated for this. Ministers and civil servants instinctively hate agitators – especially when they are right, as the IWA has been.'

Munk submitted his short-list to Aickman: Grant Ferris, Smith, Rolt, Robert himself, with Lowles as a possibility. To this Robert added Sir Alan Herbert, Peter Scott and Christopher Clifford. Munk said that there were two people whom he did not wish to see on the board – Charles Hadfield and Lord Lucan (who had frequently, as a front-bench Labour spokesman, opposed the IWA in Parliamentary debates).

Shortly afterwards, Clifford resigned from his position as managing director of Royal Worcester and Robert succeeded in obtaining an interview for him, as a candidate for the authority's chief executive, with the Permanent Secretary at the Ministry. The prospect, however, was so vague concerning the likely date of appointment, its status and remuneration, that Clifford soon accepted another senior position with Bristol Pottery, though placing a clause in his contract that he would be permitted to undertake part-time work for British Waterways.

During the summer of 1961 Robert was deflected from these issues by another highly absorbing activity. He had been engaged by Henry Heinz of the American baked-bean empire to organise a most extraordinary and daringly original orchestral tour of the Thames: from Oxford to Westminster, the American Wind Symphony Orchestra of sixty musicians was to give eleven open-air concerts from an elaborate floating platform that was to be towed by tug down the river.

With the English climate to contend with and lack of precedent to help, it was a rather eccentric enterprise saddled with diverse and unforeseen difficulties, and the problems were magnified by the vessel itself. The 'dream boat' had been designed by an American architect, Louis Kahn, and had to be built within an impossible time-scale of eight weeks at a Deptford yard. It would be the largest craft to navigate the Thames as far as Oxford; it looked magnificent, but it was extremely cumbersome to steer and provided no shelter for anyone.

The first concert was planned for 4 July at Battersea. By the second week of May there were intractable problems about obtaining in time the complex hydraulic gear required to raise and lower acoustic screens, one 100 feet long, the other 60 feet, behind the orchestra. There were also seemingly insuperable difficulties over finding a fireworks contractor willing to organise the massive displays that were to take place after each concert. Accommodation had to be found and booked for the orchestra and support crew at each venue along the Thames.

In late May Robert needed extra assistance and brought in a friend and IWA member, Marianne Kaye, an Austrian Jewess who had narrowly escaped to safety in Norway at the outbreak of the war. Somehow, no doubt inspired by Robert's incredible energy and zeal for any event that combined the arts and waterways, everything came together on the night. 'It all happened as planned – or very nearly,' he reported. During a none-too-bright summer, only the concert at Marlow had to be abandoned before its conclusion; the others attracted crowds rising from 4,000 at Richmond to 10,000 at County Hall, London. Those attending remembered for ever the brilliant sound and visual spectacle created by the white-jacketed musicians playing under the illuminated canopy, like a great seashell, and the dazzling climax as the fireworks exploded into a panoply of rainbow colours reflected in the gleaming waters of the Thames.

Shortly afterwards, Robert and Felix, who had also been helping with the concert tour, retreated for a holiday of recovery to the little island of Raz, linked by a causeway to Alderney in the Channel Islands, owned by Marianne's husband, Ernest Kaye. The experience turned out to be less romantic and restful than anticipated, largely because of the crossing from Portsmouth in a small run-down coaster, the *St Ernest*.

On arrival at the harbour, they found that the ship was being extensively repaired after breaking down on the inward journey and, being the only passengers, they languished for three days in Portsmouth, sleeping on the hard narrow benches in the saloon. On the third evening, after they had eaten an Indian meal of dubious character in the town, the captain suddenly announced their departure. As the ship left the shelter of the harbour it was worryingly apparent that a severe storm was rising. The little vessel was tossed and bounced like a plastic toy in a bath, the two passengers were violently sick and terrified, and Felix's small dog Sarah was thrown uncontrollably all over the cabin. 'It was so bad as to be almost ludicrous, and lasting for about twelve hours, mostly in darkness – it was precisely like the typhoon in Joseph Conrad,' Robert said afterwards. A week later, the *St Ernest* went down with all hands lost at sea.

Robert was much more enthusiastic about the two successful performances that he arranged of his favourite mechanical device, the Noakesoscope. A screening of its slides opened the inaugural meeting of the Friends of the National Film Archive, and proved so popular that Sir Arthur Elton, the chairman, arranged a further evening's entertainment jointly with the Victorian Society, at the Lyric Theatre, Hammersmith. John Smith was among the guests invited afterwards to a party given by Audrey Bowley to mark the opening of her antique shop in the King's Road, Chelsea.

The Transport Bill, published at the end of 1961, provided for the break-up of BTC into its component parts: railways, docks and waterways. For the first time in more than a century the unholy and ruinous alliance between rail and canal was to end. The nearly 2,000 miles of Britain's waterways which, over the years, had been acquired by a variety of railway companies for reasons of commercial competition, allowed to decline, then under nationalisation in 1947 brought under the massive rail-ruled conglomerate, were at last to be returned to a separate, yet-to-be-created authority responsible solely for inland waterways.

It should have been marvellous news. It should have represented the triumphant culmination of the campaign for which IWA had been fighting for so many years. Yet the government, in drafting the Bill, had once again failed to tackle the real issue.

The Transport Bill was an extremely complex document, a nightmare of Parliamentary draftsmanship which had to take into account the entire precedent of statutory and case law under which the country's transport systems had evolved. Even though the plight of the waterways was so severe, the real reason for instigating this change of policy was the serious decline of the railways in the face of competition from motorway traffic. The wheel of fortune had turned full circle, and it was now the turn of rail to find itself unable to compete economically.

The steady erosion of branch lines since 1950 had still not been sufficient to restore prosperity to the railway network. Now the country was poised to face the savage cut-backs recommended in the plan produced by Dr Richard Beeching, drafted from ICI to take over where the generals had failed, soon to become first chairman of British Rail. The Beeching plan, rather like the Rusholme recommendations for waterways, concentrated on modernising the few main national routes at the expense of the branch network.

Even though the wheel had turned full circle, waterways were still trapped unfairly in its gyration, crushed under the weight of the more powerful railways. The Transport Bill had been construed in such a way as to deal with the problems of rail rather than solve the entirely different waterways situation. There is a fundamental difference between the two systems: whereas the owner of a railway track must normally operate all services, a waterway more nearly resembles a road – open, within reasonable regulation, to all. 'What usually happened when we called the Ministry's attention to the impact of their proposals was that they denied our interpretation, and conceded that it was correct only under heavy pressure and after endless negotiation,' Aickman explained.

Under the Bill, an Inland Waterways Authority (still, at this stage, to be so called) was to be established. It was to be given a five-year period of grace in which the government would subsidise its operations to a maximum of £10 million; thereafter, it would be expected to be self-financing. Adoption of this policy was the main reason for introducing other contentious changes in the law which were designed to protect the new authority and enable it to operate profitably.

Under clause 43 the Authority was empowered to make such charges for its services and facilities 'as they think fit' – the granting of such an open unregulated power to a monopoly was unparalleled in the transport industry. Even an attempt by Conservative MPs to modify the proposal by adding the words, 'reasonable charges', was frustrated by party conflicts.

When the debate reached the House of Lords the amendment received wide backing until the government called upon Lord Hailsham, 'who emitted such clouds of legal obscurity as to confuse the issue with complete success', reported Robert. 'The peers said that they did not know which way up they were, and supported the government accordingly.'

The effect of another clause was even more far reaching in that it virtually removed the obligation under the original statutes to maintain the right of navigation at all times and to all users. The new authority was to be relieved of this responsibility for five years in the case of all waterways which were not in a navigable state during the period of six months prior to the vesting date, and consequently they were not required to improve the standard nor held liable for damage resulting from the unnavigable state.

'As the clause stands, it, in my opinion, provides for the extinction of the public right of passage on the whole system during the interim period without rhyme or reason and is as it stands, indefensible,' E. W. H. Christie, the Association's legal consultant, advised Aickman.

If there was any doubt about the government's policy on this issue, it was clarified by John Hay, Parliamentary Secretary, in a letter to Charles Longbottom, MP: 'The clause has been included in the Bill as a protection to the Authority against the risk of being compelled to undertake costly and unnecessary works for which the taxpayer would have to foot the bill,' he wrote. He confirmed that the effect of the clause was to absolve the new authority from failure to maintain any inland waterway in a navigable condition, except for those considered to be already navigable during the specified six-month period. The government's plans were further defended on the entirely spurious grounds that the Bill only applied to the nationalised waterways – as though they represented a small and insignificant proportion of the national network.

The Bill was a purely mechanical legal device to transfer

power from one nationalised corporation to another. There was no acknowledgement of the years of study and research invested in looking for a solution to the waterways problems, and the recommendations of the government's own instruments, Bowes and IWRAC, were disregarded. Far from any safeguards for the future development of waterways being given, the new authority was to have a clean slate from which had been wiped off the statutory rights of navigation.

In the debates and select committee hearings, Grant Ferris kept up a persistent, doughty campaign for the retention of statutory rights until he incited Marples's personal anger. 'Marples was very, very furious with me and wanted to fight me physically in the corridors of the House,' he recalls. Finally, he was compelled to recognise that 'politics is the art of the possible' and to accept a compromise position when the Minister threatened, 'If he doesn't shut up, I'll put the whole thing in the holding company and scrap the board altogether.'

The ministry's policy received strong endorsement from the Conservatives' legal *eminence grise*, Lord Hailsham, who felt that there had been a great deal too much passion and suspicion about the controversy. 'The structure of the organisation imposed by the Bill seems to me by far the most rational the canals have enjoyed for very many years,' he wrote to Christie. 'I do not think that good business management – which is what they appear to need – is necessarily ensured by an exact maintenance of the legal *status quo* which appears to be an incitement to litigation rather than a guarantee of sound management.'

It was just the kind of viewpoint to be expected from the person who had greater experience than anyone else in the legal process of Parliamentary government, yet Robert Aickman was more than justified in regarding the Bill not only with the utmost suspicion but also as a measure which removed the consumer's only effective defence against a state-run monopoly.

'We will shortly be faced with the situation that the waterways will be accessible only under licence from the

Authority,' he wrote to John Smith, 'which will be categorically empowered to charge as it thinks fit, and of which the governing body will be appointed entirely by the Minister, to whom alone all appeals against the governing body will lie.'

These fears were further fuelled by the attitude of Ernest Marples when pressed for a decision on the Kennet and Avon by Lionel Munk, who drew his attention to the strong support for the canal expressed at a public meeting of local residents, rather than boaters. 'In considering an important problem of this kind I must try to avoid being prejudiced by sectional pressures and organised displays of "public indignation",' Marples replied.

Munk, who had so diplomatically tried to conform with IWRAC's policy of compromise, was outraged by the Minister's cavalier treatment of such a crucial issue. 'I might not be unduly impressed by "organised displays", but I am most certainly impressed by public opinion, especially when it is so continually and frequently expressed on a large scale as in the case of the K. and A. canal,' he retorted.

Marples, who had refused to allow publication of IWRAC's recommendations, was equally infuriated when this correspondence was published.

There seemed to be little doubt about the government's real intentions when the annual – and, of course, it was to be the last before reorganisation took place – BTC Bill was placed before Parliament only a few weeks after the Transport Bill was published. As already feared, it sought the closure of nineteen sections of statutory navigation, including the entire 45 miles of the Chesterfield, all 11 miles of the Grand Western, all 9 miles of the Buckingham arm of the Grand Union, the top 5 miles of the Erewash, the Stockport branch of the Ashton, the Burslem branch of the Trent and Mersey, Dudley tunnel and City Road basin. Soon afterwards, the Saltisford arm of the Grand Union at Warwick was added. In proposing these abandonments, the Minister was over-ruling IWRAC's recommendations to keep open the Chesterfield, Erewash, Buckingham and Dudley sections.

John Hay, again, defended the closures in a letter to

Gilbert Longden, MP, claiming a saving of £35,000 out of BTC's total annual loss of £600,000 from inland waterways. To restore them to navigable condition would have cost £700,000, compared with 'redevelopment' estimates of £250,000. This viewpoint was challenged by several IWA members.

'Mr Austin repeats the popular fallacy that it costs more to close a canal than to maintain it (these canals are not, incidentally, being "abandoned" – British Waterways will still be legally responsible for their future maintenance for purposes other than navigation). This belief is just not true,' Hay wrote to Charles Longbottom. 'Economics in the maintenance of canals which have been closed to navigation can be achieved by such means as lowering water channels, savings on bank repairs, and replacement of worn-out locks by weirs. Bridges can be replaced by culverted embankments.'

A difference of view on the comparative costs between maintenance on the one hand, and restoration or closure on the other, particularly with regard to the Stratford, escalated into an acrimonious exchange in which the Parliamentary Secretary, unusually, was prepared to enter into the argument. According to John Hay, BTC had given different sets of estimates ranging from £119,000 for 'total elimination' of the Stratford to £18,000 capital expenditure to turn the canal into a stream (though this would still require annual maintenance).

Restoration, British Waterways had estimated, would amount to £134,000 to raise the Stratford to commercial standards, compared with the National Trust's budget (based on voluntary labour) of £42,000 – though the Minister added that commercial traffic would not be precluded if it found that it could use the restored route.

The argument was academic, yet the correspondence rumbled on in a very bad-tempered way over many months. Finally, Aickman accused the government, in the wake of their disastrous by-election defeat by the Liberals at Orpington, of being out of touch with public opinion and urged Hay to go and see for himself. 'If you had paid it a quiet and private visit when the National Trust moved in, you would have seen for yourself the absurdity of the figures which have been given to you.'

Disillusion with the government's handling of transport policy even reached the ears of William Watt in Philadelphia, who regularly corresponded with Aickman, keeping him briefed on the massive investment being put into modernisation of the North American commercial waterways. 'I see that one of the great myths of English history, that of the incorruptible, untouchable, and altogether wonderful British civil service, of which every US schoolchild has been taught by teachers to whom the institution seemed little short of divine, is now just a myth – a myth or an outmoded bit of ancient history,' he wrote.

Robert set him straight on one point. The civil service was not corrupt in the American way – it was just appallingly conservative. If a civil servant took a risk, acting on his own initiative, he was liable to be reprimanded if it failed; whereas, conversely, if it succeeded, then he could not be rewarded.

In Britain, concern over the lack of a positive national transport policy became so widespread that Lord Stonham formed a National Council on Inland Transport with about 100 corporate members (associations and large companies), representing some 12 million people, and Robert Aickman joined as vice-chairman. The Council sought to establish a transport policy which would benefit the whole community, 'replacing the present chaos by order', by having a balanced system with each type of traffic using the form of transport most suited to it; in fact, it wanted to see a more economic appreciation of the real cost of roads which enjoyed a huge hidden subsidy.

In a 6,000-word memorandum to the Prime Minister the National Council stated:

If the present trend continues unchecked, and road traffic, both lorries and cars, continues to increase, the state of the roads in, say, ten years time will be too ghastly to conceive. By then the Beeching plan will have transplanted the railway system, so that no alternative will remain but to demolish more of our town centres and cover yet more of our countryside with tarmac.

To this prophetic analysis, Harold Macmillan replied: 'I think it is difficult to pass judgement until we have the result of Dr Beeching's traffic studies, which will help us, among other things, to establish much more clearly than we do at present what functions the railways are in fact best fitted to discharge.' Lord Stonham ruefully observed that 'while the PM is awaiting Dr B's findings, substantial rail closures are continuing'.

Robert Aickman also played an active role in the defence of the railways as vice-president, along with John Betjeman, of the Railway Development Association, assisting in the formation of branches around the country, chairing a public meeting on 'The Case for Railways' at Caxton Hall, Westminster in April 1961, and frequently addressing audiences on the subject. The *Bulletin* invariably contained, under the heading 'Motor Moloch', horror stories of the numbers of people killed and injured on Britain's roads, along with news of the ever-growing invasion of the environment by vehicles.

As the future of the waterways was once again bounced playfully between the two sides of the Westminster debating chambers and the Transport Bill ground remorselessly through its inevitable stages until it suffered the final indignity of the 'guillotine', cutting off further discussion, in other parts of the country significant advances were being made by individuals prepared to go out and fight for their rights.

The Royal Assent was given to the Transport Act, and soon afterwards the official opening of the lower Avon was celebrated over the Whit weekend, the climax of twelve years' devoted voluntary effort, marking the first restoration of a navigation in the twentieth century. On Saturday morning, 9 June 1962, an armada of boats set out from Tewkesbury and arrived in Pershore in the afternoon for a thanksgiving service in the abbey. The following day, with the party swollen by many official guests, the flotilla continued upstream to Evesham, where it was greeted with a civic reception.

'Mrs Smith' in the end contributed £6,000 out of the £20,000 total that the restoration cost in materials, all the labour being given on a voluntary basis. Apart from the army, work had been limited to weekends, but it had continued over *every* weekend, with Douglas Barwell calling upon a force of nearly 250 people.

He was aware of each person's individual skills and talents and deployed them accordingly; he himself, as the engineer in overall charge, was on emergency calls at all time. His family had trekked down to the Avon most weekends and holidays, and his wife had catered for the work force and handed out the beer that was provided every lunchtime.

'Once the river is open to Evesham, Evesham is a port,' Barwell had forecast in early days – and afterwards proved it by sailing his cruiser from the town across the Irish Sea.

From the opposite side of the country, Arthur Cavender told Aickman that the Great Ouse Restoration Society was hoping for Ministry approval of a scheme to renew Cardington lock – which would open navigation to Bedford – and the river board believed that they would obtain government funding as part of a flood-protection project.

Even more encouraging was the rate of progress being achieved in restoring the Stratford canal. David Hutchings – a man driven by a single ideal and intolerant of bureaucratic delays and interference – set himself a challenging timetable: to reopen the canal within three years and within the very tight budget allocated. His slogan was: 'Boats to Stratford before the Russians reach the moon.'

The first twelve months' schedule demanded that the canal should be navigable to Lowsonford by the end of March 1962. 'After near heroic efforts by our volunteers to install the bottom gates of locks 27 and 29 under the most arduous conditions, this boat [the 70-foot *Emscote*] reached Lowsonford on 28 March at about 9.30 p.m. in a snow storm,' David recorded.

By September better weather and lighter evenings had enabled Hutchings to make an incredible advance so that, at the end of the month, the bottom gate of lock 38 at Preston Bagot had been installed, completing restoration of the

heavily locked section of the canal from Lapworth. Ahead
lay the long, single-locked pound where the water was
carried in aqueducts over roads at Wootton Wawen and
Bearley. Then there remained a final thicket of sixteen locks
as the course fell sharply at Wilmcote down into the Avon
valley and Stratford town.

To match this extraordinary speed of working, lock gates
had had to be produced at the rate of one a week; and, in
fact, over one particular weekend, two gates had been fitted.
Repair of lock chambers and side weirs was also nearly
finished, and dredging almost completed as far as the
Edstone aqueduct. By the end of September, in fact, the
canal was navigable for more than half its length and half the
locks had been repaired – the programme was on budget and
slightly ahead of schedule.

Confidence was running so high that, even though there
remained a daunting amount of work, plans were being
made to celebrate the first-ever restoration of a canal in royal
style. Since the reopening in 1964 would coincide with the
fourth centenary of Shakespeare's birth, approaches were
made to Peter Hall, the young and highly successful director
of the Royal Shakespeare Company, and the concept of a
joint event was warmly taken up by Dr Levi Fox, head of
the Shakespeare Trust. Clarence House indicated, though it
was too early to make it official, that the Queen Mother,
who was Patron of the National Trust, would accept an
invitation to play a leading role as the guest of honour.

CHAPTER 118

Boats to Stratford Again

Twelve months before the deadline for completing the restoration of the Stratford canal, David Hutchings warned Lionel Munk in April 1963 that there was a definite danger that they might not be able to achieve the target. An appallingly severe winter had been followed by an exceptionally wet spring, seriously hampering work everywhere, and these difficulties had been compounded by the discovery that the locks in the southern half of the waterway were in a much worse state than the northern ones that had already been repaired. The atrocious conditions had deterred volunteers and David made a desperate plea for more workers.

'Fortunately none of us were experts, or we should have known it was impossible,' was the way in which David summed it up afterwards – and it was this attitude of mind that carried him through this most desperate period. Despite the problems, he refused to defer the target completion date.

The winter of 1962–3 was so severe that it was blamed for dealing the final death blow to canal-carrying, although, in fact, there was so little life left in the corpse from the years of political and bureaucratic procrastination that it was already virtually beyond revival.

Work on the Stratford restoration was never totally halted – because Hutchings would never allow such a thing to happen – but progress was slowed to an insignificant rate for many weeks. Even a one-ton dragline dropped from a height of forty feet could not penetrate ice eighteen inches thick, so dredging was impossible. Attempts to pump out the Edstone aqueduct failed when the water froze in the pipes. Over one particular night, six inches of ice formed where work had been going on the previous day; hammers and pickaxes could not smash it, and it had to be sawn up in blocks. Diesel engines were invariably awkward to start and there was a constant threat that vehicles, if they became bogged down in mud, would be frozen into the ground before they could be moved.

On top of everything else, the RAF and army personnel, who had formed the bulk of the weekday work force, had to be transferred to snow-clearing duties on the roads. Looking for an alternative source, Hutchings turned to the Prison Commissioners and, within a short time, he had gangs of what were to prove some of his best workers sent from Winson Green gaol. By March he had six star prisoners who regularly worked an eight-hour day, six days a week.

Over the course of that dreadful winter almost no progress had been made on locks and, with twelve months left, Hutchings was faced with 17 of the total of 36 locks still to be restored. It was found, moreover, that 10 – and not 8 as previously forecast – of the Wilmcote flight of 12 locks would require extensive rebuilding. In all cases at least one wall had to be entirely demolished and reconstructed, and in some cases both sides of the chamber and the approach walls had to be rebuilt. The work was heavy and required a degree of technical skill. In addition, access to these particular locks was poor and became much worse in wet weather – often as much as 200 tons of debris had to be carted away, as well as tons of new bricks and other materials brought in.

The locks, which had been empty of water for many years, had been badly distorted from side-ground pressure, made worse by the settlement of the clay soil in this area, and exacerbated in winter by the action of frost breaking up building materials. In these cases there was no alternative but the total demolition of the wall until the faulty section had been eliminated and sound foundations reached. This work was carried out using compressors, even explosives in really bad cases, followed by pressure hoses and wire brushes. Heavy mesh reinforcement was then erected and a continuous steel bar laid horizontally and fastened to the mesh with anchor points; concrete, using up to three mixers at a time, was poured into the space between the mesh and the ground. As most of this work was done by unskilled and inexperienced prisoners, methods suitable for them had to be evolved. With speed the vital factor, there was, regrettably, no time to spare for the aesthetic finishing, such as refurbishing Victorian brickwork, that David Hutchings would have preferred under better circumstances.

The solid oak gates, some as much as sixteen feet in length and weighing up to four tons, were extremely difficult to handle and were dropped into place by an RAF crane. A record was set up in the spring, when work restarted, and the four gates for locks 54 and 55 were measured, made by a firm in Henley-in-Arden, delivered and installed – all within ten days.

Dredging also became increasingly demanding and difficult over the last section of the canal within the town itself. From one of these locks eighteen old bicycles were retrieved (today, it would have been supermarket trolleys), while a great quantity of rubbish had been thrown into the canal where it was crossed by the A34 Birmingham main road. Here the mud was over four feet deep, a greater mass than anywhere else on the canal, and a poor towing-path through a narrow cutting added to the problems. The Royal Engineers solved this by making a new path, but elsewhere, under the series of town road bridges, the debris had to be removed by hand shovel.

By September David Hutchings was planning to start on the old canal basin, immediately above the river Avon and set in front of the red-brick 1930s Royal Shakespeare Theatre. In the first half of the nineteenth century Bancroft had been a busy inland port with a second basin dug in 1827, surrounded by eleven coal wharves and wharves for lead, glass, corn and timber. The construction of a horse-drawn tramway, with its own narrow bridge over the Avon, across the Cotswolds to Moreton-in-Marsh, had turned Stratford into a thriving centre of trade, and annual coal tonnage exceeded 10,000 tons. The coming of the railways in 1860 soon killed off the canal traffic; the second basin was filled in and the original one turned into an ornamental lake with a fountain. When the new theatre was built in the 1930s, after the turreted Victorian building had been lost in a fire, the remaining derelict wharves were cleared away, except for one timber wharf on the side of the Avon, and a footbridge placed across the old barge lock between the basin and the river at a height that prevented any future passage of boats.

Stratford council had shown remarkably little enthusiasm for the canal's restoration and there had been talk of diverting the route away from Bancroft by cutting a new channel to enter the Avon above Clopton bridge; at this late stage, there was no hope of any assistance from the council in clearing and renovating, and the National Trust decided that the shortest way to avoid an argument was to replace the footbridge – strictly, the council's duty – at their own expense. Once again, the Prison Commissioners came up with the answer. The new bridge was made from timber and steel at Wormwood Scrubs – the first bridge ever to be constructed by prisoners – placed on site by the Royal Engineers and installed by the inmates of Winson Green.

As the third winter approached, Hutchings renewed his call for help. 'Appeals for volunteers have been virtually ignored by – even particularly by – those people and organisations most likely to benefit from the opening of the canal and it should be clearly understood that, in spite of the progress made over the last few months, i.e. an average of two weeks to restore each of the locks on the Wilmcote flight, there is no reason whatever for complacency.'

Planning for the ceremonial reopening continued regardless of David's worries. Jack Rathbone, the Trust's Secretary, had taken charge of their arrangements and he had the splendid idea that the official reception should take place at another of their properties, the magnificent, historic country house, Charlecote, standing in parkland on the banks of the Avon – 'provided that guests can approach by river'. There was a snag in that the house lay several miles up the river, which was no longer used as a navigation; nevertheless, he explored the idea with the River Severn Board and Hutchings before being forced to give it up.

Robert Aickman, simultaneously, was making manoeuvres to ensure that the IWA was not overshadowed by the Trust and found an ally in Levi Fox ('like a don at a Redbrick university') who, though officially responsible for the Shakespearean fourth centenary event, seemed to be receiving little support. The unique combination of the canal reopening – and it was *the* one that had originally aroused his interest in waterways – and the historical event appealed to Robert's sense of the dramatic and to his entrepreneurial skills. Here was an unrivalled opportunity for blending both arts and boating into a festival of national importance which would repeat, and even exceed, the triumphs of Market Harborough.

Drawing upon his recent experience in organising the American orchestra's tour of the Thames, he envisaged the Avon alongside the theatre being used as a superb natural arena for performances on a floating platform. At Robert's instigation, David Hutchings, who had taken on the additional task of chairman of the organising committee, made a series of approaches to orchestras in Birmingham and London, though finally the choice settled on the Bournemouth Symphony Orchestra, then under the direction of a top international conductor, Constantin Silvestri.

Before long the suggestion arose that the festival would be enhanced by the inclusion of some professional ballet. No sooner proposed, than arranged – for Robert had become chairman of a small touring company, Ballets Minerva, directed by Edward Gaillard, a dancer of some repute who had appeared in the film *The Red Shoes*. Robert's involvement stemmed from a chance conversation at an IWA meeting and he had helped to steer the company, then struggling, on to a firmer financial footing, obtaining for them an Arts Council grant, and he enjoyed being part of a friendly and lively enterprise, which he regarded as being like J. B. Priestley's Good Companions.

The site for the festival proved to be an altogether more troublesome affair. The Association anticipated that at least a hundred boats would be converging from all parts of the country and, from the outset, they assumed that the ideal moorings would be on the public recreation ground opposite the theatre, providing a spacious and prestigious location, yet away from the town itself. The local council had a different view; refusing this site, they offered a far less satisfactory one on flood-prone rough meadows above Clopton bridge. Despite a further attempt to persuade them, the council refused to change their minds, and the whole event was in danger of collapsing until the Royal Shakespeare Theatre made a magnanimous offer: the boats could be moored alongside the land they owned between the theatre and Holy Trinity collegiate church, and the festival could take place on the smooth green lawns of the beautiful riverside gardens – once the fine family home of Flowers, the brewers.

The fascination and demands of organising such a major event brought a welcome relief to Robert from his latest severe disappointment over the composition of the British Waterways Board – at a late stage, it had been decided to keep this known and recognised name. It had been brought into existence on 1 January 1963 with 'two elderly gentlemen', as Aickman described them, heading the board of directors: F. S. Arney, formerly General Manager of the Port of Bristol Authority, as part-time chairman, and Sir John Hawton, retired Permanent Secretary of the Ministry of Health, as full time vice-chairman. It had been rumoured that Sir Geoffrey Lowles was in line to become chairman, but he had died the previous September. Within a few months, in fact, Hawton took over as chairman and a 38-year-old chief executive, A. M. Allen, was brought in from the Atomic Energy Commission. Apart from Admiral Parham and Sir Reginald Kerr, who were retained as non-executive directors, the only person with any kind of personal knowledge of the inland waterways to join the board was Charles Hadfield – ironically one of only two names on Munk's 'black-list'. John Smith's cynical doubts about the selection of the board members had been proved absolutely right, and the opportunity was missed of giving dynamic leadership to the new initiative.

Although Hadfield had not taken any active role in the waterways campaign since joining the Central Office of Information, he had written a book called *Introducing Canals* in 1955 in which he had set out his own blueprint for their future: the remaining commercially successful routes were to be improved and developed and given a guaranteed life; the remainder should be separated from BTC, taken over either by the National Trust or by individual trusts like LANT, and provided with a pound-for-pound grant from public funds for an agreed number of years with assistance from local authorities and technical help from BTC.

At about the time that he was taking early retirement from the Civil Service to join with David St John Thomas in establishing the publishers David and Charles, he heard of the prospect of British Waterways Board being created and applied through the 'old boy' network to the appropriate senior official for his name to be considered for the Board. There was some surprise about this since 'you are not supposed to apply to government boards yourself!', he admitted, but he was seen and his record placed on file. A few months later, suddenly, he received a telephone call at lunchtime, asking him to see the Minister that evening. He caught a train and arrived at 6.30 p.m. Marples, sitting at a boardroom table with a bottle of burgundy from his own French vineyards before him, asked Hadfield whether 'he was one of these cranks?'. 'I hope not, Minister, but that is for you to judge,' he replied. After an hour's conversation about the waterways, discussed over the wine, the meeting ended with Marples asking Hadfield to contact him whenever he wished. The next morning, he was telephoned to be told that he had been appointed to the Board.

Arney's appointment as chairman was diplomatically welcomed by Grant Ferris, who told him: 'You have one supreme advantage, that you are taking over from a body which has become extremely unpopular.' But he was not surprised when Aickman refused his invitation to have dinner with the new Board and the Ministers. 'Hadfield is a man who likes canals dead, and is uneasy when people disturb his dreams by trying to bring them to life,' Robert replied, adding that Marples had 'destroyed all the ancient public rights in the waterways'.

A far more serious rebuff to the new set-up was Vivian

Bulkeley-Johnson's decision that it would be necessary to close down Willow Wren, the last major commercial fleet. He explained that for many years he had hoped against hope that a policy would be adopted of ranking canals as the third force in the country's transport system and that some positive form of encouragement would be given, initially, in helping to expand commercial traffic. 'Now, owing to the composition of the new Board and all that we have heard of its intentions, it is obvious that we can no longer continue the fight,' he wrote to Robert. 'There comes a time when it becomes criminal to go on throwing good money after bad.'

In the ten years of the company's operations the Bulkeley-Johnsons had invested nearly £100,000 behind their belief in the importance of waterways transport. The company had been started in 1953 after Leslie Morton heard Robert Aickman's lecture at the Royal Society of Arts, stressing the importance of a vigorous carrying business to ensure the survival of the canal system. Enthused by this message, Morton had visited both British Waterways and the Ministry, and undaunted by their cool reception, he had returned to Aickman who had introduced him to Vivian Bulkeley-Johnson.

Within a year, Willow Wren was already in operation with three fine pairs of boats and crews to match them: *Warbler* and *Wagtail* (Fred and Gladys Horne), *Redshank* and *Greenshank* (Jack and Rose Skinner) and *Mallard* and *Shoveller* (Alf and Frances Best). Braunston was acquired and developed as the operating base, the fleet rose to a total of about twelve actively working boats, including *Avocet* and *Dabchick* (Jack and Doris Monk), and with keen and enthusiastic marketing many regular contracts were acquired, breaking new ground. As Willow Wren's management used the fleet as a flag-waving exercise for the waterways campaign, they sought and undertook carrying work all over the country, just to prove that the canal network could meet a great variety of demands – though this, under the out-dated tolls system, was often impracticable and uneconomic.

Despite the initial disillusion over the British Waterways Board, a change of attitude – or, at least, public relations –

became apparent soon after it was set up. The first overture was made by Sir John Hawton, who told Aickman, 'I am sure that we shall need all the help that we can get, and I am sure that you can give us a lot.'

Robert accepted his invitation to meet and came away with an impression that Hawton had absorbed the key issues that he had pressed: making existing waterways viable by a specific and declared policy of multiple use (leisure, commercial and amenity); setting up an inquiry into modernisation; averting the extinction of commercial carrying; and avoiding the past iniquities of the annual Transport Acts.

Aickman made a particularly strong plea for the abolition of the tolls system and immediate introduction of annual licensing, as Willow Wren had been given a stay of execution. Although the Bulkeley-Johnsons had personally pulled out, they had transferred the boats and Braunston lease for a nominal sum to a new company under Leslie Morton, who planned to run it as a co-operative. The boatmen would no longer receive a basic wage, but would instead hire the boats and take responsibility for them while the company provided them with cargo. The key to success depended on BWB introducing annual licensing.

Hawton, at last, after a further meeting with Aickman and Morton, made a small concession, though in the most guarded manner. He explained that the new Board needed some more time to work out the lines of policy for waterways; in the meantime, naturally, they did not wish to decide on a particular piece of the pattern before they could see the whole. It would be wrong, for instance, to commit themselves to a decision on the National Trust's avowed interest in taking over the Caldon canal.

'Nevertheless, here is Morton actually in the field and wanting only the chance to prove his experiment,' he continued. 'I should not want us to be in the position of actually stopping him trying . . . Perhaps the best thing is, while we are working on the broader pattern, to make some immediate interim arrangement for trying out a licensing system for a time.' The facility – at £25 per boat per annum, as recommended by the Bowes Committee – would be limited to

Morton, and possibly Michael Streat, and it was not to be assumed that it prejudged policy either way. There spoke a former civil servant.

This decision, hesitant though it was, was one of the very few taken by the new authority to adopt the improvements which had already been recommended, after extensive study, by earlier review bodies. While policy across the broad pattern, as the chairman stated, had been placed in the pending tray, canals throughout the country, whether commercially successful or not, were continuing to erode and decline as no positive measures were being taken to encourage revival; the harsh fact was that the fate of the Kennet and Avon, the Ashton, Chesterfield and many others hung just as much in the balance as before, except that their future now depended on a new organisation about which little was known and which had retreated behind a smokescreen of policy review and research. All action had been suspended; at best, it was a ceasefire pending negotiations, or a renewal of hostilities.

John Smith thought that Sir John Hawton was 'quite a hopeful figure – although I do think he tends to say things simply because he thinks one wants to hear them'.

This state of suspended animation was set to continue, in fact, through most of the five years' grace that the government had granted. Reporting on their second year, BWB was still proclaiming:

> The need for a clear and understood policy has certainly not diminished in urgency since last year. Practical difficulties have for many years arisen because those who are interested in one or more of the many aspects of waterways use are uncertain where they stand. These difficulties arise still: they arise increasingly.'

The period of ceasefire, while the waterways continued to deteriorate, caused renewed dissension within the IWA. Lionel Munk, at the setting-up of BWB, had adopted a policy of giving the new authority the chance to prove itself and its intentions without being subject to the kind of public pressure that had been applied to BTC in the past. Robert Aickman agreed to go along with this attitude for a time; yet, inevitably, he found it increasingly difficult to contain his impatience and frustration over another prolonged period of inactivity when he had campaigned so assiduously for so many years for solutions which, he believed, were obvious – and inevitable – if the waterways were to be saved.

The gap between the two men – and Munk had not only been involved in the campaign for fewer years but also had a personal stake in the commercial outcome as the owner of Maid Line Cruisers – started to widen perceptively. The Kennet and Avon became a source of dissension as Munk placed a top priority on its restoration (partly because it would extend the cruising waters of the Thames valley) whereas Robert was still fighting in principle for every canal, especially the Ashton.

Munk was, in fact, trying to negotiate a rather sensitive and complex deal with BWB over the K. and A. He felt that a voluntary trust on its own would not have the resources to take on the entire restoration over eighty-six miles and more than a hundred locks; instead, he was looking for a combination of volunteer effort and BWB technical in-put. Sulhampstead lock, the first western barrier, was selected for this initial experiment in joint enterprise, and an appeal for £20,000 was launched on the basis that BWB would be co-operating. Munk saw it as a test case of BWB's genuine intentions.

Aickman was not alone in fearing the outcome of negotiating with an authority which had failed to commit itself to any definitive statement of policy. Michael Macfarlane wrote to him: 'While on the subject of Lionel, I am horrified by his attitude on the K. and A. I gather that you have long given up on this subject, but it is only now that I realise that the entire movement is in jeopardy from the pride of one man.'

Munk himself, during this honeymoon period with the new authority, thought that IWA should adopt a stance along the lines of the RAC and AA on roads – accepting that the Association was no longer aggressively campaigning to change policy but rather playing a pragmatic role in seeking to safeguard and improve users' interests within a recognised structure.

'If their policy is satisfactory and if a sound deal can be arranged, then IWA would tend to become something akin to the AA, whilst maintaining a watching brief in case of future trouble,' he told Robert. 'The members want the canals safeguarded for the future. In my opinion, most of them do not want a continuation of strife, *if strife is not necessary*.'

Robert tried very hard, against his natural inclinations, to come to terms with this attitude, agreeing with Lionel that publicity should be 'dampened', although he argued that BWB officials so far had shown only a difference in emphasis, not in policy. In contrast to Munk, he still received letters from members asking the Association to campaign more vigorously.

To one of them, Roger Calvert, he replied: 'I incline to the view that at the moment the situation is quite hopeless . . . I think that an immense public disillusionment lies ahead.' He felt, increasingly, that waterways were no longer a special case. The nation as a whole so lacked a coherent transport policy that the only realistic solutions could be achieved by forming a small, tightly knit pressure group of 'well informed radicals' who would call for a transport revolution. He himself did not wish to be a member of such a group – he had given enough of his life to such work.

At the same time, Munk was suffering from self-doubts which were in contrast to his confident public profile. In a closely-typed four-page letter to Robert, in March 1963, he confessed that he felt unrecognised in many ways for the efforts that he had put into the movement: for his work as national chairman, his particular campaign for the Kennet and Avon, his role with the Association of Pleasure Craft Operators, his representation on the Royal Yachting Association committee, and his time spent in visiting and encouraging branches. To Robert, as editor of the *Bulletin*, he complained about the lack of prominence given to his various activities; with Robert, as a colleague, he shared a mutual frustration over members who not only failed to recognise their efforts but also criticised their failure to achieve results.

Two months later, Munk decided that he wished to resign, while 'hoping to maintain the friendliest of relations with everyone', and he proposed to announce this at either the next council meeting or the AGM. He assured Robert that he had 'no ambitions to take over, or partially take over, your role'.

'Yes, there is trouble: and it is the same old trouble once again,' Robert admitted when Crick Grundy sympathetically inquired about the state of affairs. 'Firstly, the demand that we should cease being rude to British Waterways, the Minister of Transport and others set in authority over us; secondly, the demand that we should concentrate on pleasure boating and cease worrying about trade.' About Munk, he added, 'I sincerely do not know what exactly he does want: it strikes me as nothing less than converting the Association into an annexe of Maid Line cruisers.'

John Gagg, during an angry exchange with Robert over a critical review of one of his books in the *Bulletin*, was another person to argue in favour of a policy of moderation. 'I would seriously ask you to consider whether IWA's methods and attitudes aren't in fact leading to such cleavages – and derision – that your own aims become more and more in peril,' he queried, 'or, to put it another way, might not British Waterways, disgusted and irritated by this constant campaign of jeers and cat-calls, harden their attitude and do things that a responsible and more sober approach might have prevented?'

This view was certainly not shared by two key Parliamentarians, reflecting the attitude of those on the receiving end. George Strauss, the front-bench Labour spokesman on transport, acknowledged that 'in the many discussions we have had on inland waterways we have discovered that the inland waterways lobby is the most powerful of all in the House' – and this at a time when the issues over Rhodesia and nuclear disarmament had reached a fierce political temperature. From the upper House Lord Methuen said of the IWA, 'we owe them an immense debt' – it was the 'body that has borne the brunt of the fight to ensure the survival of our inland waterways'.

The hiatus in waterways policy also spread to the National Trust, which had become withdrawn and strangely silent. Robert felt that John Smith – now chairman of the powerful general purposes committee – was 'inaudible and invisible'. The Trust had, unexpectedly, been offered as a gift, by its private owner, the river Wey navigation in Surrey, linking the Thames and the Basingstoke canal. Robert, upset by the lack of contact, proposed to Jack Rathbone that a joint National Trust and IWA committee should be formed to co-ordinate such developments.

This prompted John Smith's return to the scene. He asked Robert to dinner, saying how much he had missed him and that the Trust was 'an organism, not a machine'. Smith, at dinner, 'could hardly have been more tiresome or less forthcoming', Robert told David Hutchings. He flatly turned down the whole idea of a joint committee. 'He is the most formidably clever man and he has such power of one kind or another that it looks to me as if the whole waterways campaign is going to end in the preservation of a few beauty spots approved by Mr Smith as industrial monuments,' he added.

Munk's reaction to the negative outcome of the dinner was to agree with Robert that the Association had been too subservient to the Trust and that, if they showed more independence, they might bring Smith 'to heel', proving that there was nothing like having a common adversary to wield together two differing partners.

Royalty, however, provided the bridge to bring together all the separate factions. When the Queen Mother formally agreed to reopen the Stratford canal, and accepted an extremely heavy programme of events, everyone buried their differences and became deeply involved in ensuring that the occasion would be outstandingly successful. John Smith briefed Jack Rathbone precisely on the people to be invited, including Sir Frederick Parham and Sir John Hawton ('for the sake of goodwill') and some 'actual prisoners', while he requested that the Stratford canal committee should be particularly well treated ('for the sake of a quiet life').

It was planned that the Queen Mother would emerge from the canal into Bancroft basin at the head of a flotilla of boats, and Smith stressed that she should be seated on a raised gold chair in the bow of the boat ('as high as possible without braining her under the road bridge') and that she should lead the procession and not be overpowered by the Royal Marines band in the following boat.

The choice of champagne caused much concern among the organisers until Rathbone had a meeting at Clarence House. The Queen Mother had no special preference, he reported, 'provided that the champagne is neither sweet nor warm'. She had agreed to the Royal Standard being flown from her boat but she requested that the salute of guns – already arranged with the Royal Navy – would not be fired. The menu met with approval: fillet of sole in aspic, roast Aylesbury duckling and fresh Evesham strawberries.

As the pressure of looking after all these arrangements on the spot bore down on David Hutchings, Robert reassured him with the opinion of Lady Cynthia Asquith (who had known the Queen Mother well and was no respecter of persons for the sake of their rank). She described her as 'very intelligent, artistically sensitive, alert and energetic'.

The programme for the concert on the river, agreed between Aickman and the orchestra's manager, was changed more than once as Silvestri pressed his own wishes. The conductor refused to perform Strauss's *Macbeth* overture, and *Romeo and Juliet* had to be substituted. Hutchings, already having to cope with these ominous signs of artistic temperament, was worried about the facilities that the Ballets Minerva would require and appealed for advice to Aickman.

'Where British orchestral musicians are bloody-minded, British ballet dancers, and all who go with them, are small children, often sweet but in constant need of motherly guidance,' he replied, adding that a few tables and mirrors for make-up would be needed.

David had one further artistic problem to sort out: he had undertaken to arrange an exhibition of paintings by his wife as part of the display in the theatre gardens. Over the past three years, despite the energy-sapping demands of the canal restoration, he had devotedly encouraged in many ways Joan's passion for art. He was deeply shocked and hurt when, in the midst of the traumas of planning for the reopening celebrations, she walked out of their home and out of their life together.

In June, too late, Jack Rathbone warned Aickman that Hutchings was thoroughly overworked and under strain. The next day David wrote to Robert, resigning from IWA: 'the reasons are purely personal and domestic'. He was particularly sorry that he would not be able to 'continue to support you as I have tried to do in the past'.

Robert responded by assigning Philip Grahame, the Association's full-time administrator, to work in Stratford immediately and right up to the time of the reopening on Saturday 11 July.

Those of the 200 boats expected for the festival who arrived early were fortunate. They could take their time at a leisurely pace over the hard-working journey down the thirteen miles and thirty-six locks of the canal; savouring the pleasures of a route that few had used this century; gently cruising past the peaceful tree-fringed sheep meadows of the rolling Warwickshire countryside, bathed in summer sunlight; admiring the charming white-washed lock cottages; squeezing under the tiny Victorian bridges whose sides were cantilevered to allow a gap in the middle just sufficient for the rope of the original horse-drawn narrowboats to pass through; glimpsing neat black-and-white thatched cottages in the village of Lowsonford, and the imposing Elizabethan red-brick and timber manor house at Preston Bagot; gliding breathtakingly over rail and road on the Edstone aqueduct; and, finally, dropping in quick succession from one lock to the next on the Wilmcote flight as the town of Stratford emerged in the Avon valley below and, beyond, the round hills of the Cotswolds appeared in the distance.

Those crews who had been more pressed for time and had come a greater distance, like the boat that had travelled 500 miles from the Leeds and Liverpool, had a tougher journey as craft were arriving in droves a day or two before the official ceremony. Although the first complete transit of the restored waterway had been accomplished by *Laughing Water* in the spring, no one could be certain how this canal, absolutely derelict only three years earlier, would sustain such massive usage over a week or two. Maintaining an adequate water supply was a serious problem as the canal depended on reservoirs at Earlswood on the northern section still under British Waterways control. The progress of the craft was monitored by army radio units at strategic sites from Lapworth down to the Avon, and a task force would dash out to deal with emergency hold-ups, perhaps caused by a broken-down boat or unfamiliarity with the conditions, before a serious blockage built up.

At the beginning of July, on the wide, sparkling reach of the river that lay above the weir and derelict lock at Lucy's mill, the boats that had started to arrive in Stratford one by one from the narrow canal began to swell into a gathering of dozens, then scores and finally into a jumbled, bobbing mass of craft, moored to pontoons from the gardens surrounding the floating concert platform, many-coloured streamers and bunting flapping in the brisk wind – a spectacle of Venetian splendour. There were craft of all shapes and sizes; among the river cruisers stood out the gleaming hull of the newest Maid Line vessel, *Robert Aickman*, named by Philippa Scott, Peter's wife, in the spring at Kingston-upon-Thames; the largest of the assembly were a pair of Willow Wren narrow-boats, each seventy feet long, *Coleshill* and *Cygnus*, bringing a consignment of Honda motor cycles which had left Japan thirty-six days before.

David Hutchings dashed hither and thither among the swirling crowds of sightseers, still enrolling 'volunteers' for many last-minute tasks. One boat-owner was told: 'We want a man with great taste and perspicacity – just hang all those flags round the stage.' Other recruits were putting finishing touches to the paint of the bottom locks as the boats continued to arrive: one bare-footed boater was warned, as he stepped on to the black beam, that it was wet – 'so it is', he remarked, examining his imprint.

Saturday, 11 July 1964 was grey and overcast, the air cooled by a strong wind, until the crucial moment when the Queen Mother, radiant in turquoise blue, arrived from the royal train at Stratford station. Then the clouds broke and the sun shone. Escorted by the Earl of Crawford and Balcarres, she was handed on to the beautiful steel narrow-boat *Linda* at the wharf behind the smart Georgian terraced houses in Tyler Street. Two other boats, *Jasmine* and *Lady Hatherton* (the latter an elegant, former canal director's boat used during the 1890s for tours of inspection and owned at that time by Hutchings), formed the procession which dropped through the last narrow lock, passed under the main road bridge, as dark and low as a short tunnel, and emerged out of the restored canal into the wide-open world of Bancroft basin, thronged with crowds, cheers ringing.

At the lock between the basin and the river, before passing under the new Wormwood Scrubs footbridge, the Queen Mother cut a blue ribbon and bells pealed out from the spire-surmounted tower of Holy Trinity collegiate church, perched on the riverside.

Between the basin and the church brilliant black and yellow heraldic banners fluttered from the theatre's skyline, a reminder that on this historic day, when the reopening of a canal nearly 150 years old had been marked, the fourth centenary of William Shakespeare's birthday on 22 April was also being celebrated with royal accolade. That same evening the Queen Mother attended a gala production of *Henry V*, afterwards watching from the theatre balcony as fireworks cascaded over the orchestra on the river barge playing Handel's *Music for the Royal Fireworks*, and the opening words of the play reverberated with still greater significance:

> O! for a Muse of fire, that would ascend
> The brightest heaven of invention;
> A kingdom for a stage, princes to act
> And monarchs to behold the swelling scene.

'Not having taken part in the Stratford project was like not having been at Agincourt,' observed John Smith later.

As the exhibition marquees were taken down, the debris swept away, and the last of the visiting boats made their weary way back up the heavily locked canal, Robert Aickman took a last lingering look down the river which flowed between cattle grazing in the meadows towards Luddington, curving under the steep tree-lined hillside at Cleeve, racing through the old mill at Welford, sneaking through the narrow arches of Bidford's ancient stone bridge and, as the course widened, idling round the gentle hillsides above Evesham, thick with regimented fruit orchards. One life-long dream, going back to his boyhood visit to the theatre, of restoring the canal had been triumphantly achieved within the incredibly short time span of three years – what, now, were the chances of completing, as often discussed, the former inter-connection between the river and canal navigations, offering continuous passage from the Severn to the Grand Union?

Although it was known that there was no serious obstacle to claiming the legal right to the upper Avon navigation, the physical task was immense and on a greater scale than with the lower Avon. The former eight locks had virtually disappeared, most of the weirs had gone, the river had changed course in places since the navigation was last used, the water level had dropped and the river was in fact little more than a drainage channel. The complications of obtaining river board agreement and clearing the statutory position would take a very long time to sort out. All of this would require a considerable fund; Douglas Barwell had estimated at least £300,000. It was on a scale exceeding anything so far attempted and far beyond the resources of the IWA, which was still struggling from year to year to raise a modest £3,000 campaign fund.

Unexpectedly, the situation was transformed and the prospect of restoring the upper Avon, though still distant, was brought more nearly into focus. Malcolm White (a fictitious name as the donor still wishes to remain anonymous), who enjoyed travelling around the waterways in his own boat, had been making generous contributions for the past two or three years to IWA, specifically to underwrite

Robert's time and to provide some compensation for his loss of earnings. About a year before the Stratford reopening, White told him that, if he was successful in repatriating capital at present tied up in South Africa, he intended to donate money to the upper Avon project.

No one, however, had anticipated the extent of his generosity (and, moreover, it was a strictly anonymous gift) until he revealed that he would donate about £90,000 on the condition that this would comprise one-third of the total cost of restoration and that the remainder would be raised from other sources. Kenneth Gill Smith insisted that the task would call for a full-time professional manager, as he believed that there would be 'stiff opposition from many riparian owners, who would require very tactful handling'.

Douglas Barwell ruled himself out of taking on a further commitment on such a scale and Malcolm White made it clear that his gift was dependent on David Hutchings carrying out the job. 'On the upper Avon I suspect the need is not only for an engineer, but, to put it more crudely, for a dedicated showman and organiser, who will sell the project to the world,' Robert told David. 'I think that you are the only possible man.'

Tentative approaches made by Robert to John Smith about the National Trust's involvement were ignored, with the result that, after his earlier frustrations over the Basingstoke, he came steadily round to the view that this time the IWA would achieve the best results by setting up their own trust, and he briefed lawyers to start the process. Hutchings, who had suffered from complete exhaustion and nervous strain for several months, would not be committed, though he insisted that, if he accepted the job at all, he would not be answerable to a large and distant committee.

A provisional committee of IWA officers with Christopher Clifford as chairman had been assembling occasionally for some months, but Hutchings failed to attend any of the meetings as he had been too busy to travel over to Clifford's home at Upton-on-Severn. 'Why could they not meet in Stratford?' he asked. The upper Avon project seemed to be drifting dangerously out of sight as months passed without any sign of positive direction.

Towards the end of 1964 rumour filtered through to Aickman that even Malcolm White was becoming disheartened at the lack of progress and expressing understandable doubts about his commitment. When the news reached Robert that Hutchings was actively seeking other jobs, he dashed down to Stratford to take charge of the situation. He approached Sir Fordham Flower, then Stratford's most respected leader, who had been an active vice-patron of the festival, and he agreed to take over the chair of the proposed trust. Clifford, bitterly upset by what he regarded as personal disloyalty, resigned from the IWA. Shortly afterwards Hutchings agreed, on a provisional basis, to oversee the survey of the river as the preliminary stage to planning and costing the full restoration, and contractors were appointed to carry out the work, which required study of every stream, ditch and land-drain feeding into the river.

In 1965 the Upper Avon Navigation Trust was formally established and the long, demanding process of reopening the river to boats was begun. The Trust, chaired by Sir Fordham Flower, succeeded in persuading Hutchings to give up his architectural career by assuring him that he would not suffer financially from the decision.

Robert Aickman had one further decision to take – about his own involvement in the waterways campaign. Now that he was certain that the upper Avon restoration could be achieved without depending on national authorities he realised that he had reached a time of life when he had, at last, to look after himself – to fulfil his ambitions as a writer and to generate some income from his work. Over the past year or so he had frequently corresponded with Munk, even more often talked late into the night, about his pressing need to recover in financial terms the time that he had been devoting to the IWA campaign. He hoped that some *modus vivendi* could be found which would enable him to continue to run the promotional aspects of the campaign and receive reasonable compensation, perhaps even in the form of a deferred pension.

His frustration with the stalemate in national waterways policy was intensified when British Waterways produced an interim report described as 'essentially one of general comment, not a final conclusion or recommendation'. There were indications in the report that official policy was gradually groping towards the right goals, yet the pace remained unbearably slow to people like Aickman, and uncertainty about the future was just as great.

'We certainly do not ask you to approve all we say in this report. But, if not judged utterly unacceptable, we shall know that we can get on with our next stage,' Sir John Hawton tentatively introduced his report to the Minister. 'We must say at once that these provisional first views will need to be tested by systematic financial investigation, not only of the course which seems to us at first sight to offer the best solution but of other courses open to us.'

There was recognition that boat licensing, in place of tolls, had crept in; that closure was increasingly regarded as an expensive measure; and that proposals for mass abandonment had gone out of fashion, though many canals, such as the Ashton, Worcester and Birmingham, Chesterfield and Caldon remained in a 'grey' category.

The real breakthrough came in British Waterways' acceptance, for the first time, of the concept of multiple use of canals, meaning that 'every useful, business, economic or social purpose to which the waterways can be put should be as fully developed as possible, and on as many of the waterways as could justify all or any of the uses sufficiently'.

When the Board introduced this as 'a quite new conception', Aickman was stung into making an acid comment to Sir Alan Herbert. 'The [IWA] formula has always been "multiple use": use of all the waterways, though obviously in varying proportions, alike for commercial carrying, pleasure-boating, water supply, and angling; also, sometimes for land drainage; usually for tow-path lovemaking and general amenity-gaping, history study, botany study and bird-watching.'

Robert recognised that the interim report had made a start, but a start only. Whatever the Board might have said to the Minister about being in a 'hurry', they were still in a 'hurry' a year later when half the five years of grace had expired, without any clear policy established. Robert perceived that he had either to take several steps back from the waterways scene or be prepared to devote the remainder of his life to it.

'I reflected that "the man who fights a dragon becomes a dragon", as the Chinese put it: and I had been in the campaign night and day for eighteen years,' he wrote. 'I decided to take several steps back.'

He made one last attempt to put some strength back into a movement that he believed had become spineless. He encouraged Michael Macfarlane, a business consultant who was ideally suited to the role, to make himself available on a full-time, professional basis as campaign manager, and in a very few weeks Aickman succeeded in raising guarantees from three sources that would have funded the position over three years. But this overture was rebuffed, causing bitter resentment and the resignation from the council of Macfarlane, David Cooper and Crick Grundy (by now manager of the Stratford canal).

In October 1964 Robert Aickman retired from his active work with IWA, though remained in his official capacity as founder and vice-president. In a long letter to Munk, he explained that he had two main reasons for resigning.

'I do not think that I am the best person to attempt the armistice with British Waterways which I agree should be sought,' he wrote. 'I consider that all I stand for has suffered too much at official hands over the past years; I do not really speak the same language (certainly not in the capacity of suppliant) as the people we have to deal with; and, by no means least, I am very doubtful about the success of the negotiations.'

His second reason was entirely personal – that he simply could no longer afford, without adequate compensation, to give so much of his time. 'To put it quite quietly, I did not think that last autumn the council (excluding you, as I think I can say with sincerity, and one or two others) took seriously enough the financial dilemma in which my work for the

Association, through years of inflation, had landed me,' he explained.

Lionel Munk, the pragmatic leader who had taken over all the reins from Aickman, paid outstanding tribute to his predecessor. 'He worked fantastically hard for us ever since the formation in 1946, and his efforts and those of others have resulted in the present position of the Association when it has never been so influential, nor so solidly based from administrative, membership and financial points of view. Robert has been a pugnacious, persistent and fighting leader of the highest calibre. A major part of the Association's present standing is to his credit.'

Robert, an idealist who sought achievements perhaps beyond realistic attainment in the modern world, and a persistent self-critic who was always driving himself to higher goals, was far less satisfied. He had seen it as a campaign to put 'man on top' – he had envisaged the waterways not just as an end in themselves but as a means for humankind to assert itself over the age of the machine and of bureaucracy.

'If the waterways campaign is not waged as part of a much wider war on anti-human elements in contemporary life I believe it will fail even to keep the waterways, let alone keep them for any purpose worth bothering about.' he concluded. 'On the other hand, I am sure that the unique success enjoyed by the Association has derived mainly from the expression its campaign gives to human needs which are submerged by all the modern agencies of welfare, commerce and din.'

CHAPTER 14

Twenty Years and After

'It is said that it takes twenty years to change public opinion: where the canals are concerned, we managed this in less than fifteen. By the mid-Fifties, no impartial observer would fail to agree with the fundamental claims of the campaign. Now, in 1966, we appear to be on the very threshold of seeing all that we have fought for becoming a reality,' wrote Hugh McKnight, who had taken over as editor of the *Bulletin*, in the edition celebrating the IWA's twentieth anniversary.

In a retrospective feature he pointed out that the concept of a voluntary organisation as epitomised by the Association had been virtually unknown in 1946. 'It seems incredible that a tiny band of idealists even considered they could take on the combined forces of Authority . . . so giving the waterways the future stability that they had lacked for more than a century.' Their initiative had pioneered the path for other kindred organisations to campaign for the restoration of the railways, theatres and many other causes.

'Who among our earlier members can fail to forget how we were savagely ridiculed for our belief that pleasure-boating on the waterways would soon develop into a national pastime, and that hire craft would grow into a flourishing industry?' asked McKnight.

His editorial concentrated on the turnaround in public opinion that had occurred, and the transformation already achieved in leisure use of canals, once nearly abandoned, like the Oxford and Llangollen. After two decades of campaigning, it was a natural time for self-congratulation, yet the overall claim was premature: the political scene remained as bleak and unpromising as ever.

With their initial five-year period of grace running out

rapidly, British Waterways had published in December 1965 a detailed survey of the system, *The Facts about the Waterways*, which gave a statistical analysis of each canal, recording in the main a dismal story of poor maintenance and uneconomic returns. It was another unimaginative and negative report, offering no positive way forward to reviving the national heritage, and concluding that an annual subsidy of at least £600,000 would be needed to keep the system going at a minimum level.

Almost the only positive point in the document was a request for an extension of the five-year suspension of the rights of statutory navigation.

> Unless there is amending legislation of some kind, the Board will, at the end of 1967, be faced with increased obligations but with resources quite inadequate to meet them . . . While the problem will become acute in 1967 it is chronic already. Questions of practical day-to-day management (for instance, those involving expenditure and budgeting) are inevitably made more intractable and obscure by uncertainty about the future.

Less than two years after Aickman's resignation Lionel Munk himself had become disenchanted with the continued prevarication of the authorities, and he announced that the council was terminating their policy of co-operation with BWB. Although they had been correct to extend a hand of goodwill originally, they now felt that the report's failure to make constructive and progressive recommendation, together with its general air of doom and gloom, forced them to readopt a more aggressive strategy.

Munk was particularly upset that his own plan, promoted in the previous year, for establishing a Waterways Trust to take over the 1,000 miles of the non-commercial (amenity) canals had been ignored, despite its complete backing from the Parliamentary supporters and the National Trust. It had been envisaged that the proposed Trust, supported by government funds, would work closely with BWB, who had simply failed to take any serious notice of the project.

'Vituperation will do our cause no good whatsoever,' Munk had cautioned in his critical appraisal of *The Facts* report. Yet the publication a few months later of a Transport White Paper (proposing a sequence of five-year reviews which meant that no security for the waterways was promised and little investment would be forthcoming) stung the Association into a verbal assault exceeding anything heard previously. 'This infamous', 'this appalling' White Paper, 'such wicked nonsense', 'Ministry deadbeats', 'our present perilous position', 'unenterprising and unimaginative officials', 'would-be Parliamentary dictators', 'meddling with inland waterways is political dynamite' – the phrases crackled and blazed from the pages of the *Bulletin*, written by a man in the white heat of anger, bitterly annoyed at the cavalier manner in which his proffered co-operation had been flung back in his face.

'Let this government know, and those ministry officials, that now they really have a crusade on their hands, and we shall never give up the fight until we have finally achieved the aims of our association – the guaranteed retention and development of the whole canal system,' Munk concluded.

Fired by the knowledge that he had the tide of public opinion swinging behind him, Munk launched the most intensive nationwide campaign yet organised: starting with an IWA membership drive and the creation of a special boat-owners' section. Every branch was urged to organise protest meetings at their local centres and to hold their own rally in 1967; Parliamentarians were to be mobilised into taking action at every opportunity; and a national conference representing all relevant bodies, such as tourism, sports and the environment, as well as boating, was to be held in April 1967. The whole programme was set to climax with a waterways week across the country in September, when saturation media coverage was expected.

It is imperative that every IWA member, every waterway organisation, every boat club, every member of Lords and Commons concerned with waterways, and every far-seeing member of the public, now co-operate with us fully, and joins us in our waterways crusade. Together we can work wonders. If we allow the authorities to divide us, we shall go down.

The crusade did work wonders. One month before the national waterways week was to be held in September a second White Paper was published. It represented such a turnaround in policy, and went so far to meet the IWA's demands, that the campaign was called off. It struck a refreshingly positive stance from the start: 'It is the government's intention that for the first time this recreational purpose of the nationalised waterways should be recognised by Act of Parliament.'

Although there was little fundamental change in the way in which the waterways were categorised from the earlier Rusholme and Bowes reports, the significant difference was that the second class was described as 'cruising waterways' and the list had been extended to include *both* the Worcester and Birmingham and the Staffordshire and Worcestershire, part of the Kennet and Avon, the upper Peak Forest, Macclesfield and Chesterfield canals. For these routes BWB was to be given 'a new and positive duty of maintaining these waterways to a standard of navigability suitable to powered leisure craft'.

There still remained a number of waterways not included in the two main groups, such as the Ashton, Caldon, most of the Birmingham Canal Navigations, part of the Leeds and Liverpool and the Brecon and Abergavenny. Described literally as 'the remainder', BWB was to allow them to be navigated, if suitable, while their future was reviewed. The possibility of restoring some of them to full navigation was mentioned, and the Minister would have the power to upgrade them in the future.

Dismissing completely the previous proposal of five-year reviews, the White Paper recognised the need to remove uncertainty and to encourage private investment. The government accepted that public funds would have to be made available for some time, and a consultative body was to be set up to give the Minister advice on those waterways with an uncertain future.

'Without doubt, it represents the greatest step forward the IWA has ever achieved,' Munk stated. He estimated that 90 per cent of the system was to be retained, and the remainder was still open to negotiation; while he was not complacent about every aspect of the report, it was apparent that the politicians and civil servants were demonstrating a new belief in and enthusiasm for the waterways.

The provisions of the White Paper were reflected to a large extent in the Transport Bill when it was published late in 1967, though IWA was forced into fighting a fierce rearguard action over the retention of several routes, notably the Ashton and Peak Forest. The Bill's worst feature was that it provided for the abolition of the public right of navigation over the nationalised waterways which dated back to the Regulation of the Railways Act 1873 and to the statutes under which each canal had been established. It had been the trump card of the IWA campaign from first to last – in the future the public would be utterly dependent on the goodwill of the politicians and civil servants of the day.

The 1968 Act, as it became, placed most of Britain's waterways, at last, under the jurisdiction of an independent authority with as much muscle power as any other state body, charged with the responsibility to maintain, develop and run them to the benefit of the users. This structure and division has remained virtually unchanged to the present time. One of the most positive measures of the Act was to enable BWB to work in partnership with local authorities and voluntary organisations, and this has encouraged restoration on a joint basis of several canals, including the Ashton and Peak Forest, Caldon, Montgomery, and Kennet and Avon, and, in the last decade of the twentieth century, there is even the prospect of reopening Standedge tunnel.

Eighteen months after the reopening of the Stratford canal David Hutchings handed over its management to Crick Grundy and took up an architectural teaching post at Birmingham University, while starting to plan for the restoration of the upper Avon. This was a project on a totally different scale from the lower river, as virtually all navigation works had disintegrated so much that entirely new locks and weirs would have to be constructed. A new river navigation was, in effect, to be designed and built.

The right of navigation was not in question, but the Trust did not own any land around the projected sites, nor was there any right of access to them. For five years Hutchings personally conducted negotiations with the landowners and, against all predictions of opposition, succeeded in obtaining consent, many sites being given free or at a nominal sum.

The river authority was a different matter. Without actually opposing the scheme, it imposed such severe restrictions on reducing the water level by lowering or even destroying the remaining weirs that the project would have been abandoned by anyone less dedicated than Hutchings. 'I can say truthfully, without being facetious, that it was our ignorance that got us through,' he stated. 'Any engineer would have baulked, he would have thought that it was idiotic to try a scheme like this, but we weren't clever enough to understand how difficult it was going to be, so we just blundered on.'

The greatest problem confronted them at Marlcliff, six months after work had started in May 1969, where they were compelled to remove an existing six-foot weir and lower the river below its natural bed. It meant cutting through the line of marl, about a quarter of a mile wide, that runs across England, passing under the river at this point. The rock proved to be too resistant for even the toughest drills used by a Royal Engineers unit, and a machine for digging granite brought down from Aberdeen was useless. Eventually, the army worked night and day for two weeks, breaking up tiny sections with a series of explosions and then scraping away with a huge machine.

The fourteenth-century stone bridge at Bidford-on-Avon presented another serious difficulty as a channel had to be excavated beneath one of its narrow arches. Built originally by the monks of Alcester, there were, of course, no plans and no one knew how the bridge was founded. After a year of negotiations with the local authority, permission was finally granted, subject to four conditions: the main road over the bridge was not to be closed for a minute; a £10,000 bond was to be placed as surety with the council; the council's clerk-of-works was to be present; and monthly progress reports were to be submitted.

After building a coffer dam, it was discovered that the bridge had no foundations beyond slabs of stone, about two inches thick, sitting on a bed of gravel. Using a mechanical digger, a channel was cut, leaving the stanchions hanging in mid-air, and steel-reinforced concrete bags were packed under them. The job was completed by laying a concrete bed, two feet thick, in the excavated channel.

'We sent our first – and last – monthly report on the sixth day and the job was finished,' David recalled. 'There was a tremendous blow-up, of course, as the authorities could not believe that it could have been done properly within six days. They didn't realise that we had three advantages: no administration, no engineers, and we weren't paying our men. If you've those sort of advantages, you can't go wrong.' The work had been carried out by prisoners and Borstal boys, supervised by Eric Pritchard, David's indispensable right-hand man, who proved to be a genius in coping with the on-site emergencies.

After his earlier experience on the Stratford, when he started on the upper Avon restoration David ruled out volunteers for this kind of work, as he needed a work force that was keen and willing to work six days a week – without pay. Prisoners provided the perfect answer, except that he never had the same group for more than six weeks so no one worked on more than one lock or weir, and each recruit had to learn the job within a few hours. Even so, two locks were each built in the record-breaking time of three weeks.

The prisoners, who queued at Gloucester gaol for the chance to come out, were trusted in more ways than one: not only were they trusted to work, and work competently, but they were also trusted to drive around on their own, picking up supplies. There was never any question of escape; they were devoted to the task. 'For the first time in their lives, in all cases, somebody gave them a chance,' said David. 'I am no liberal – if they committed crimes, they should be in prison – but for the first time, they were working for the community because someone believed they could do something.'

By mid 1971 six of the nine new locks on the upper Avon had been built, and a vast amount of landscaping completed; there were boats on the river, which was already being run as a navigation with income from licences. 'My philosophy on this river, as on the canal, was to get it open as quickly as possible with minimum, safe standards, and then after it was open, with the money then earned, to work back, improving and developing,' stated Hutchings.

Less than five years after starting on the tremendous task, the river was once again open to navigation from Evesham up to Stratford, and on 1 June 1974 Robert Aickman, who had become chairman of the Upper Avon Trust, welcomed the Queen Mother on her return visit to the town for the formal reopening celebrations.

Aickman's last major involvement with waterways restoration was not destined to end so happily. In 1974, shortly before the Avon's royal opening, Robert visited the river Derwent in Yorkshire and, with Dr Graham Smith, honorary secretary of the Derwent Trust, and his wife Heather, toured the twenty-eight miles of river from its tidal confluence with the Ouse to the head of navigation at Malton.

Robert was greatly impressed with three factors: firstly, it was one of the most beautiful rivers in the country, flowing through lovely countryside past fine estates; secondly, the charming Victorian navigation was still in a fairly good state of repair, only one of the five locks needing to be rebuilt; and thirdly, there was already the Trust, led by Graham Smith, with the enthusiasm and vision to carry out the scheme.

Compared with the scale of the task just finishing on the Avon, the Derwent appeared to be a straightforward proposition which could be carried out within about three years for a budget of around £100,000. Since Robert felt that, within a few months, the Avon would have become 'a light from the past, no longer a beacon to the future', he agreed to become chairman of the Trust.

One lock, at Sutton-on-Derwent, had already been restored by the Derwent Trust and agreement reached that a lock would be built within the new barrage across the mouth of the river. The English Tourist Board had indicated that it would meet half the cost of the restoration, and the scheme had the support of the Sports Council and local authorities. Knowing that they had such widespread public and official backing, the Trust decided to adopt the correct course of action by applying for Parliamentary powers to run the navigation to ensure that, once the restoration was completed, it would be operated, like the Avon, by a properly constituted body. Almost at once, the proposal ran into implacable opposition from the water authority and the delay, while negotiations took place, extended from weeks to months and finally years, allowing a so-called conservation group, which had not existed originally, to emerge and gather strength, opposed to boats on the river.

Robert Aickman died several years before the issue unexpectedly turned into a challenge against the very rights of navigation on the river. Unfortunately, the Derwent had an exceptionally complex and obscure legal history, although there could be no doubt that it had been used for navigation for centuries. In 1989, after a lengthy hearing, a judge found that the right no longer existed, but the decision on the most important issue – whether a waterway was a highway for the purposes of the Rights of Way Act – was reversed on appeal in 1990. The future remains uncertain, however, since the House of Lords has given landowners permission to appeal. Meanwhile, there has been no one to look after the river, which has become silted and clogged with weeds, and the old navigation structures have fallen further into dereliction.

The Derwent highlights a development which has caused concern elsewhere as there has been growing opposition from local groups, nature conservationists in particular, to the reopening of navigations, and boaters now find themselves unexpectedly blamed for 'polluting' the countryside. Proposals, for instance, to restore the Avon between Stratford and Warwick, and the higher Severn above Stourport, have run into serious difficulties, and severe restrictions on the number of boat licences have been imposed on the now restored Basingstoke.

It is an extraordinary and inexplicable twist in the tale of Britain's waterways restoration, which started in 1945 when only a handful of enthusiasts cared about a natural heritage forgotten by the public and government alike. It passed through a period when 'saving' the waterways became recognised as the banner-bearer for the environment, and now in the century's last decade it has reached a stage at which, in the eyes of some, the waterways appear to be *too* successful.

Tales of Love and Death

From the first meeting at Tardebigge in 1945 to his retirement in 1964, Robert Aickman had devoted nineteen of the best years of his life to the waterways campaign. He had worked tirelessly, with little thought of his own career, travelling up and down the country, attending countless meetings and events. He had become known to nearly everyone who had played a part in the movement, yet he remained an enigma to many. He had a withdrawn and shy personality, which meant that few had any real knowledge or understanding of his character.

In April 1965, Robert penned, as one of a series of valedictory pieces, a brief autobiography for readers of the IWA *Bulletin*, concluding with the advice: 'Those, if any, who wish to know more about me, should plunge beneath the frivolous surface of *The Late Breakfasters*.'

This novel was his first published work since *We are for the Dark* had appeared in 1951. The manuscript had been doing the rounds of the publishers without success when Robert was contacted by Herbert van Thal, who had just set up a literary agency, London Management, and asked if he had 'anything in his locker'. Within ten days of receiving it, van Thal had sold the book to Victor Gollancz. The book, published in 1964, was dedicated to 'Herbert van Thal – MAGICIAN'.

Released now from most of his waterways involvement, Robert applied his energies to establishing the career as a writer that he had always envisaged. In the remaining seventeen years of his life he had a further eight books (seven collections of ghost stories and the first part of an autobiography) published, five by Gollancz; he edited a very successful series of eight collections of ghost stories for Fontana paperbacks; and a further five books (including the second part of his autobiography) have appeared posthumously. In the relatively short time span of less than two decades Robert Aickman established a highly regarded place among the great writers of a peculiarly English literary form, the ghost story.

Aickman thought that there were only about thirty or forty first-class ghost stories in the whole of Western literature. He drew a sharp distinction between science fiction on the one hand, the horror story on the other. 'The writing of science fiction demands primarily the scientific aptitude for imagining the unrealised implications of a known phenomenon', while 'the horror story is purely sadistic; it depends on the power to shock'.

A good ghost story, Aickman believed, drew upon the unconscious mind, in the manner of poetry; it needed to offer neither logic nor moral, and it was an art form of exceptional delicacy and subtlety. 'The good ghost story gives form and symbol to themes from the enormous areas of our own minds which we cannot directly discern, but which totally govern us; and also to the parallel forces of the external universe, about which we know so little, much less than people tell us,' he wrote in one of his introductions (which offer some of the best analytical criticism of the genre available) to the Fontana series.

He confessed that, although they were called ghost stories and he knew of no better name, readers were aware that, in many cases, no actual ghost appeared. Some people, he said, hoped that there were ghosts; some people hoped that there were not; most people managed to combine both of these aspirations, hoping and dreading at the same time, as exemplified by the question put to a Madame de Deffand:

'Do you believe in ghosts, madame?'

'No. But I fear them.'

Aickman's own first collection of stories, *Dark Entries*, was published by Collins in 1964, shortly after the novel, and immediately confirmed his individual style and deftness of touch in handling this most precarious of literary forms. His own approach was invariably to establish at the outset a

clear and recognisable everyday situation, likely to be known
to any reader, who would be taken, as though hand in hand,
along an accustomed pathway before unexpectedly reaching
a point of no return like a man, on the morning of his death
sentence, taking a reassuringly familiar walk around the
prison yard until he enters a door never before opened and
takes his final, fatal step.

The danger of the genre, as Aickman recognised, was that
an inept word or out-of-place reference, a shade of emphasis
wrongly applied or a clumsy phrase could shatter the gossa-
mer web of illusion that had to be spun around the reader –
and any such unintentional mistake could turn a tale of the
unexpected into a parody arousing smiles of derision.

In his work Robert found a way of giving physical
substance to the disturbance of the psychic. He went beyond
the conventional ghost story into the realms of the spirit and
mind, writing of deep-seated disturbances, often sexual, full
of post-Freudian analysis. Most of the relationships were
peculiar and bizarre and frequently influenced by a psychic
unease that emerged from the buildings and landscapes.

He was incredibly adept at drawing from his own experiences, much from his IWA years, and extracting out of them
a previously unthought-of level of perception. The location
for the plot of 'Meeting Mr Miller' was the third-floor flat,
very like the Gower Street one, of a penniless young writer
in a house otherwise occupied by miscellaneous offices, from
which disturbing sounds emanated while he made love to
the woman from the basement flat.

'My Poor Friend' took a cynical and bitter look at the
work of Parliament through the eyes of the organiser of a
voluntary pressure group who was seeking help from a
lobbyist, finally driven berserk among the labyrinthine corridors of Westminster and the artificial façade of ceremonial.
'Everybody nowadays thinks it is a bad joke that the Member
of Parliament can almost never decide how he will vote, but
is compelled, none the less, to spend most of his Parliamentary life attending "debates" based fundamentally on the
premise that he can so decide and is, therefore, accessible to

argument,' Robert wrote (rather unkindly in view of the personal support he had enjoyed).

Aickman's endless hours spent at tedious, drawn-out public meetings in cold, draughty halls were parodied in 'A Roman Question', in which the speaker was forced to stay with a committee member in his dim and dingy semi-detached house in a remote Birmingham suburb. The tawdry tinsel of a local repertory theatre was pulled back in the sad story of 'The Visiting Star'. Women were depicted time after time as young, beautiful and sensual, attainable, but only briefly, the passion invariably fleeting and insubstantial.

The stories are punctuated with Aickmanish opinions, presented by the characters in them. 'I hate the state one got into during the war. But then . . . I hated the war altogether.' 'Of course, the Jews are like that; once a friend, always a friend.' ('The Clock Watcher'.) 'It is during the long middle years [of marriage] that the feeling of all-round frustration is consciously dominant.' ('A Roman Question'.) 'There is no one it is easier to like than a first-class woman secretary.' 'It is not in every case possible to choose. Often our present is decided for us by our past.' ('The Late Breakfasters'.) 'You live surrounded by the claims of other people: to your labour when they call it peace; your life when they call it war; your celibacy when they call you bachelor, your body when they call you husband.' ('The View'.)

Aickman compared the writing of a ghost story to composing a poem: the mood could not be summoned, or even expected; though 'exercises' could be practised, he personally found that 'the muse of the supernatural' seemed to prefer a moment when he was thinking of and concentrating on something quite different. Even so, his own method was thoroughly systematic. He liked to write without interruption for about three hours, preferably in the morning, when he would break and enjoy some female company.

His need for utter privacy and peace in creating the right environment for writing caused various difficulties. In 1973, after protracted legal battles, he was forced to leave Gower Street and moved, rather surprisingly, to the Barbican, then only just taking shape as a planners' dream residential village in the heart of the City of London. Felix, who suggested it, felt that he would be attracted by the arts complex of theatre, concert hall and art gallery, but they were not yet built and she has admitted that it turned out to be an unfortunate choice.

Robert tried his best to disguise his flat's uncompromising contemporary design. 'The modern square box of a Barbican apartment has been skilfully arranged to look like the wing of a minor country house. His writing studio is lined with old books, editions of ghost stories, and velvet curtains where mysterious draughts blow,' as a national newspaper described it. But the noise defeated him. Sounds reverberated and echoed harshly around the large, windy concrete courts; much worse, and previously unknown, an adjoining telephone exchange produced a weird, high-pitched mechanical whine and the neighbours indulged frequently in loud screaming matches.

Robert started to move peripatetically around London in search of quieter venues, combined with the desire to write in surroundings other than his own home and to have company on hand when he had finished. For two years he regularly used a spacious semi-basement room in the Redcliffe Gardens home of his friends and former IWA workers Ann Pym (sister of Lord Pym, the former cabinet minister) and Mary George. When Mary retired from the Electrical Association for Women, the arrangement was no longer practical and he sought the refuge of Margaret Rawlings's little-used London house, but shortly afterwards, in 1976, he met a neighbour in the Barbican, Jean Richardson, who was also a writer, of children's stories. As she worked most days in the rights section of a publishing firm, Robert soon found a perfect haven in her flat only a few steps away.

Much winter reading beside the fireside lay behind the process of selection for the Fontana collections. He himself took immense delight in reading his own stories aloud when friends gathered together, and 'Ringing the Changes' was his personal choice for boating trips. On completing the drafting of a new story, he made a practice of crossing London to read it to Felix, not so much to ask for advice or approbation, rather simply to sense the feeling of reaction.

The only work of non-fiction published (by Gollancz in 1966) in his lifetime was *The Attempted Rescue*, a sardonic, brutally perceptive and brilliantly amusing account of his own childhood and life up to 1939. The second part of his autobiography, covering the waterways crusade, was often promised but did not materialise until after his death. It was published under the title *The River Runs Uphill* (by J. M. Pearson in 1986), but it suffered from over-revision, which took out the guts and the freshness that illuminated the first book. For some unexplained reason, sadly, he never tackled the kind of objective, descriptive book about the waterways scene for which he was so well qualified in every way. If he had tried, as he did in a single chapter contributed to a composite book about rivers, he could have written a fascinating travel book.

'In a sense Robert was a writer all the time,' said Jean Richardson. 'His whole life style was an artistic one, he was reading and thinking and looking at things with a writer's eye; the fact that a relatively small amount went down on paper doesn't take away from the fact that his life was directed towards this end.'

For the first ten years of his writing career Robert had hoped that his stories would be published in the far larger north American market, where he had already become known to devotees of the ghost story. In 1976 he found himself unexpectedly wooed from two directions at once by Kirby McCauley, a literary agent, and by Herbert van Thal, who had belatedly decided to open his own New York branch. *Cold Hand in Mine* was published in the USA that year, followed later by other books, and he was awarded the Oscar of ghost-story writers, the World Fantasy Award.

Aickman suffered from depression, at times deeply, and his stories reflect this in their atmosphere of all-pervading doom, the knowledge of impending catastrophe that cannot be avoided. He believed that the ghost story helped readers to become reconciled in part with death, 'not only by suggesting that all of us, or many, or some, survive it, but also by justifying the death institution itself, illuminating it as an instrument of justice'.

His natural flair for writing ghost stories was underpinned by an awareness of the supernatural. 'He had a very great interest in the occult from a psychological and spiritual aspect, though he certainly said that he had never seen a ghost,' Ann Pym recalled. As a young man he and Mary George had spent a night, planned with great anticipation, at Borley Rectory, known as 'the most haunted house in England'. Afterwards, Robert had been disappointed to report to Harry Price, who had conducted many scientifically controlled experiments there, that there had been no positive happenings beyond their overall sense of unease and an unexplained pebble that hit Mary.

England, he believed, was the metropolis of the supernatural, as of lyric poetry: out of any gathering of twenty people it would transpire that one had had a paranormal experience. 'What is more, there will regularly be among the twenty a further person who has been through something considerably more upsetting than the tale told by the first speaker; so upsetting that the person does not care to talk about it, except sometimes to a single individual of proven sympathy.'

Robert made himself available to give counselling to people disturbed by psychic experiences, and he took painstaking trouble in discussing their sensory feelings with them. In 1978 he told one woman living in north London (and he advised her to obtain an additional opinion from a clergyman) that 'it is not a matter of disturbances emanating from outside, but of disturbances emerging unconsciously from within you . . . The view I take is that owing to intense stresses within you (there has been quite enough to cause them), odd things happen in your vicinity without your directly causing them. No one really knows how this comes about, but it seems to be a fairly frequent occurrence. It is somewhere between psychic investigation and psychiatry: not quite one and not quite the other.'

In any sphere of activity in which Robert was interested it seemed that he had a natural ability to take the lead. He was chairman of the London Opera Club and a founder member in 1962 of the Delius Society, but his most significant contribution to the arts was the five years he spent as chairman of Balmain Productions, parent company of Ballets Minerva.

He was first introduced to the struggling company by IWA member Stanley Wilcox (father of television's Desmond Wilcox) and he went with Audrey Bowley to see them dance at Folkestone. Although twenty or so members of the company lived on a veritable shoe-string (prima ballerina Kathleen Gray helped the choreographer's mother to stitch costumes), they were so enthusiastic that Robert felt they deserved much wider recognition. While Audrey, Mary George and Ann Pym built up a large and influential subscribing list of friends of the ballet, Robert worked on his Arts Council contacts and succeeded in considerably raising the grant as well as obtaining support from the Wolfson Foundation.

The company now had a previously unknown financial stability which enabled them to commission outside choreographers for new works including, *Christmas Carol* and Byron's *Manfred*, and for a time they were at the forefront of British touring companies. Then something went wrong. After a poor performance at Hackney, Ann Pym said, 'Something isn't suiting the artist in Eddie [Gaillard]; I don't know what it is, perhaps basically the Arts Council. I expect Robert would think so, and it would be hard to find him wrong.'

Aickman greatly resented the presence of the two Arts Council representatives at council meetings, although in theory the grant was made 'without any strings'. The dancers felt that they were being taken over, body and soul, and losing their artistic freedom. The larger financial backing, in truth, had put a severe strain on the company to compete beyond their resources. After a clash of opinions about the future, Robert and his friends resigned in November 1967.

From the age of five, when he was first taken by his father, Robert remained an ardent theatre-goer, rarely missing anything of importance on the London stage, almost always accompanied by a female friend, each of them paying individually for their own ticket. He carefully preserved the programmes, which were stored in three vast Victorian cupboards, originally salvaged from his grandfather's house and laboriously carted from flat to flat (he moved from the Barbican to a third-floor flat at Gledhow Gardens, SW5 in 1978). The collection of 3,000 programmes was accepted, after his death, by the Victoria and Albert Museum.

Since he had never cooked a meal in his life, he frequently dined out, either with friends or at one of his favourite Soho and Chelsea restaurants. With Ann Pym and Mary George he shared a birthday club to which each of them contributed regularly, keeping proper accounts; then, on each anniversary, they went out to eat at a place chosen by the birthday member, sometimes in an obscure quarter of London.

Excursions into the country to historic houses, the Basingstoke canal and Epping Forest, were a favourite weekend pursuit – planned meticulously by Robert, who gave precise directions to his female driver. He was able to pick out a perfect picnic place from the Ordnance Survey map and arrive there at the right time without any fuss. 'I don't think I ever remember a picnic place that wasn't interesting or beautiful or in a quiet situation,' recalled Ann. 'You always felt that if you went back it wouldn't exist without Robert – or you would have great difficulty in finding it! Certainly, it could never have been the same – he always made it a special occasion, even in wintry weather.'

Wherever he went, Aickman preferred to have the company of women rather than men; he simply felt more at ease without the competitive instinct engendered by the presence of another male. During his two decades of working for IWA he attended hundreds of events – boat rallies, branch dinners, exhibitions, protest meetings and so on – at which, in many instances, he would be a principal speaker and would invariably be supported by an attractive woman. As the female friend was often different whenever he met the same group of people, he earned a reputation that was envied by some, scorned by others.

The enigma was that few women found him particularly

attractive in a physical way. His attraction stemmed from his hypnotic personality and the breadth of his interests. He had the fluency to communicate his passions for theatre, music, visual art and the environment to his friends, and to share these enthusiasms with them without creating a patronising impression. 'He had a sort of Svengali effect on women,' Eric de Maré thought.

His relationships with women were frequently platonic, though with some he became deeply involved emotionally to a degree that caused at times severe hurt and upset to both sides. In the view of Jean Richardson, 'Friendship with Robert could be rewarding, but you had to be prepared to take the rough with the smooth and some of the rough could be very rough indeed.' After the final, traumatic break-up with Elizabeth Jane Howard, Robert insisted that her name was not mentioned in his presence; in consequence she became estranged from their mutual friends, like James and Anthea Sutherland, for some years.

Later in life Robert liked to keep each of his women friends in separate compartments so that they did not meet each other; each had a particular role according to their personal tastes, one, for instance, accompanying him to the lyrical music of Delius, another to the drama of Wagner.

Felix, who had a longer and closer relationship with Robert than anyone else, explained that he was not 'a feminist and certainly not a womaniser – he just liked women's company because he found their minds more receptive and perceptive. He enjoyed the spice of flirtation which gives an edge to a conversation. He was stimulating to talk to because he made you feel that he was really interested in what you had to say – and he was genuinely interested.'

The reverse side of his personality – one which often created misunderstandings among casual acquaintances – was that he was exceptionally shy. Although he was a confident and fluent public speaker, he was much less capable of routine day-to-day contact. He had few social graces, and he was not prepared to indulge in small talk, partly because he would not compromise by paying compliments if he felt them to be unjustified. He rarely stayed to speak to Mrs Harrison, who cleaned his flat once a week, preferring to leave a written note, sometimes complaining angrily about the breakage of some minor piece of crockery.

Many of his friends saw him as rooted in the past and not suited to living in the modern world; as though he never quite escaped from his eccentric, isolated and classical upbringing, dominated by a much older father. The material benefits of modern technology meant nothing to him since, for instance, he never possessed a radio or television set, or learned to drive a car. The fact that he was out of touch in these conventional ways gave him a detachment that enabled him to make penetrating judgements about people and situations, but there were other times when errors of judgement occurred.

Aickman's leadership of the waterways movement has remained a controversial issue, some seeing it as arrogant and inflexible, others as positive and determined. It could be argued that a less abrasive and aggressive stance would have encouraged better communication with the authorities and a compromise solution at an earlier date, but this would almost certainly have been at the cost of sacrificing precious miles of canal (such as the Ashton, Peak Forest, Caldon, and probably even the Kennet and Avon) and, in any case, there were no signs from the authorities that this was desired (and Robert kept his ear very close to the ground through his many contacts). Moreover, subsequent history demonstrated that when Lionel Munk tried, genuinely, the compromise route, it failed and he was forced, frustrated and angry, to return to the attack.

It is easy with hindsight at this stage to criticise a past strategy and to claim that smoother methods could have been used. The facts are, however, that no one else worked so hard and for so little personal gain, no one else maintained so resolute a belief in the justice of the cause and its ultimate success when it looked unattainable, and no one else stayed the course for so long. All those who worked with Aickman, even his critics, acknowledge his charismatic personality and his flair as a publicist, while his admirers accept that there were flaws to his character.

John Smith, who gave up his voluntary role with the National Trust to found the Landmark Trust which has successfully saved scores of Britain's priceless architectural 'follies', has a lifetime's experience of public campaigning. 'To further a cause, you have first to gain attention, particularly from those in authority,' he said. 'There are two ways of doing this: you can cajole and influence and generally stroke their ears, or you can attract a person's attention by punching him on the nose. Robert belonged to the latter school of thought with this important refinement – he made the opposition look ridiculous as well.'

Charles Hadfield, who realised after the IWA's second official meeting that he would not be able to work with Aickman, did not come across him again personally, but he heard him speak in public and was impressed with his effect on an audience. 'Up to 1950, he was the only man who could have done it, but the moment he made this disastrous mistake of recasting the objectives of the Association and firing people who didn't agree with it, he lost his head and increasingly used his speaking ability to convince people of things that were rubbish.'

A powerful and effective campaign for the waterways had had to be mounted in the 1950s in order to swing public opinion behind the cause, in Peter Scott's view. 'Robert was the moving spirit of the IWA: he was a marvellous, most extraordinary man. Tom Rolt was a great character, too, and amusing, but Robert had the brains. I think a personality split was almost inevitable.'

After Tom Rolt moved to Talyllyn, he and Aickman did not meet for eighteen years. Tom only stayed with the railway for two years, though he remained a vice-president of the Preservation Society for many years. He then returned to the attractive house of Cotswold stone, at Stanley Pontlarge, where he had lived as a child, a warm and rambling family home. There he concentrated on writing books, including his autobiographical account of his involvement with the waterways campaign (*Landscape with Canals*) and highly readable biographies of two engineers who had important impact on rivers and canals, Thomas Telford and

Isambard Kingdom Brunel. After his divorce with Angela came through, he married Sonia Smith and they had two sons, Dick and Tim, who lived together at one time on a houseboat at Oxford.

In June 1969 both Rolt and Aickman were invited by John Smith, who was then High Steward of Maidenhead and a Member of Parliament, to a party on the restored Jesus College, Oxford barge which was being taken upriver from a boatyard at Teddington to its future mooring near Brunel's famous railway bridge at Maidenhead. It was a lovely afternoon and a convivial occasion, but the two men stood obstinately ignoring each other on opposite sides of the beautiful college barge until Sonia could bear it no longer.

'It seemed an ideal occasion to bury the hatchet – after all, it had been nearly twenty years since the row. So I went over to Robert and greeted him. He responded so cordially that I was encouraged to suggest that he met Tom again. But he didn't move from his place, leaning against a rail. So I went back to Tom and coaxed him, and they managed it and had quite a good conversation. So for the first time in all those years, suddenly the two principal founders of the IWA were talking again.'

Although it was to be their only meeting before Tom died five years later, they had a good correspondence when Robert spontaneously, possibly as an olive branch, suggested that Tom should write a philosophical book on the theme of change creating a lower quality of life, but Tom was too busy to tackle it. 'Had Tom and Robert remained friends I have no doubt that they would have shared a great deal,' Sonia feels. 'Many of the same things they loved. Although they fell out, they had many values in common.'

Tom was a member of the Science Museum Advisory Council and vice-president of the Newcomen Society for the study of the history of engineering and technology; he was awarded honorary degrees by the universities of Newcastle and Bath and was a Fellow of the Royal Society of Literature. As to waterways, on the twenty-fifth anniversary in 1971, he (and Charles Hadfield) were invited to rejoin the IWA. He made one last voyage along his favourite Llangollen canal and across the Pont Cysyllte aqueduct a few months before his death at the early age of sixty-four.

The wheel of Aickman's life seemed to have turned almost full circle when, two years before his death, a chance meeting (which Robert must have felt to be preordained) brought him together with his old classics master from Highgate school. T. L. Twidell was returning one day from a visit to Shaftesbury when he happened to enter into conversation with another train passenger who turned out to be Robert's cousin. As a result, the master and pupil re-met and found that the years had not diminished their respect for each other, nor their mutual interest in the occult, and they met again several times and exchanged thirty letters in the short time remaining.

'Fifty years ago, he gave me pleasure with his weekly essays, then written over a weekend by Classical V, and his were all of alpha quality,' Twiddell wrote in his obituary of Robert in the school magazine. 'As of one of them I commented "Aickmanish", so of one of his "strange tales" fifty years later I made the same comment.'

Another meeting, though arranged and not by chance, to which Robert attached the greatest importance was with Elizabeth Jane Howard. By this time, in late 1980, he was gravely ill with cancer, while Jane was herself alone again, having not long before separated from her husband, Kingsley Amis, and left their large family home in Hampstead. 'He was very brave, he had an awful time and he was very stoic, he was moving and I felt very sad for him,' she said. 'Felix was a tower of strength and devoted to him. Over his life, he did engender a great deal of affection as well as a great deal of hostility. I certainly have never known anyone like him.'

When Robert had become seriously ill during the autumn of 1980 he refused to enter hospital or undergo any formal medical treatment. He placed himself in the hands of a homeopathic doctor who prescribed daily injections of natural fluid that he found extremely difficult to administer himself. When he became virtually bedridden he was looked after at home with immense loving care and comfort by his devoted friends Felix, Audrey, Ann and Jean, all sharing in a rota and, in fact, only getting to know each other for the first time. He was taken to hospital for the very last days and died on 26 February 1981.

With punctilious forethought, maintaining to the last a lifelong perfectionism in organising events, Aickman left precise instructions for his funeral. His will detailed a lengthy list of bequests, ensuring that each of his treasured friends was remembered by a gift from the estate of one of Robert's possessions, such as an original oil painting, that they had admired. A large body of friends gathered at the Royal Society of Arts on 22 April 1981 for a memorial tribute at which Sir John Smith, Sir Geoffrey de Freitas (IWA president), and Sir Peter Scott spoke of his work for the waterways, Elizabeth Jane Howard and Margaret Rawlings gave readings, and musicians played some of his favourite pieces, including works by Delius. It was an occasion that he would have admired – beautifully conducted, with much laughter and applause and no false sadness.

Among the many obituaries that appeared, Crick Grundy in *Waterways World* asked the question: why did Robert Aickman undertake his stupendous and apparently thankless task for the waterways? He found the answer in a paraphrase of Robert's own writings. In the waterways he had discovered a field of activity 'large enough, but not too large, and infinitely worthwhile, where he might make a counter-demonstration against the moulding of man into little more than a machine and, by so doing, might capture a redoubt to be held indefinitely by a few like-minded people. In his autobiography he tells us that he failed, but in many of us he lit a flame which will not be extinguished, and our lives are the richer for having known him.'

As Sir Peter Scott pointed out at the memorial tribute, Robert Aickman, surprisingly, had not received any official recognition from the nation for the immense contribution that he had made in leading the restoration of a heritage which had been almost lost and which had now become an irreplaceable asset in an environment that was being constantly eroded.

His formal memorial is a simple bronze inscription set in an elegant brick podium alongside the lock that bears his name on a beautiful and peaceful reach of the river Avon. The true memorial to his life's work can be seen in Britain's 3,000 miles of living waterways and in the progress that is being made by others, who have taken up his lead, in continuing the restoration of abandoned canals throughout the country.

Bibliography

Unless otherwise stated, these titles were published in the UK.

Aickman, Robert and Howard, Elizabeth Jane, *We are for the Dark* (Jonathan Cape, 1951)

Aickman, Robert, *The Story of our Inland Waterways* (Pitman, 1955)

——*The Late Breakfasters* (Victor Gollancz, 1964)

——*Dark Entries* (Victor Gollancz, 1964)

——*Powers of Darkness* (William Collins, 1966)

——*The Attempted Rescue* (Victor Gollancz, 1966)

——*Sub Rosa* (Victor Gollancz, 1968)

——*Cold Hand in Mine* (Victor Gollancz, 1975)

——*Tales of Love and Death* (Victor Gollancz, 1977)

——*Painted Devils* (Scribners (USA), 1979)

——*Intrusions* (Victor Gollancz, 1980)

——(posthumous)*Night Voices* (Victor Gollancz, 1985)

——(posthumous)*The River Runs Uphill* (J. M. Pearson, 1986)

——(posthumous)*The Model* (Arbor House (USA), 1987; Robinson, 1988)

——(posthumous)*The Wine-Dark Sea* (Arbor House (USA), 1988); Mandarin (1990)

——(ed.)*The Fontana Book of Great Ghost Stories* (Fontana, 1964) (7 further collections published 1966 (twice), 1967, 1969, 1970, 1971, 1972)

Edwards, L.A., *Inland Waterways of Great Britain* (6th edn) (Imray Laurie Norie & Wilson, 1985)

Faulkner, Alan, *Willow Wren* (Waterways World, 1986)

Hadfield, Charles, *Introducing Canals* (Ernest Benn, 1955)

——*British Canals* (7th edn) (David & Charles, 1984)

Howard, Elizabeth Jane, *The Beautiful Visit* (Jonathan Cape, 1950)

Hutchings, David and Higgins, David, *The Upper Avon Navigation Guide* (Hutchings, 1977)

Mackersey, Ian, *Tom Rolt and the Cressy Years* (M. & M. Baldwin, 1985)

McKnight, Hugh, *The Shell Book of Inland Waterways* (David & Charles, 1975)

Owen, David, *Water Rallies* (J. M. Dent, 1969)

Perrott, David (ed.), *The Ordnance Survey Guide to the Waterways* (Robert Nicholson, 1983)

Ramson, P. J. G., *Waterways Restored* (Faber & Faber, 1974)

Rolt, L. T. C., *Narrow Boat* (first published 1944) (Methuen, 1984)

——*High Horse Riderless* (Allen & Unwin, 1947)

——*Sleep No More* (Constable, 1948)

——*Green and Silver* (Allen & Unwin, 1949)

——*Inland Waterways of England* (Allen & Unwin, 1950)

——*Thames from Mouth to Source* (Batsford, 1951)

——*Navigable Waterways* (Longman, 1969)

——*Talyllyn Adventure* (David & Charles, 1971)

——*Landscape with Canals* (first published 1971) (Alan Sutton, 1984)

——*Landscape with Machines* (first published 1977) (Alan Sutton, 1984)

Scott, Peter, *The Eye of the Wind* (Brockhampton, 1968)

Official publications

British Transport Commission, *Canals & Inland Waterways: Report of Board of Survey* (BTC, 1955)

British Waterways Board, *The Facts about the Waterways* (HMSO, 1965)

Lower Avon Navigation Trust, *Gateway to the Avon* (11th edn) (LANT, 1984)

Ministry of Transport, *Government Proposals following the Report of the Committee of Enquiry into Inland Waterways* (HMSO, 1959)

——*British Waterways: Recreation and Amenity* (HMSO, 1967)

——*Transport Act 1968* (HMSO, 1968)

APPENDIX A

Inland Waterways Association's memorandum to the Minister of Transport, March 1947

This was the first public statement of IWA's policy, and it is notable for its breadth and clarity. If only the Minister of Transport, to whom it was presented, had pressed BTC to implement its terms, twenty years of campaigning and political in-fighting would have been avoided. The Association's members were years ahead of the authorities in envisaging the multi-use of waterways (through commerce, leisure-boating, sport and tourism) and in asking for rationalisation of toll charges. In view of IWA's subsequent internal fight, it is noteworthy that the policy set out in this memorandum is clearly in favour of retaining and restoring *all* navigations.

1. That existing navigations should be kept in first-class order both for commercial and pleasure traffic.
2. That navigations no longer in use owing to deterioration by neglect should be restored.
3. That no navigation should be abandoned until the Bodies representing all of the following have been consulted: (a) commercial users, (b) users of the waterway for sport and pleasure, (c) defence services; and, in addition, local authorities and Catchment Boards affected, and the Ministers of Health, Agriculture and Fisheries, and Town and Country Planning.
4. That the system of tolls should be reviewed in order to standardise and simplify charges and to rationalise the system of rates for through traffic.
5. That a systematic policy of dredging should be carried out which should aim to achieve a minimum depth of five feet on all waterways carrying through traffic, as obtains in France and elsewhere.
6. That a review of the width of canals should be undertaken with a view to extending the range of larger craft.

7. That a review of costs per ton-mile of water transport should be undertaken in order to ensure the diversion of as many loads as possible from over-burdened rail and road systems to the waterways.
8. That steps be taken vigorously to promote the use of the waterways for recreation and by tourists, including visitors bringing foreign exchange to this country.
9. That working conditions of boatmen and their families should be improved in many cases, particularly as regards food rationing arrangements and the system of wage payments.
10. That very much better and more extensive supplies and facilities should be provided for the repair and construction of all craft suitable for inland waterways.

APPENDIX B

Report of the Board of Survey
(*British Transport Commission, 1955*)

This was the way the waterways were classified by the Board of Survey and approved by the British Transport Commission. If this plan had been carried out, the countrywide network would have been decimated (thus deterring any growth of commercial traffic and the later development of round routes enjoyed by today's boaters). Canals for immediate execution included the Oxford, Stratford, Llangollen and Macclesfield, which are among the most popular tourist attractions now. Total mileage to be abandoned was greater than indicated as it did not include canals and branches whose future was undecided.

Group 1: Waterways to be developed
(Total mileage – 336)

Aire and Calder Navigation (including Ouse Lower Improvement)
Gloucester and Berkeley Canal and the River Severn
Grand Union Canal (Regent's Canal Dock and Brentford-Berkhamsted)
Sheffield and South Yorkshire Navigation
River Lee (below Enfield Lock)
River Trent
River Weaver

Group 2: Waterways to be retained
(Total mileage – 994)

Ashby Canal (used section)
Birmingham Canal Navigations
Calder and Hebble Navigation
Coventry Canal
Fossdyke Canal
Grand Union Canal (above Berkhamsted)

Kennet and Avon Canal (River Avon section)
Kensington Canal
Leeds and Liverpool Canal
Oxford Canal (northern section)
River Lee (above Enfield Lock) and River Stort
St Helens Canal
Shropshire Union Canal (Main Line)
Staffordshire and Worcestershire Canal★
Stourbridge and Stourbridge Extension Canals
Stratford-on-Avon Canal (northern section)
Trent and Mersey Canal
Worcester and Birmingham Canal★
Ure Navigation

Group 3: Waterways having insufficient commercial prospects to justify their retention for navigation
(Total mileage – 771)

†Ashby Canal (upper part)
Ashton, Peak Forest and Macclesfield Canals
†Barnsley Canal
Bridgewater and Taunton Canal and River Tone Navigation
Chesterfield Canal
†Cromsford Canal
Dearne and Dove Canal
Erewash Canal
Forth and Clyde Canal (including †Monkland Canal)
Grand Western Canal
†Grantham Canal
†Huddersfield Canal
Kennet and Avon Canal (Reading to Bath)
Lancaster Canal
Manchester, Bury and Bolton Canal
Monmouthshire and Brecon Canal
†Nottingham Canal
Oxford Canal (southern section)
Pocklington Canal
Ripon Canal
†Shropshire Union Canal (Welsh section)

★ 'No need to retain for transport purposes both the Worcester and Birmingham
Canal and the southern section of the Staffordshire and Worcestershire Canal
which form alternative routes from the Severn to the Midlands system.'

†Shropshire Union Canal (Montgomery and Shrewsbury
  sections)
Stratford-on-Avon Canal (southern section)
Swansea Canal
Union Canal (Scotland)
Witham Navigation

† 'Already formally closed to traffic or abandoned . . . There are also certain arms
and branches of canals in other categories, such as the Rufford branch of the
Leeds and Liverpool Canal and the Aylesbury arm of the Grand Union, which
serve little or no useful transport purpose, and should be placed in this category.'

APPENDIX C

Transport Act 1968: Section 104; Schedule 12

The classification under the 1968 Act has remained unchanged to the present day, so this is still the statutory basis of British Waterways Board. It places, at least in theory, undue emphasis on estuary and port-linked navigations. The major Scottish canals appear in this list after being excluded by the Board of Survey, who wished to transfer them to the Scottish office. The 1968 Act only gave the names of waterways listed under Parts 1 and 2; all the rest came under the amorphous heading of 'The Remainder', so the survival of canals like the Huddersfield Narrow and parts of the Birmingham Canal Navigation, the Kennet and Avon, and Leeds and Liverpool depend to this day on the goodwill of the government in office.

Part 1: Commercial Waterways

    Aire and Calder Canal
    Calder and Hebble Navigation (part)
    Caledonian Canal
    Crinan Canal
    Sheffield and South Yorkshire Navigation
    New Junction Canal
    Trent Navigation
    Weaver Navigation
    River Severn
    Gloucester and Sharpness Canal
    River Lee

Part 2: Cruising Waterways

    Ashby Canal
    Birmingham Canal (main line)
    Birmingham and Fazeley Canal
    Calder and Hebble Navigation (part)

Chesterfield Canal (part)
Coventry Canal
Erewash Canal (part)
Fossdyke Navigation
Grand Union Canal (including Northampton branch, Aylesbury arm and Hertford Union)
Grand Union (Leicester section, including Market Harborough arm)
Kennet and Avon Canal (parts)
Lancaster Canal (part)
Leeds and Liverpool (most)
Macclesfield Canal
Oxford Canal
Peak Forest Canal
Ripon Canal
Shropshire Union (including Llangollen Canal)
River Soar
Staffordshire and Worcestershire Canal
River Stort Navigation
Stourbridge Canal
Stratford-on-Avon Canal (northern section)
Trent and Mersey Canal
Trent Navigation (part)
River Ure
Witham Navigation
Worcester and Birmingham Canal

(*Note*: This is a summary; the Act gives precise details of the limits of navigation.)

The Remainder

The Act did not specify other waterways owned by British Waterways Board and coming within this category. They included:

Ashton and Lower Peak Forest Canal
Birmingham Canal Navigations (most)
Brecon and Abergavenny Canal
Bridgwater and Taunton Canal
Caldon Canal
Chesterfield Canal (part)
Erewash Canal (part)

Huddersfield Canal
Kennet and Avon Canal (most)
Leeds and Liverpool Canal (part)
Monkland Canal
Montgomery Canal
Pocklington Canal
Union Canal

Index